The MODERN ARK

The Story of Zoos:
PAST, PRESENT AND FUTURE

VICKI CROKE

SCRIBNER

SCRIBNER
1230 Avenue of the Americas
New York, NY 10020

SCRIBNER *and design are*
trademarks of Simon & Schuster Inc.

Designed by Brooke Zimmer
Set in Columbus Monotype
Manufactured in the United States of America

1   3   5   7   9   10   8   6   4   2

Library of Congress Cataloging-in-Publication Data
Croke, Vicki.
The modern ark : the story of zoos : past, present, and future /
Vicki Croke.
p. cm.
Includes index.
(alk. paper)
1. Zoos—History. I. Title.
QL76.C76 1997
590'.7'3—dc21   96-48901
CIP

ISBN 0-684-19712-x

For my mother and father

ACKNOWLEDGMENTS

WRITING A BOOK is supposed to be a lonely activity, but I found that, like a Cecil B. de Mille production, it requires a cast of thousands—friends and family who'd do anything to help and total strangers who care deeply about their field and will do anything to provide the writer with accurate information.

I have been touched by so much generosity of spirit that I have learned as much about kindness as I have about zoos.

First, I want to thank Roger A. Caras: mentor, idol and friend. Roger and his wife, Jill, have shown me the planet—the Arctic Circle, Africa, the Galapagos Islands and Australia. Roger has introduced me to a world of deep thought and compassion. I am grateful for his help, humbled by his achievement and honored by his friendship.

To Henrietta Aladjem or "Chief." She is the science writer and seer who has guided and believed in me since I was a sickly and skinny fourteen-year-old suffering from lupus.

To Louise Kennedy: talented writer, gifted editor and tolerant neighbor. If the book could have been published with Louise's margin notes, it would have a real shot at the best-seller's list.

To the Biandos—John, Charles, Andrew, Linda and David—for their enthusiasm and love.

To Dorothy Greelis for the single-malt scotch and the wheaten wolfhounds. To Amy Macdonald for the suppers and gossip. To Sean Mullin for the computer handholding.

I also want to thank:

Perry Knowlton, my learned agent, who is elegant in the city, rugged in the country, and always a good friend.

Hamilton Cain, who showed me the way to more vivid writing.

John Lehnhardt, of the National Zoo, who invited me into his magic sphere of elephants, spending a great deal of his time coaching me until I got it right. I not only gained a great resource, I hope I've also acquired a friend.

Tony Vecchio and Anne Savage of the Roger Williams Park Zoo in Providence, Rhode Island, who opened their zoo and their minds to me. If all is right in the world, Tony is the wave of the future—a forthright and modest man.

Vernon N. Kisling Jr., who was my guide and safety net on the history chapter.

Kathi Travers, my partner in zoo crime.

Rick Barongi, Dianne Ledder, Carol Carniaux, Jane Hartline, Steve Cohen, Linda Corcoran, Georgeanne Irvine, Werner P. Heuschele, John Seidensticker—all zoo people who lent opinions and, in many cases, guest bedrooms.

Wilson Harris for a home in Atlanta.

I want to thank my dear friend Bernadette Rossi Lehr, who even in death taught me about life.

To Lacey, my grand and noble Irish wolfhound, who stayed by my side until this book was finished. To Tess Trueheart, her great-niece, through whom her legacy will continue.

And to Scott Beckman, my love.

CONTENTS

Contents

INTRODUCTION

As I stood watching a small group of orangutans at the Los Angeles Zoo on a bright December day, the keeper, Rosemarie Weisz, invited me to come back later and visit with them more closely in their night quarters.

The orangutan exhibit itself told me very little about orangutans and how they live in the wild. In fact, watching the handful of red apes sitting on a rough, barren mountain of gunite gave a false impression of them. Orangutans are fairly solitary in the wild (except for mothers with infants and courting males), and their habitat is dense, wet jungle. Later, as the chill of evening set in, I did learn an important lesson about the heart of the zoo.

Back in the grim night quarters, I fell in love with a handsome thirty-year-old redhead named Louis. Male orangs weigh up to two hundred pounds, have long, shaggy red fur and sport balloonlike round cheekpads on a fleshy face. Each orangutan, housed in a separate, barred area, was taking a night meal of fruits and vegetables.

"Louis is a gentleman," the keeper said. "You can go see him." Louis was drinking warm cider from a paper cup, and unlike any animal I had ever seen, he was sipping it, savoring each mouthful like a sophisticated vintner. Suddenly, Louis extended his huge catcher's mitt of a hand between the bars, palm up. "He wants to hold your hand; it's OK," Rosemarie called out as she checked on the others. I placed my puny hand in the center of his and then began to massage his fingers and palm. Between sips of cider, Louis groaned with pleasure. I felt as though nature itself reached out, held my hand and touched my soul. Louis's devoted keeper laughed sympathetically and said, "Oh, Louis, another female for your harem." A female orang nearby hurled an apple at my thigh.

It is rare for a zoogoer to have such an intimate experience, yet this truly is why we flock to zoos in such great numbers—120 million a year in the United States. Even in the decrepit L.A. Zoo, which is finally being renovated, one comes to realize that zoos are intrinsically a celebration of life. These magnificent animals, no matter the setting, are sparks of light in a dark world. The zoogoing experience strikes a primitive, visceral and, yes, even spiritual chord. At the zoo we can see that we are as tall as the giraffe's knee, or that the polar bear's paw is larger than a human head. Seals swoop around the tank with an agility that makes us smile.

At Chicago's Lincoln Park Zoo, I watched a massive silverback named Gino leap and lunge around his exhibit with Bahati, a tiny three-year-old baby gorilla, in exuberant, gentle play. On a cold and rainy day in Tacoma, Washington, when the zoo was empty, I jotted down notes in front of a glass-paneled underwater viewing area. When I glanced up from my notebook, I noticed a set of eyes fixed on me. Then for half an hour a female fur seal named Duffy mirrored my every move as I ran, turned, twirled, dodged, feinted and exhausted myself. At New York's Bronx Zoo I shivered in deep snow as three heavily furred young snow leopards stalked and chased one another through the creamy drifts of their frozen habitat.

My best zoo encounters were all about feeling. What we take

away in our heads from zoos is questionable, open to interpretation, but what we take away in our hearts is irrefutable. E. O. Wilson, Harvard's famed entomologist, calls this response biophilia—the arguably genetic longing most of us have for nature.

But zoos are a funny institution. Throughout time they have told us more about their respective cultures than about the animals they house. The bellicose Romans gathered exotic animals for combat spectacle, filling amphitheaters with water to battle hippos. For the Greeks of Aristotle's time, appreciation for wildlife became a scholarly pursuit.

What will our zoos tell future generations about our culture? We certainly live in a technological age: We can create periodic rainshowers in artificial indoor rain forests, and zoo animals are fed optimal diets and given great medical care. But the crossroads for zoos today is one in which the scientific path meets the moral, ethical and spiritual paths. How do we score on understanding the essence of nature? Do we have reverence for all living things? Do we respect the web of life? Are we humane enough to allow our captive wildlife a full range of natural behaviors?

Thoughtful members of the zoo community are speaking out. And they are telling us that it takes more than a frozen and thawed egg and sperm to make a cheetah. The essence of an elephant cannot be distilled in a test tube. The life of a chimpanzee cannot be read in a petri dish. We now know animals on a cellular level, but that is not enough. There are cultures and quirks and secrets in the animal world that pass undetected beneath our scientific gaze. We cannot preserve animals in sterile solution. We must save their place in the web of life, too.

"Biodiversity is not a 'thing' that can be saved," David Hancocks, executive director of the Arizona-Sonora Desert Museum, told the American Zoo and Aquarium Association (AZA) in 1995. "A tiger is a thing that can be saved, but biological diversity is a complex and dynamic ecological relationship between plants, animals, and microbes in a biotic community." Good science tells us that we should keep social animals in groups, provide water to aquatic creatures and allow predatory animals to stalk. We grasp these things on an intellectual level, but it requires a moral imperative to institute it.

Around the planet, as animals disappear and habitats shrink, humans flock to zoos. In a society increasingly disconnected from nature, the zoo provides a venue for us to link souls with wildness. If we continue to lock beasts up in barren enclosures, the heart of darkness will belong to mankind. Just as bear-baiting seems barbaric to us now, so will confining wild animals in cement bunkers seem to our grandchildren. Cut off from its place in the world, an animal appears as only a shadow of its true self. I am a great believer in zoos, but my faith was sorely tested while researching this book.

At the world-famous San Diego Zoo, I observed an African civet, described by a zoo sign as a "nocturnal thicket dweller," pace around a sunny cement pen. In zoos across the country—the National Zoo, Cincinnati, Bronx, Chicago's Brookfield Zoo, San Diego—I have witnessed polar bears, sloth bears, American black bears and spectacled bears in small cement grottos. At the Philadelphia Zoo, a Siberian tiger named Abigail paced in an almost hypnotic trance inside a green-tiled cage, backing up to one wall, leaping forward and building speed before getting to the far wall and then repeating the procedure. At the Minnesota Zoo in Apple Valley, a female moose swam through a pond in the middle of a large, wooded area, yet this beautiful scene was overshadowed by the sight of so many animals—particularly the large Amur leopards—inside the zoo's main building, a gloomy cement maze of small exhibits.

As I traveled around the country, I saw clearly that even the best zoos are challenged by the needs of their residents. We recognize ourselves in the faces of the gorillas—and it's boredom we see written there. Our hearts ache for the sleek, powerful tiger as he grimly paces the same steps out and back, over and over, in order, pharmacologists say, to release the body's built-in opiates—endorphins in his brain—in the same way humans get a "jogger's high." We are saddened by the sight of elephants—standing in barren enclosures created by humans determined to create safe, sterile environments—stamping their feet or bobbing their heads, cut off from vegetation by bars or wire, cut off from risk, chance, variability and the rich, complex tapestry of social life and familial bonds.

Zoos today are decidedly more natural-looking than ever before. Plants, bushes, trees and grass fill our sightlines, but are usually kept out of reach of the animals by barriers or zap wires. Zoos are still prisons for some animals, such as the polar bear, who can easily travel forty-five miles in a day across frigid tundra. These are among the most difficult animals to maintain in captivity, and enrichment experts say that a really good polar bear exhibit simply does not exist anywhere in the country.

While zoo exhibits are becoming more "naturalistic," there isn't one such exhibit in the United States that would claim its inhabitants are prepared to survive in the wild. To truly mimic nature would introduce too many hazards and present too many problems. Real grass and dirt and trees can harbor bacteria and are easily ripped out by strong animals. Gorillas in Atlanta, Georgia, destroyed $20,000 worth of plantings in the first month of living in their new outdoor enclosure. Interaction between separate clans is often violent. Allowing predators to stalk prey would mean enrichment for one creature but death to the other (Detroit Zoo's Steve Graham's attempt at this was met with an uproar). Spacious, lush ranges full of trees and rocks guarantee that certain animals will wander out of public view. Keepers report that if there is an obstruction between the public and an animal, the animal will always hide behind it, so such obstructions are usually removed. Still, a few zoos are brave enough to allow this: Minnesota for its tigers and Roger Williams Park Zoo in Providence, Rhode Island, with red wolves.

The image of "the new zoo" launched a marketing bonanza in the eighties and nineties. But how much of that PR is for real? In 1993, at the start of this project, I attended the annual conference of accredited zoos. For a solid week, I heard about the most fascinating and innovative programs in reproduction, enrichment, conservation and education. Across the country, though, I found mostly bored animals in small enclosures. In fact, right in the city where the conference was held, Omaha, Nebraska, I visited a tiger about whom I had read so much—one of the very few test-tube tigers in the world. This celebrity cat, now grown, was kept in a tiled exhibit no larger than a small bathroom. We are so dazzled by the biology that we forget about the animal itself.

There are beautiful bits and pieces of the "new zoo" spread across the country, however. The two-acre gelada baboon exhibit at the Bronx is so large and well planned that its inhabitants can socialize and gather food just as they would in the wild. On the vast acreage of the San Diego Wild Animal Park (not the zoo itself), rhinos, giraffes and waterbuck can mingle at a watering hole among flamingos, in a scene straight out of Africa. And the new bear exhibit in the Northern Trail of the Woodland Park Zoo in Seattle is by far the best in the country. A large, open area is strewn with bear toys—trees and logs and boulders—and crowned with a stream and deep pool (which allows underwater viewing) stocked with trout. It keeps two bear cubs, Denali and Keema, active. Even Fannie, an arthritic old Kodiak bear, was inspired before her recent death to create a daybed for herself out of the vegetation in the new exhibit—a new behavior for her.

AND YET THE challenge for zoos extends beyond the exhibits. The wildlife of this planet is under siege, and zoos have the opportunity to rescue it through education, conservation and reproduction. Children watch wildlife documentaries with spectacular footage of powerful, tawny lions running down prey, but how does this correspond to the lethargic lions heaped in the corner of a cage? A friend who went on safari with me commented that, despite a lifetime of visiting zoos, she felt she had never truly seen a giraffe until she observed them moving in synchronized fluid strides across the vast veld. The giraffe is not an oddity but a beautiful brushstroke on the living landscape. Zoos are no longer the only place children and adults learn about wild animals. The savvy zoogoer has seen, through wildlife documentaries, these animals in their natural environments. Zoos cannot compete with slick, quick-cut nature programs, which race from birth to sex to gory death. But good zoos today can carve out a niche that fits intelligently into the spectrum of people's experience. Much of the effort of the Roger Williams Park Zoo to save cotton-top tamarins has involved teaching the people of northern Colombia about these monkeys.

We cannot save the world's biodiversity through captive breeding, but we can help. As populations dwindle, certain genes will be lost. If we can't save huge numbers of animals now, at least we can save their genetic material to revitalize future generations. In 1930, there were 5 to 10 million elephants in Africa; in 1989 that figure was reduced to 600,000. It is impossible to calculate the variety of genetic material that is gone forever.

The Arabian oryx and the black-footed ferret, once on the brink of extinction, have been captured, selectively bred and, when their numbers allowed, reintroduced to the wild. Yet they are among only a handful of species whose return has been successful. There are another hundred troubled species—such as the cheetah, the okapi and the orangutan—for which scientists, working through species survival programs, are studying nutrition, health, behavior, DNA fingerprinting, artificial insemination, egg harvesting and embryo transfer in an effort to bolster their numbers and ensure their health. A few years ago, as soon as a Sumatran rhino died of colic in San Diego, a team of vets removed mature eggs from her ovaries and stored them in a tank of liquid nitrogen. At the National Zoo, golden lion tamarins are learning to climb vines in an "outward bound" program designed to prepare them for release into a reserve in Brazil. And at the Brookfield Zoo in Chicago, a computerized cytogenetic analyzer is helping to unlock the chromosomal secrets of the rare Humboldt penguin. Billions of dollars have been pumped into the renovation of the country's zoos, and the image of the new zoo is as fresh as its new face: the zoo as the modern ark, preserving endangered species and maximizing genetic diversity. As technology improves, many other animals will be helped by Species Survival Plans (SSPs) administered by the membership and accreditation organization, the American Zoo and Aquarium Association.

But even the breeding of wildlife in captivity is surrounded by controversy. We can rejoice in the birth of a baby at the zoo, an adorable lion cub, an unsteady zebra foal or a glistening seal pup, but then we also must understand that zoo births often mean the death—euthanasia or occasionally sale to hunting ranges—of older animals, who must make way for the younger, more appealing zoo attractions.

No zoo wants to be in the death business. The deep reservoir of medical information that zoos maintain is critical to helping animals in the wild. Today, conservationists and field biologists turn to the zoo community for help in managing wild populations whose diminishing habitats are becoming megazoos. The zoo world has stepped in to inoculate gorillas against measles and to prevent the spread of anthrax in Zambian hippos. Techniques for immobilization, anesthesia, assisted reproduction, parasite treatment and vaccines are being perfected in zoos and administered in the wild.

Where will these animals go? Habitat destruction is by far the most dangerous threat to wildlife today, looming large, casting its shadow across all these noble efforts. There are twice as many Siberian tigers in captivity as there are roaming the Russian steppes. One of the most serious charges against zoos is that they are stingy with money for conservation efforts. So what should the zoos, many of them financially strapped, be doing about this?

Zoos today are scrambling to reinvent themselves. Even now, after spending billions on renovations in the 1980s, much of it misspent in flashy, glitzy exhibits that already look run-down and outdated, zoos continue to confront an identity crisis. The New York Zoological Society (NYZS) has decided to christen its zoos "conservation areas," combining its conservation arm with its zoological parks. It even for a time called itself NYZS/The Wildlife Conservation Society, before just settling for Wildlife Conservation Society (WCS). One of the wealthiest and savviest of zoo organizations, WCS has read the writing on the wall and has moved quickly to distance itself from the dark, sad concept of the old zoo. What WCS wants to present is a scientifically advanced organization working at home and abroad to understand and preserve nature. And they are doing just that.

WCS knows that if zoos are serious about saving species, they must actively save wild places. This is the model for the future of zoos, but they stand alone, with few zoos coming close in stature, outreach or reputation. A look at serious field conservation projects run by accredited zoos shows the majority belong to WCS.

We cannot expect to fix the problem by renaming zoos conservation areas or referring to cages as enclosures. And zoos cannot continue to ignore critics. Zoo visionary David Hancocks has written: "Zoos as they presently exist are not sufficient for the coming century." The AZA may scoff at the reports of animal rights groups, but it cannot or will not provide data on the percentage of zoo animals who suffer from stereotypic behavior, the ratio of antiquated cages to modern enclosures or the number of keeper deaths that occur each year. The brightest members of the zoo community are calling for honesty and integrity in facing these challenges. The change must be fundamental—reinvention, not renovation, is the buzzword of tomorrow.

I am one of the tens of millions of zoogoers who love animals and want a zoo experience that is exciting, educational and untainted by guilt. I want to see animals who are free to roam and interact and *behave*. I want to know that my local zoo is part of a global force that is working to right the wrongs in our relationship with the animal kingdom. There is an inherent problem with the concept of zoos: Wild animals don't belong in cages. Appreciating wilderness and wildlife has nothing to do with bars and wire mesh and electrical fencing. The essential message—that we must respect nature—is a commonplace in zoo brochures, but to have real meaning it must be embedded in every aspect of the zoo itself.

From their inception, zoos have given human beings the chance to view amazing creatures up close. The relationship throughout much of history has been one-sided. Capture and captivity meant early death for most. With better diet and medicine, that equation has begun to balance out. Most zoo animals were bred in captivity and not the wild. Most zoo animals live longer than they would in the wild. And we have more to give them than monkey chow and dewormers. The best zoo of the future will be a monument to humanity as well as zoology.

One of my most gratifying experiences happened on safari in 1991. While sitting high on a hill, I watched a massive lone bull elephant drink from a watering hole below and then amble across the dusty plain until he was a dot on the horizon. Zoos have a vital role in our society, but they must never forget that the beauty, elegance and power of nature is etched most eloquently in its freedom.

1

BEYOND THE BARS:
SAVING THE WHOLE ANIMAL

Despite the thick pane of safety glass, there is something electrifying about being dwarfed in the shadow of a placid silverback gorilla. And the excitement is heightened when that gorilla is Willie B. at Zoo Atlanta. His story is about the resilient spirit of one creature and the transformation of the world around him.

Willie B. is impressive. At thirty-seven, the 450-pound, silverback lowland gorilla is in the prime of his life. He stands six feet tall, and his neck measures forty inches around. He is the dominant male in a group of three females, one of whom, Choomba, gave birth to Willie B.'s first offspring, a female named Kudzu, in early 1994. His days in captivity at Zoo Atlanta are spent in activities much like those in which he would engage in the wild. He forages for food, socializes, grooms and rests.

But life has not always been so sweet for Willie B. There are 650 gorillas in captivity worldwide, and Willie B.'s upbringing is not unusual. Born in the wild in 1958, this social primate lived for twenty-seven years in what amounted to solitary confinement. Alone in a concrete box with metal bars, he never saw another gorilla, only the faces of zoogoers who often jeered or screamed at him. Willie B. would lie on his side, one arm over his head, legs crossed and eyes staring blankly out into nothing. With little to occupy him, he grew fat. Zoo Atlanta director Terry Maple has described the old Willie B. as the "loneliest gorilla in the world."

Many gorillas raised in a "hard zoo" environment throw or eat feces; some constantly regurgitate their food and then reingest it. In his book *Zoo Man,* Maple says visiting gorillas in these old settings "was like visiting a mental ward: the occupants were seen as crazy and self-destructive." Maple wanted to create a "soft," natural environment for Willie B. that would allow him to forage and socialize like a wild gorilla.

On a muggy morning in May 1988, Willie B.'s world changed. He cautiously explored his new outdoor habitat that morning until the strange feeling of raindrops drove him back inside. Within the crowd of hard-bitten zoo experts, emotions ran high. Willie B. now enjoyed an outdoor habitat with trees, grass and blue skies. The next year, he was carefully introduced to some female gorillas (who for a short time dominated the socially unskilled male). Two months after meeting Kinyani, he copulated for the first time. Willie B.'s impoverished life became enriched: Companionship, bright sunshine and the sound of birdsong replaced solitude, fluorescent light and the clanking of metal doors.

A full 10 percent of Zoo Atlanta's acreage was devoted to the new gorilla enclosure—26,000 tons of soil moved, 3,500 trees and shrubs planted.

Today, Willie B. spends his afternoons in front of a huge viewing area. As he munches on carrots or apples or raisins, zoogoers can sit on carpeted stadium steps and observe him. Well-muscled and thickly furred, Willie B. sits at arm's length from zoogoers. When he turns and peers directly into the glass at the crowd, instead of jeers, there are whispered gasps of delight.

It doesn't take a zoologist to see that life is better for Willie B., but despite all the talk of the naturalistic zoo revolution of the 1980s, a high percentage of zoo exhibits are antiquated. According to Sue Pressman, a zoo expert who has surveyed American zoos for the Humane Society of the United States and the World Society for the Protection of Animals, only a third of U.S. zoo exhibits can legitimately be called naturalistic and enriched—and that may be a generous estimate. Tony Vecchio, the director of the Roger Williams Park Zoo in Providence, Rhode Island, tours zoos across the country on a regular basis. His assessment comes close to Pressman's. He says that he has a critical eye and would tinker with 95 percent of the exhibits he sees, but adds, "I would consider only about 30 percent of them unacceptable." Vecchio estimates that "50 percent of the zoos probably have an entire area or building that would be considered antiquated." While the zoo can be an intriguing place to visit, it can be an awfully boring place to live.

The AZA, the organization that accredits the country's zoos, has not surveyed the naturalistic terrain. The group's expert on conservation and science, Michael Hutchins, says he could not venture a guess about these percentages. "There are a lot more, certainly, than there were even at the beginning of the 1980s," he says.

What shapes a zoo environment is the architecture—the physical structure or landscape of animal habitats (as well as the visitor services)—and the range of activity made possible for the animals. Sometimes a zoo benefits from its location. The Philadelphia Zoo is set on a flat, walkable plot of land with plenty of shade trees. In the summertime, zoogoers can stroll comfortably around the grounds. Yet the ease and serenity of the land contrasts sharply with some of the old enclosures—the echoing, tiled cat house and the sterile chimpanzee cages.

When we go to a zoo that is filled with active animals in natural environments, we leave feeling happy, and we may not even be able to put our finger on why that is. Driving away from the eighteen-hundred-acre San Diego Wild Animal Park, one feels a deep sense of satisfaction. The vast, scrubby terrain dotted with trees, softened by rolling hills mirrored in watering holes and teeming with African and Asian animals is a portrait of pristine beauty.

Too often, however, we leave a zoo feeling uneasy, maybe even depressed. None of the animals appeared sick, the cages were clean, but something was missing. The Los Angeles Zoo, despite the hard work of a talented staff of keepers, is a good example. A mostly municipal institution in a huge city, the 113-acre zoo needs a major overhaul. Chimpanzees live out their lives on a mountain of gunite rock that looks as if a cement truck accidentally unloaded there. The material is cold to the touch in winter and scorching in the summer. There is no shade, nothing soft to sit on. The zoo is participating in the captive breeding program for giant elands—magnificent spiral-horned antelope that stand a breathtaking six feet at the shoulder. Six of these animals scuff around a small, dusty corral. Many of the electronic interactive devices don't work. An endangered maned wolf—red-coated with outlandishly long black legs—paces the perimeter of his round pen.

TODAY, WHEN WE SEE photos of America's "old" zoos, we shake our heads. In the bad old days, "natural" meant painting jungle scenes in gorilla cages and ice floes for the polar bears. Our view of the natural world is much more sophisticated today. In zoos we imitate the rainstorms of the tropics, the light cycle of the arctic regions, the sounds of the savanna. But much of this is just high-tech mural painting. Man is a visual species, and though today's zoos may look very different to us, they may not feel any different to the animals. The rough, molded gunite of some new gorilla pavilion probably doesn't feel or smell like the wild to gorillas.

Such enclosures are often safe, sterile magician's props that provide only the illusion of nature. And the animals know the difference. Trees at the London Zoo are augmented with fake foliage to look denser to visitors; monkeys lick water from the real leaves after simulated rainstorms, but they leave the fake leaves alone. The Roger Williams Park Zoo reports that some of its birds will not nest in artificial trees. AZA's Michael Hutchins isn't surprised. "I suspect that a lot of the artificial trees are not built with the specific needs in mind for particular animals." Small wonder that William Conway, director of the Bronx Zoo, has said, "The most dangerous animal in the zoo is the architect."

The eighties revolution was based on more than a billion dollars' worth of renovations nationwide. In the January/February 1994 issue of *Museum News,* National Zoo director and quirky visionary Michael H. Robinson asserts, "Zoos have changed almost beyond recognition in the last fifty years. Penitentiary-style bars are a thing of the past; open habitats and naturalistic enclosures are the order of the day everywhere." If only it were so. Old exhibits are still in use, and old mistakes are still being made even in new exhibits. According to a paper written by David Shepherdson, probably the top behavioral enrichment expert in the world, "Many of the practical problems encountered when trying to enrich existing zoo environments are a consequence of exhibit design flaws or traps, and many of the exhibits being designed today are repeating these errors. These range from the design of drains which do not allow the use of natural substrates [grass or dirt] to enclosures which do not allow access for heavy machinery to replace climbing structures, logs, vegetation, etc. Theatre sets are designed for easy scene changes, zoo enclosures frequently are not."

Did the massive amount of money spent on zoos in the flush decade of the eighties change the lives of the animals in any significant way? For some animals, the revolution brought more space and more functional habitats. But for many, it brought only eye-catching displays and high-tech graphics. In the $26 million, three-acre African Pavilion at Boston's Franklin Park Zoo, a pair of bongos—large, striking African antelopes with a red coat and white stripes—are confined to an enclosure the size of a living room. A leopard in this pavilion paces in circles in a cramped, rocky habitat.

Henry Doorly Zoo in Omaha, Nebraska, is home to the largest indoor rain forest pavilion in the world, the Lied Jungle. But the central, imaginative, open and airy habitat is spoiled by frightfully small glassed-in habitats along the walls. Clouded leopards, a golden cat and golden lion tamarins (squirrel-size monkeys from South America) are among the animals pressed into tiny exhibits.

What one wire service reporter called "glassed-in caves," the rest of us might call claustrophobia-inducing terrariums. Some 317 mammals, birds and reptiles, plus about 300 amphibians and fish, live in 35,000 square feet of "display management area." Despite this sad situation, this pavilion has been cited in countless magazines as one of the best in the country.

For many zoo directors, more space simply means more animals. But providing more space for animals is one of the best things zoos are doing today—and for enrichment experts that means psychological as well as physical space.

A Trunk Full of Memories

THE BOREDOM OF some zoo animals involves two issues. One is ethical: Is it morally acceptable to maintain wild animals in peak physical condition but in a state of behavioral bankruptcy? The other is practical: When we talk about preserving endangered species, how much of that animal are we truly preserving: just pure protoplasm, or the whole animal, including mothering skills, navigational abilities, love calls and survival techniques? Scientists are sorting out which behaviors are "hard-wired," or instinctive, and which are "soft-wired," or learned. Cowbirds raised in isolation can still sing or recognize a love song, yet hunting seems to be an alien concept to captive-born cheetahs. An elephant is more than a trunk, baggy gray skin and a few thousand pounds of bone and tissue and blood. A complicated mammal resides in there.

Elephants have been known to adopt abandoned baby elephants, to care for the sick and injured, to communicate with each other over long distances. Orphaned elephants are known to wake up screaming and to refuse food. We can't freeze the concept of elephant—or that of any other animal—in a tank of liquid nitrogen. John Seidensticker of the National Zoo in Washington, D.C., states plainly that "It is not enough to produce genetically diverse babies;

we must also produce and maintain behaviorally competent animals who can thrive in the wild."

The zoo environment must be enriched for two reasons: It is morally and scientifically sound to do so. Michael Hutchins says enrichment helps with the conservation goal of modern zoos; it makes "people feel better about watching animals"; and it produces animals that are "psychologically healthy and more likely to be able to reproduce and integrate into a social group." And today, some of the brightest scientists in the zoo world are focused on this situation. They don't grab the media attention that frozen embryos and exotic test-tube births do, but their work is just as vital to the future of wild animals.

"The high-tech stuff is very attractive and very exciting—my God, we can't save all of these animals, so let's freeze everything down. What has been a fear of mine, and, I think, of many of my counterparts, is you can't freeze behavior," says Jill Mellen, Conservation Research Coordinator at the Metro Washington Park Zoo in Portland, Oregon. "If you want to preserve an animal, they are obviously more than just their genetic components. Learning and even culture can be so important to these animals."

Mellen admires the people she calls "sperm cowboys," and she works with them on saving animals, but, she says, "Their goal is that this is a last-ditch effort. If we are freezing everything down, we have lost the battle and we're well on the way to losing the war." Mellen works to preserve behavior and to make life comfortable enough for animals to mate without artificial assistance.

Zoo animals are free from parasites and predators, and their meals are packed with every element their bodies need. Infant mortality rates are much lower than in the wild, and these animals are so fit and robust that they often reach sexual maturity earlier and cycle faster. But what about other needs?

Mellen's colleague at the Metro Washington Park Zoo, David Shepherdson, gained fame as an enrichment expert at the London Zoo before coming to Portland. Shepherdson's role at the zoo is to make life more interesting for the occupants. Though this zoo still has many cages that are antiquated on the outside, they are brimming with activity on the inside.

As Shepherdson has put it, "Enrichment can usefully be thought of as a way of increasing the psychological space available to captive animals."

Shepherdson feels the situation is quite critical, and writes in one paper: "An elephant's rich array of diverse individual and social behavior is as much a part of what makes it an elephant as is its trunk and its huge feet. Since behavior is a consequence of interactions between both genetic and environmental factors, failure to reproduce an environment that is at least functionally equivalent to that of the wild will inevitably result in the loss of many forms and patterns of natural behavior." Lessons passed from generation to generation are never learned and, as Shepherdson points out, have the potential to be lost much faster than genetic diversity.

Shepherdson's and Mellen's work is not a "clean science." With genetics, it's easier to measure a quantity of semen, easier to define success—a live birth. But how do you measure a hyena's happiness or a frog's feeling of fulfillment? Scientists must sort out fact from anthropomorphic fiction.

One thing is certain: Zoos can and must improve. This is a scientific community that has studied every aspect of the animal world yet still displays creatures in regressive ways. Small cats, such as ocelots, fishing cats or jungle cats, are a good example. As Mellen has written in a research article: "In strong contrast to the complex environment in which small cats have evolved, the captive habitat for these animals typically provides relatively little or no cover. Solitary in nature, these cats are routinely housed in pairs." Mellen goes on to say that they are also often caged near big cats, "which they may perceive as potential predators." And small cats, which in the wild feed throughout the day on small prey such as birds and rodents, are generally fed once a day in zoos.

John Seidensticker and the Bronx Zoo's James Doherty have written that "A surprising number of 'solitary' carnivores is maintained together in zoo exhibits as male-female or same-sexed pairs. . . . For some species, this is simply wrong behaviorally; adults are never found together except briefly for mating." Some generally solitary animals may remain with siblings for an extended period of time. But what is the animal's normal social contact, and what is being represented by the exhibit? These two zoo experts stress that the zoogoer should be informed.

Throughout the scientific literature, we learn that zoo animals, removed from the complex environments for which they have evolved a rich range of survival skills, are forced into a state of "reduced welfare." All too often, our prized captives develop disturbing and harmful patterns of behavior to replace normal ones.

What Is Normal?

THERE IS A JOKE in the zoo world that if members of animal rights groups ever witnessed the savagery of the wild, they would shut it down. Animals in the wild spend most of their time eating, avoiding being eaten and confronting stressful situations that involve mating or rivalry.

Determining what is normal seems rather basic: animals that swim or dig or fly in the wild should be able to do so in captivity. The question, unfortunately, is much more complex. To understand a species or an individual's dance of life, we must also comprehend the rhythm and the steps. Many frogs need a rainshower to spark sex. Elephant matriarchs lead their families on a circuit of survival in a shifting environment—they move in sync with nature to find food and water. It is perfectly natural for a polar bear to gain an enormous amount of weight—779 pounds in the case of one female recorded—over several months to compensate for a previously poor hunting season, or to wait patiently for more than an hour at a seal's breathing hole, kill it with a blow from a massive paw and lethal bites to the head and spend fifteen minutes washing up in snow or water to cleanse herself of greasy seal blubber. Two zebra stallions in the wild could spend an entire day battling for a mare. Caracals (handsome reddish or sandy-colored small cats with black ear tufts) will come into estrus if living conditions suddenly improve (clearly a survival adaptation to their harsh desert living conditions).

Behavior varies from clan to clan and from individual to individual. There are even "cultural" differences among animals. Asian elephants greet one another by blowing gently into each other's trunks, while the larger Africans will stick their trunks into each other's mouths. Among wild chimpanzees, there is a wide range of behavorial differences. Only those from Western Africa have perfected a nut-cracking technique using branches or stones as hammers and flat rocks as natural anvils. Jane Goodall's famous chimpanzees of Gombe groom by facing a partner and using their free hand to hold an overhead branch, while the chimps living in the Mahale Mountains one hundred miles away use the free hand to hold the hand of the partner. Gombe chimps fish for driver ants with twigs, while the Mahale chimps won't touch them. The Mahale chimps do, however, eat carpenter ants, which the Gombe chimps do not eat. And chimps from the Tai forest in Ivory Coast hunt in a much more organized and cooperative way than their eastern relatives. These nuances serve to make the task of cataloging behavior more difficult.

It takes time, money and insight to discover the simple complexities of what "normal" is. Jill Mellen is working with a large grant from the Purina Company "to go around to all zoos and ask what's a normal cheetah, snow leopard, tiger, and begin to develop techniques with a large pool of healthy animals, instead of waiting till we're in trouble and rushing in to work with the few remaining, and maybe less than healthy, members of a species."

There are two approaches that combine to determine what constitutes a normal animal. One is to measure hormone levels in the urine, which may indicate stress levels, and the other is simply to observe the natural behavior of animals in the wild and compare. Some differences may remain, however, as animals that are in captivity should modify their behavior to cope with their present environment.

One indicator of contentment has been an animal's willingness to breed, but many farm animals and dogs in puppy mills breed under the worst conditions. Are the lions and anteaters who are so willing to reproduce in captivity simply those that are fit for cages and perhaps unfit for the wild? Many animals are kept off exhibit in order to spark breeding behavior. We hear over and over from keepers how animals do not enjoy being watched under any circumstances and simply will not mate if disturbed by the public. This seems perfectly normal.

What Is Abnormal?
The Prozac Generation

DEFINING WHAT IS abnormal can be equally complex. Zoo animals may exhibit behavior never witnessed in the wild. Gorillas do not throw feces in the wild, but it happens all the time in captivity. Several zoo elephants—Ruby in Phoenix, Starlett O'Hara in Atlanta—paint on canvas. Clearly, elephants have never been observed at an easel out on the veld. But evidence suggests that Ruby enjoys the activity, and her keepers claim that the color choices and patterns in her paintings often reflect her environment. For this highly intelligent animal, a very "unnatural" activity may provide a healthy dose of stimulation.

But there is a much darker side to the strange activities of some zoo animals. Clearly, keeping animals in penitentiary- or sanitariumlike conditions often results in hostile, aggressive, withdrawn or neurotic behavior. And certain species—the cunning or intelligent or exploratory—are especially prone to it. These include polar bears, tigers, leopards, elephants, chimpanzees and gorillas.

In the wild, animals spend a great deal of time resting, but in captivity, they often take rest to an extreme. In zoos, unhappy animals sleep or eat too much, they overgroom or become overly aggressive, they may starve themselves or refuse to breed, they can display hypersexuality and be naive or neglectful parents. Certain animals, such as gorillas, may eat feces, something they do only occasionally in the wild, during periods of bad weather. But the unhappiest animals routinely perform ritualistic acts that seem to indicate a disturbed state: pacing, regurgitation and reingestion, rocking and head bobbing. Although rarely seen in the wild—in a highly stressed macaque monkey, for example, or an orphaned chimpanzee—unhappy zoo animals will often self-mutilate. Polar bears, who can travel hundreds of miles a year while hunting in the wild, have been known to scrape their paws raw and bloody in painful and constant pacing in their zoo cages.

Chimpanzees, so like us, can suffer greatly in an impoverished environment. According to a 1990 Regional Proceedings paper of the American Association of Zoological Parks and Aquariums (AAZPA), the list of bad behaviors is long: "Among the most obvious are severe problems with aggression and the associated trauma wounds, and so-called abnormal behaviors which include undesirable behaviors like coprophagy, repeated regurgitation and self-mutilation which are potentially harmful to the animal's health." Problems with breeding and parenting are added to this list.

Elephants can behave strangely. Ruby, the painting elephant, when isolated for seven years and deprived of company, displayed some disturbing behavior. She would take some of her own grain and set it out to lure ducks into her enclosure; as soon as one got close enough, Ruby would stomp it into the ground with one of her enormous feet. And to the dismay of zoo officials, she also masturbated often.

Zoo officials vehemently disagree, but according to a recent survey conducted by the Born Free Foundation (a British charity that monitors animals in captivity), mental illness among zoo animals is rampant. Somewhat anecdotal, the 1993 study took three years to complete and involved one hundred zoos. The group says it found a bulimic gorilla in Barcelona, bulimic chimps in Sacramento, a psychotic baboon in Cyprus and a bear that constantly pulled its hair out in Rome. The director of the study said, "Our evidence confirms that deprived of their natural environment, social structures and outlets for many of the skills for which they have naturally evolved, animals exhibit abnormal behavior."

Zoos may balk at terminology such as "madness" or "mental illness," but no one in the community is happy with neurotic, repetitive behaviors technically known as stereotypy. Shepherdson says the Born Free study is meaningless and nonsensical, carried out by "untrained observers."

A little harder to shrug off would be the words of experts. John Seidensticker, curator of mammals at the National Zoo, looked at surveys in the literature and estimated in a 1991 *Zoo Biology* article that fully 60 percent of captive bears perform stereotypic behaviors. Even Smokey the Bear *(Ursus americanus)* suffered from it at the National Zoo.

And then there is the serendipitous assessment from Dr. Nicholas Dodman, a brain chemistry expert at Tuft's University School of Veterinary Medicine. Dodman visited the San Diego Zoo in 1994 with his family. While everyone else was awed by the vast array of spectacular creatures, the scientist says he was shocked by this "stereotyper's heaven." Everywhere he looked, he saw bears pacing, elephants swaying and giraffes bobbing their heads. This man, who is unlocking the chemical mysteries of such behavior in domestic and zoo animals, claims at least 30 percent and perhaps as much as 50 percent of the animals he observed at the San Diego Zoo were indulging in this disturbing activity. His impulse, he says, was to move to San Diego to study the phenomenon, but he quickly realized that "you could go to any zoo and see the same thing."

Officials at the AZA will not even hazard a guess at what percentage of animals at accredited zoos behave this way. Michael Hutchins wrestles with these issues himself. I asked the AZA's expert if he knew the extent of the problem. "I don't really know," Hutchins says. "I can tell you, though, if animals are housed in an appropriate environment in captivity, they don't develop stereotypies." Hutchins thinks getting a fix on the scope of the problem would, in fact, "be a valuable study," but, he says, it would have to include all the variables: "Where did the animal come from? Was it mother-reared or hand-reared? . . ." Hutchins says there is no doubt that these behaviors "are compensation for a less than adequate environment."

But it is true of even the best zoos. A sea lion at Roger Williams Park methodically swims a certain circuit of his tank upside down, touching the same point on a glass panel to turn every time. A gorilla at the Bronx regurgitates half-digested food into her hand once a minute and then eats it again, shaking her head violently before each episode. A polar bear at the Brookfield Zoo paces five steps out and five back, over and over again.

A study (released in the summer of 1993) by British ethologist Marthe Kiley-Worthington, who visited fifteen British zoos over two years, found that elephants spent 22 percent of their time head-bobbing or biting bars, bears spent 30 percent of their time pacing and camels wagged their tails, stamped their feet and shook their heads in frustration.

THESE BEHAVIORS appear to serve no purpose, though they may be exaggerated forms of functional acts such as walking or grooming. And although why this happens is not quite known, it is believed that these animals, perhaps because of boredom, are tapping into the body's built-in opiates (endorphins that produce a "jogger's high") to achieve the same level of brain chemicals they would have in the wild. In fact, when endorphin-blocking drugs are used on these animals, their stereotypic behavior stops or is reduced temporarily. Dr. Dodman has worked with dogs who lick themselves raw; horses who "crib," incessantly biting at stall walls, causing gastrointestinal problems; a zoo bear who paced ritualistically; and a regurgitating/reingesting zoo gorilla. He believes these may in fact be similar to some behaviors in humans—obsessive/compulsive disorders (OCDs) or the ritualistic patterns of those locked in prisons or asylums (self-mutilation, obsessive exercise). In fact, treating dogs who lick themselves sore with the same drugs used in OCD patients does alleviate the problem.

This is cutting-edge science at its most intriguing. What scientists know is that dopamine is the neurotransmitter that connects thought with action. In the film *Awakenings,* the patients had no dopamine and therefore couldn't move at all. Too much dopamine and a human or animal will be agitated and aggressive, indulging in stereotypic or self-destructive behavior. Dopamine, then, is key to stereotypic behavior. We also add serotonin, a chemical released through exercise that has a calming effect (a self-produced mood stabilizer). Now bring endorphins to the cocktail and we have the complicated puzzle pieces for stereotypy. Yet we are still having trouble fitting them all together. Giving these animals endorphin or dopamine blockers or Prozac, in various combinations, works.

One would expect that when administering endorphin blockers, the animal would initially increase its stereotypic pattern in a desperate attempt to get a "fix." And Dodman says that is exactly what happens. "Like if you substituted someone's real cigarettes with very low nicotine cigarettes, you know they'd be sucking like idiots trying to get more until they realize that there is no buzz and the behavior would extinguish over time. We did observe that with dogs' lick granuloma [excessive licking of one spot]. When we gave them the drug, there was an exacerbation of the licking, followed by suppressions." It is believed that endorphins are the reward in stereotypy.

There are those who believe that some of these behaviors—pacing, for instance—may simply be normal reactions to abnormal settings. Polar bears cover an enormous amount of ground on their hunts, so perhaps, some specialists suggest, pacing is mere exercise. Jill Mellen watches various species of cat for hundreds of hours and believes pacing is not always as sinister as we think. "From an anthropomorphic perspective, it seems to me that these cats come out and investigate the environment, and the males pee on everything, and then they pace. . . . In the wild, what they do is go hunting and patrol their territory. And if you get too close to it, your neighbor beats the bejesus out of you. So it's a little nicer, dull, deadly dull at zoos, but it's nicer. My speculation is that pacing is a coping mechanism."

Shepherdson says, "I feel that a lot of cats have a tendency to pace at a certain part of the day—certainly just before dinner is clearly a sign of frustration, I would say. But whether that frustration is beyond the bounds of acceptability, I'm not sure at all. We get excited before a big meal if we're hungry, but you wouldn't say that that was suffering. I think that's very different from the polar bear that may spend 75 percent of its time pacing around in circles to the extent that it wears its pads out so they're bleeding. I really don't think those are the same behaviors."

Several people in the zoo world compare this behavior to humans who swim monotonous laps in a pool, or joggers who sprint around a track. Wrong, says Dodman. A more accurate comparison would be to "some people who run seventy miles a week on stress fractures in summer and winter, in hail and snow, despite doctor's orders. These people are *addicted*. If they don't have their run, they can't function." Washing your hands is fine, Dodman says, "but when you do it sixteen hours a day, it's a problem."

Personality type and genetics may play roles, but one thing is clear: the more sterile the environment, the more likely this behavior. In the words of Heini Hediger (director of Zoo Zurich in Switzerland during the middle part of this century and professor of ethology at the University of Zurich), "It should first be said that stereotyped movements are a sure sign of wrong treatment." He describes the scenario in which this pattern can begin. A "predatory animal" (large carnivores seem especially prone to this behavior) becomes agitated waiting for the keeper to arrive with meat. The animal stands at a lookout and then anxiously paces away and back to look again. Without activities to occupy him, Hediger says, the animal performs this way longer and more often; he shortens the route, often in a circle or figure-eight pattern, and sometimes accompanied by a strange head movement at turns. Indeed, Dodman has found that, in domestic animals, it is the overachievers, the Type A's, who exhibit these patterns. It is the horse "who spends half his time with his head up looking to see who's coming" who cribs. And it is the focused and attentive Labrador retriever who may lick himself raw. Should we be surprised if the great opportunists of the animal world begin to show some unhealthy displacement activity when they are cooped up?

Clearly, that is what is happening, but Dodman feels there is a lot of stereotypic behavior among a wide range of animals in the zoo. Elephants swaying, giraffes bobbing their heads or wild pigs biting at chains may not be as obvious to the casual visitor, but these are ritualistic, compulsive activities nonetheless. And because most of this behavior is the displacement of an activity with real function, all species tend to exhibit uniform stereotypies. Bears, who would cover a lot of ground, pace; monkeys, who would groom, self-mutilate; sea lions, who would hunt for fish, glide through the water in the same pattern, always touching the same points at the ends of the pool.

Some stereotypic behavior is less serious, according to Hediger, but still points to a need for enrichment—a bigger enclosure and more activities. "Lack of occupation of the captive animal," Hediger pointed out in 1950, "is an urgent problem of animal management, but is capable of solution." Part of the goal in enriching the lives of animals would include making life comfortable enough for them to breed and then normal enough for them to care for their young. Clouded leopards are quite fickle about breeding in captivity, and large males have been known to kill even receptive females. For gorillas, good parenting has been a problem. Gorilla infants must often be rescued from their uncomprehending mothers, who lack the necessary skills. When the infant is removed and raised by humans, the cycle continues. It can be broken, however, if young females are placed in large social groups where they can observe experienced mothers. While wild elephants grow up watching births and even helping in delivery, captive elephants have rarely seen such an event. At the National Zoo, one elephant apparently tried to kill her baby in an effort to appease the other frightened elephants in the barn. The squawking infant had spooked all of the animals, who had never before witnessed a birth.

"Stereotypic behavior, coprophagy, inactivity, and excessive aggression have been attributed to the stress of captivity and may, in some cases, directly interfere with reproduction by reducing the diversity of social behavior," Shepherdson says, and "enriched environments have successfully reduced the incidence of these behaviors."

Simply changing the environment, however, doesn't always change the behavior. As Dodman says, "When you take the animal out of the context in which the stereotypy originally developed, it continues to do it." The pacing animal who is provided with a new, enriched habitat will often continue to pace. For some reason, once these neurotic behaviors are in place, they seem to become "hard-wired." Dogs or fish that have been confined over a long period of time will pace or swim in the same limited pattern even after being released.

Sometimes it takes a combination of environmental enrichment plus a prescription for something like Prozac to cure a stereotyping animal. Since Dodman has turned life around, chemically, for some animals, I asked him if the institutions holding these animals were doing anything to make their lives physically as well as chemically better, which is an ethical dilemma for Dodman. He can stop many of these behaviors cold with a little pill, but does that mean we can keep these animals in a chemically altered state and proclaim their behavior normal? The drug firm Eli Lilly has provided free Prozac to a zoo in at least one case. Imagine the market for them—all those zoo animals across the continent, all those large animals, like bears and gorillas, who require higher dosages than humans.

What all the science and all the studies have shown is something any zoogoer could have pointed out years ago: Depriving animals of a natural life, both socially and physically, causes them to behave in disturbing ways, ways that might be labeled "crazy." For a truly impoverished existence, it takes a chemical "jump start" and space and activity for a normal life to restore some zoo animals to the majestic creatures they were meant to be.

Solutions

AT THE LOWRY PARK ZOO in Tampa, Florida, chimpanzees use twigs to "fish" honey and jelly out of an artificial termite mound, in the same way they would gather real termites in the wild. At the Metro Washington Park Zoo in Oregon, a polar bear enters his exhibit, and with his sensitive nose (which can detect food at twenty miles) held high in the air, explores his surroundings. Within seconds, he dislodges a shiny red apple from beneath an old rotted log with a swat of his massive paw. A speaker system allows zoogoers on the other side of the glass to hear his juicy lip-smacking and loud crunching. A spectacled bear at the Los Angeles Zoo remains occupied for long periods of time with a special peanut puzzle. The bear hangs out in the crook of a tree occupied with an indestructible, hard plastic boomer ball that has been drilled full of holes and filled with peanuts. Sloth bears at this zoo insert their snouts into holes in tree stumps to vacuum out applesauce and raisins. At the Roger Williams Park Zoo, recordings of wild cotton-top tamarins are played for those in captivity. As they would in nature, the zoo tamarins respond to the sound of an intruder by standing alert, hair on end, and giving their own long calls.

Life can be made a lot sweeter for zoo animals with enrichment activities that permit them to spend a great deal of time foraging for food. Active animals are healthier and spend less time involved in unhealthy activities: Studies have proven that foraging decreases stereotypic behavior. And active, enriched animals seem to grow smarter with complex behavioral calisthenics. Black-footed ferrets raised in an enriched environment were able to kill hamsters more efficiently than ferrets raised in standard pens—and this with no previous prey-killing experience. Shepherdson points out that guide dogs raised in enriched country environments were later better equipped to deal with city hazards than dogs actually raised in the city.

It seems that these behaviors don't just take up time, they also boost confidence and sharpen problem-solving abilities. Zoo animals look for food and then actually find it. For the first time they appear to have some control over their environment, a factor Shepherdson feels is important to psychological well-being.

These notions are hot topics at zoo conferences, but they rarely translate into zoo policies. As I toured the best zoos in the country, I saw only little evidence that anyone was interested in enlivening the scene for the animals. A polar bear sniffing out fruit at Shepherdson's zoo in Portland. Another munching on a freshly cut tree branch at the Brookfield Zoo in Chicago. A tiger wrestling with a ball in a pool in Philadelphia.

Rick Barongi, a former director of the San Diego Zoo children's zoo who is currently planning Disney's five-hundred-acre Animal Kingdom theme park outside Orlando, Florida, says, "Enrichment sounds like a good thing. Someone designs it and hands it over to the keeper and the keeper doesn't maintain it" because he or she is too busy with other chores. Tony Vecchio says that "It's very labor intensive." At his zoo in Providence, saki monkey exhibits are constantly being revised; bushes and vines are changed to make the space novel for the animals. But that means life can't be routine for those who would like it to be so—the saki keepers who feed the animals and clean the exhibit every day.

In addition, it is remarkably difficult to find new places to hide food in small exhibits. I was hiding a biscuit for my dog in the living room every night. But after six months, I ran out of clever spots. The dog no longer has to rely on her nose, she simply races over to the traditional biscuit drops and picks it out.

As tough as enrichment can be, we have known about its importance for a long time. In 1925, Robert Yerkes wrote about the importance of work and play in the lives of primates. In the 1950s, Heini Hediger took up the torch and wrote extensively about keeping zoo animals occupied. In *The Fall of the Wild; The Rise of the Zoo,* Robert Bendiner quotes Hediger as saying, "Many animals turn stupid when shut up in cages and left to themselves. Healthy activity of the occupational therapy sort can be a real benefit to them."

John Seidensticker of the National Zoo has written that Hediger grew frustrated by 1970 because his ideas were so rarely put into practice. In a zoo paper delivered in 1978 at the AAZPA annual conference proceedings, Michael Hutchins, David Hancocks and Carolyn Crockett note the aberrant behaviors of animals kept in sterile cages and point out that though Heini Hediger was discussing "in detail" how to improve this condition, his advice had largely gone ignored.

Today, Hediger is enjoying something of a rebirth. David Shepherdson quoted from Hediger in a 1991 zoo paper he delivered, stating that "the standard by which a zoo animal is judged should be according to the life it leads in the wild." We've come back around, full circle, to the notion of naturalness. But in between, there have been some odd and decidedly unnatural experiments in behavioral enrichment.

Singing Bears, Robo Marmots, Flying Meatballs, Primate Poker

IN THE 1970S, Hal Markowitz concocted a number of zany activities, based on operant conditioning techniques, to make life more stimulating for the animals of the zoo in Portland, Oregon. His work and the mechanical devices he created are now legendary, including flying meatballs for servals (a Teflon rod on a pulley system ran at various heights over the heads of the cats; jumping up and hitting the rod would result in the delivery of a lump of "Carnifare") and self-operated showers for elephants, assembled with assistance from a local car wash manufacturer. When the chain was pulled, it activated a tepid shower for twenty seconds. Each week, the elephants were given several opportunities to use the device.

Markowitz also set up a system by which a fish would be shot into the polar bear pond every time one of them "vocalized" into a receiver. By nature the polar bear is a silent hunter, using few vocalizations in the wild. The theory was that the bears would learn to growl into the system, then dash to the pool. But whenever the female, Iceter, saw the ten-year-old male, Esco-mo, lumber into position to growl, she would head for the delivery area and have a fish catapulted directly into her mouth. The device was modified, and over time, Markowitz recorded healthier animals who were less aggressive to one another.

Markowitz's work with gibbons and other animals, who would receive their full daily rations no matter what they did, proved that many animals do prefer to work, at least in part, for their food. Given a choice of being served food or actively attaining it, they will choose activity. In the wild, gibbons spend a great deal of time in treetops brachiating, or swinging, from one branch to another, eating as they go. At the zoo in Portland, the animals spent most of their time on the floor of a sterile cage with pipes and rope as trees. Markowitz implemented a food reward system high up in the cage. When a light flashed on in the exhibit, the animals could press a lever on one side of the exhibit and then swing over to the other to receive a food reward. The other gibbons could steal food, as the female polar bear did from the male, but that rarely happened here. The gibbons learned to avoid being "robbed" through careful timing and positioning. The most athletic gibbon, Harvey, however, often allowed his mother to receive his reward. Later the public was allowed to participate, with a coin-operated machine that would start the device—the zoo collected $3,000 the first year. Diana monkeys at the zoo worked for plastic poker tokens. By pulling on a chain when a light came on, they received the tokens, which they could put into a vending machine to receive food.

Markowitz inspired other zoos to experiment as well. At the Brookfield Zoo in Chicago, tigers who appeared to be feeding at the carcass of a deer were actually sitting down to a fiberglass dummy and operating a lever disguised as a rib, which would dispense meatballs. Mountain lions at this zoo could stalk and chase a mechanical woodrat or yellow-bellied marmot. Capture of the prey meant a reward of horsemeat.

And ostriches that had been working for peanuts, by pecking a key, were accidentally given a trough of "free" peanuts. After eating a little of the booty, the huge birds returned to the work apparatus and began pecking for peanut delivery.

All these innovations ceased in the late seventies. The devices were expensive and unnatural, and their maintenance was time-consuming. Though Markowitz's studies showed the animals gained physically and mentally from these contraptions, critics charged that the animals were merely being rewarded for new abnormal behaviors. Mountain lions could hunt prey in zoos two hundred times a day, according to Colin Tudge in *Last Animals at the Zoo,* which they would never do in the wild. Eventually, these behaviors became tricks, which, repeated over and over, continued to exercise the animal physically but provided no novel problems to solve. Furthermore, the animals often outsmarted the machines. Jeremy Cherfas reports in *Zoo 2000* that a kiwi (a chicken-sized flightless bird) blocked up a sensor hole in its feeding machine, which resulted in the continuous dispensing of an endless supply of worms.

Today, zoos are still struggling to enrich the lives of animals. In the case of primates, the devices seem much more sophisticated, but for big cats, some of Markowitz's old ideas are being revived.

Enrichment, Nineties Style

ENRICHMENT MIGHT not have the highest priority at today's zoos, but many people are working, even on an informal basis, to make life better for captive animals. At one end of the spectrum is David Shepherdson, employed full-time in Portland as an enrichment expert, and his colleague Jill Mellen, who are focused on naturally unlocking the mysteries of reproduction. At the other end, Georgia

Doris, a toy designer at Mattel Corporation, volunteers her expertise to help with enrichment at the Los Angeles Zoo by, among other things, designing a cricket dispenser for the long-muzzled primates called drills.

This field can't be formulized with static rules—enrichment needs to evolve, as the environment does for wild animals. People can map basic concepts and create neat devices, but no one can institutionalize or write a formula for creativity. The work is intense and ever-changing, and it is among the most interesting in the zoo world right now.

How do we decide which animals need enrichment? Clearly, highly intelligent and social animals, like chimps or elephants, require special treatment. The need is also clear for opportunists— cunning animals like polar bears, sea otters or mongooses who, in the wild, explore a territory, take advantage of different feeding opportunities and appear to learn from experience. Surprisingly, however, even the lowly wildebeest benefits from enrichment. In the wild, most hoofed animals spend as much as a third of the day foraging, but in captivity they are often fed nutritionally balanced concentrates. Shepherdson has written that this may account for "abnormal behaviors seen in captive ungulates, such as licking of fences and stereotypic lip, neck and tongue movements." These animals benefit from chances to forage—hay, straw, leaves, even branches whose bark can be stripped away. Shepherdson also reports that many ungulates will play with or manipulate small logs or plastic balls left in enclosures. The bottom line is that all animals in captivity need enrichment.

And the way to provide that enrichment can be very complex (mechanical lures for big cats) or absurdly simple (dirt for a digging animal). It can involve foraging activities (hiding food in the enclosure) or it can simulate natural light conditions. Sometimes the conclusions of scientists seem shockingly obvious. Shepherdson wrote in 1991 about the "large, significant and very positive effect" on the life of a small Asian fishing cat when her pool was stocked with live fish.

Another development is the mixing of species that would come into contact with one another in the wild, allowing more efficient use of space within an exhibit (treetop inhabitants in with land dwellers). It increases the chances for the zoogoer to observe species with different activity periods, and it offers unique opportunities for interspecies interaction. In the gelada exhibit at the Bronx, baboons, Nubian ibex, rock hyrax, blue-winged geese, Cape teal and other waterfowl coexist peacefully and simulate the Afro-alpine life zone of the Ethiopian highlands. A mixed-species exhibit is a more comprehensive and realistic glimpse of nature. It communicates better to the zoogoer how the world actually functions.

But as anyone with a dog and a cat knows, zoos need to be careful when mixing species, because the enclosure forces animals to associate more closely than they would in the wild. At the Henry Doorly Zoo in Omaha, I watched a gibbon harassing a hornbill whose wings had been clipped. The gibbon chased the bird and occasionally got close enough to pull some feathers. The harried hornbill could not fly away, as it would in nature, or find any safe haven from the agile primate. The gibbon's enrichment came at the expense of the hornbill.

The National Zoo reports rock cavies attacking marmosets; marmoset-on-marmoset violence: black-tail marmosets bullying pygmy marmosets; and black-tail marmosets ousting dusky titi monkeys from their treetop perches. At the Brookfield Zoo, zebras bullied topi antelope, pursuing the animals around the exhibit. The topis joined the giraffes at the more peaceful watering hole habitat.

Today, zoos are playing with a new notion: exhibit rotation, in which various species would be alternated in exhibits to create what one proponent calls "habitat theater." Rotation would offer stimulating scents and a varied environment, though it also has the potential to transmit disease.

It may simply not be possible to simulate the surprise of the wild without risk, but that is precisely what zoos are trying to do. Interaction, novelty, foraging competition are all part of what keep wild animals sharp, but obviously those elements can mean disease, injury or starvation to some. Can life be exciting and risk-free? Enrichment experts hope the answer is yes.

Large Carnivores

WE CAME UPON the two young male cheetahs, probably brothers, just before the searing heat of the afternoon blanketed the flat Serengeti Plain. They were lying down when we arrived, but grew restless. A handful of impala stood a hundred yards off, facing the cats. The cheetahs ambled in different directions, rejoined one another and nuzzled. They appeared quite casual. But without warning they bolted, two spotted arrows churning dust up over the scrubby green terrain. The impala were too far away and much too alert and both cheetahs flopped down, chests heaving after sprinting a short distance.

Common sense would dictate that zoo cheetahs, as capable as their wild kin of seventy-mile-an-hour sprints, should be given a sporting chance to run. And lure coursing is a good solution. This equipment, which races a lure around a zigzagging course, has been used for years to run sight hounds such as greyhounds, salukis, whippets and even huge Irish wolfhounds. The apparatus is fairly simple and consists of a motor and up to a half mile of fishing line, looped around pulleys staked into the ground. The lure is often just a simple plastic bag. The course's layout can be changed often and with ease. The Brookfield Zoo employs pieces of meat or fur to lure course its wild dogs. The National Zoo uses a traditional plastic strip lure to coax its cheetah to run up to thirty-five miles an hour.

Running after plastic is certainly not the same as hunting, but it appears that hunting does not come naturally to many cheetahs. Tony Vecchio, director of the Roger Williams Park Zoo in Providence, Rhode Island, tells the story of another zoo that put rabbits into the cheetahs' pen when the zoogoers had gone home. It was awful, Vecchio relates: These cheetahs were unskilled hunters, and the rabbits screamed as the inefficient killers scratched and bit them. Today, at Vecchio's zoo, you will find a large gunite mound (which camouflages nighttime pens inside) in the otherwise grassy cheetah exhibit. As they would in the wild on a termite mound, the two male cheetahs here climb this rock to scan the horizon (and even to defecate high up, as free cheetahs do). Cheetahs hunt by sight, and this elevated area is one simple enrichment device they use often.

In other big cats, the hunting instinct may be quite sharp, but clearly the public would not stand for live prey animals. But there are other ways to motivate cats. Food can be hidden around enclosures. Tigers enjoy plastic boomer balls. And even catnip can enrich an environment.

During a workshop on behavioral enrichment, one group of participants took rope and hung a hunk of meat still on the bone inside the tiger enclosure in a zoo in Guatemala. "And," Shepherdson says, "one of the tigers just raced out as soon as it was released and latched onto it, growling fiercely, just like it was catching prey, and hung on to it for about thirty minutes and wouldn't let go. Every time the other one came near, it would start growling and tearing at it again. And he couldn't get it down, but just clung on to it." It was stimulating for that tiger and very impressive for the people watching. Shepherdson says it was probably one of the few times zoogoers saw a tiger "showing its ferocity and strength." We don't do that sort of thing in the United States, Shepherdson says, because of fears of injury—the tiger could "get its claws stuck or eat the rope"—or because the public may object, "which I think is ridiculous."

Introducing novel items to animals is a typical enrichment scheme, but, surprisingly, it often backfires. Shepherdson says he put live trout in a pool for a female tiger, and the huge beast didn't even notice the fish. "So we reduced the level of the pool," Shepherdson says, until "there was only six inches of water left. She finally went into the pool and the trout started swimming towards her . . . she was terrified." The researcher says he is "constantly surprised by how frightened animals are of new things." On another day, a white bucket in the penguin pool spooked the whole group of tuxedoed birds.

Animals are individuals, and once again, we see that enrichment experts must attempt to mimic the endless variety of stimuli in the environment and then tailor activities to the sometimes surprising capabilities of their captives. Vecchio marvels at the strength, agility and assurance of his cheetahs. Hardly dulled-out zoo cats, these animals have sailed over barriers constructed to common cheetah enclosure standards. These impressive animals have been found surveying the zoo from the roof of a visitor viewing area outside their enclosure, and they have dispatched live chickens like skilled predators. The spirit and spunk of the Serengeti cheetahs is alive and well in Providence.

Bears Go with the Floe

ARGUABLY THE TOUGHEST captives at the zoo, polar bears are clever, no-nonsense hunters who have adapted to harsh Arctic life. Among all the animals in the zoo, this is the one keepers say they can count on to kill—quietly, efficiently, in a heartbeat. They are massive animals—weighing 1,500 pounds, and standing 12 feet on their hind legs. They can gallop at 35 miles per hour on heavily furred feet bigger than a human head (9 by 12 inches and weighing 40 pounds) and engineered with skid-proof pads covered in soft papillae. They can kill a 500-pound seal with one swipe of these massive paws and eat 150 pounds a day. Polar bears have 4 inches of blubber in some places to fend off the cold. They are great navigators who can swim 60 miles straight or walk great distances—even a female with cubs can cover about 20 miles a day. Their eyes are somehow impervious to snowblindness (it is not from a third eyelid, as some have reported). And though a polar bear's eyesight is as good as a human's, the bear relies on a sharp sense of smell. During seasonal periods of starvation, it is believed they switch their metabolism over to an internal hibernation, which frugally closes the loop and recycles waste material so even while burning body fat they continue to build lean body mass and bone.

It is also believed that with their black skin and transparent hair (it reflects visible light and appears white), they may in fact be efficient collectors of solar energy.

Polar bears are smart, learning from mistakes and maximizing every opportunity to feed. By any standard they are magnificent creatures built for an endless land where snowy earth meets the seemingly frozen sky. The lion may no longer be considered king of the jungle, but in the forbidding and frigid world of the ice cap, the polar bear still reigns supreme.

But few zoogoers have this impression of the polar bear. Our urban picture of the polar bear is not so handsome. The Arctic Circle appears desolate to us, so we create a barren and sterile cage for polar bears—a rough surface painted white and a swimming pool. In captivity, polar bears pace, rock and bob their heads.

David Shepherdson has some interesting ideas on the subject. First, staggering the bears' feeding time cuts down on the pacing that builds up around a single feeding time. Hiding fruit or even chopped vegetables can occupy this problem-solving predator. Keepers can toss mackerel, frozen in blocks of ice, into the pool. And polar bears even enjoy toys like hard plastic floats or boomer balls.

Sue Pressman, an animal welfare lobbyist, tells the story of watching, with a friend and a zoo director, a polar bear pacing near his bathtub-sized pool. The zoo director defended the scene by saying it wasn't known scientifically how much space a bear requires to live and swim. "I'm just a housewife," Pressman's friend ventured, "but I'd guess he should at least be able to do a stroke or two." Shepherdson says he has not seen a polar bear exhibit that works, but thinks it is possible to build one. "It would probably be very expensive," he adds, "but I'd pretty much give them an exhibit that you'd think of more as a brown bear exhibit than a polar bear exhibit—a big area of dirt and trees and stuff and a pond. You wouldn't be able to have underwater viewing because it would be dirty." Shepherdson points out that polar bears are closely related to brown bears and show some similar behaviors in summer, such as digging. Colin Tudge reports that one female polar bear at the Edinburgh Zoo even climbed trees when she was put into the brown bear enclosure. If zoos can't offer polar bears hundreds of miles and live prey, they must at least provide some alternative stimulation. But Shepherdson's suggestion would mean building an exhibit for the bears and not the public. And that's the rub. So far, zoos have been more interested in presenting the "look" of the Arctic than in enhancing life for the bears. Aesthetic naturalism wins over functional naturalism.

Early polar bear cages had cement floors and steel cages. Today, the better enclosures, such as the one at New York's Central Park Zoo, offer places to hide and include water and vegetation.

But there are other factors. Polar bears may need an expansive view of their surroundings. At the small New England Science Center in Worcester, Massachusetts, two polar bears have failed to develop the stereotypic pacing from which so many suffer. It is believed that their enclosure, placed high on the side of a hill and affording a panoramic view of the surrounding area, may be the very accidental key to success.

The Port Defiance Zoo in Tacoma, Washington, is often cited as having the best polar bear exhibit in the country. The large enclosure contains a rushing stream, sand and gravel areas and a deep pool. A huge window permits visitors to stand right next to a massive polar bear and even to smell the fish on his breath through an open panel high above. Even here, though, the stereotypic behavior of one bear remains firmly entrenched. So even the best polar bear exhibit in America does not appear to be good enough. Tudge and others believe a good polar bear exhibit would cover several acres and have hills and trees, some portion off public viewing, dirt and grass for digging and a pool for swimming. As yet, no zoo is rushing to lavish such space, money and time on its polar bears.

But all bears are tough to keep in captivity. When I complained to Roger Caras, naturalist and author of more than sixty books on animals, about the dismal bear enclosures at the Cincinnati Zoo, he asked, "Have you seen any bear exhibits you thought were good?" The answer, at the time, as he knew it would be, was no, though later a brand-new bear exhibit at the Woodland Park Zoo in Seattle would stun me and the zoo professionals who came to see it.

In the wild, brown bears, black bears and sloth bears spend a great deal of time exploring, foraging and eating a wide variety of foods. In captivity, generally, there is no room to roam, nothing to dig or root around in and no dispersed foods to seek out, just a once-daily, unappetizing lump of feed called omnivore chow.

This is an issue that John Seidensticker, curator of mammals at the National Zoo, has explored (with Kathy Carlstead and Robert Baldwin) in articles in scientific journals such as *Zoo Biology* and *Behavioral Processes*. One article begins simply and to the point: "The high incidence of stereotypic behaviors in zoo bears suggests that the environment of these animals lacks essential stimuli for guiding normal behavior." It is estimated that about 60 percent of zoo bears exhibit these troubling behaviors. Seidensticker points out that American black bears spend up to eighteen hours a day foraging. Brown bears in Europe are active 45 to 60 percent of the time, both day and night. And 94 percent of a North American brown bear's active time is spent foraging. We take these active and curious opportunists and put them into small, empty boxes. Seidensticker found that bears at the National Zoo were active the same amount of time as their wild counterparts, but the bulk of their activity was spent grimly pacing (40 to 60 percent) not exploring or foraging (12 to 20 percent). Seidensticker says that even if we can't change enclosures overnight, we can transform them through more creative feeding. The current system—a boring, unvarying diet, often fed in one portion—does not encourage healthy foraging activity, but it is the cheapest and easiest way to feed a bear. According to a Seidensticker study, 83 percent of zoos nourish their bears in this way. "Only 8 of 67 zoos feed in the manner most time-consuming for bears: scattering food thoughout the exhibit up to 3 times daily." In the wild, being an omnivore means enjoying a dazzling menu with a wide variety of foods whose availability shifts seasonally—fruits, nuts, acorns, berries and insects.

Seidensticker recommends feeding bears in a more natural way, smaller portions of a more varied diet, with food placed in ways that take into account real bear behavior: "Black bears use the forepaws and claws for digging, raking, debarking trees, lifting and turning over objects, or for delivering a killing slap to small animals or insects." Brown bears unearthing roots and tubers dig with forepaws and plow with their noses. They hunt small mammals by excavating and chasing them. Sloth bears dig and tear open logs or termite mounds, and they climb fruit and honeycomb-bearing trees using their huge claws. Their rubbery lips help them to suck insects out of their colonies.

Seidensticker's experiments with food dispersal proved what makes sense intuitively. When food is hidden, bears explore and forage more—much more, in fact—and pace less.

Despite the unnatural setting, bears may be quite eager to act in a natural way. Seidensticker has noticed a fascinating seasonal shift in the activity of a male American black bear at the National Zoo. In late spring, free-ranging bears search for mates; they switch gears in late summer and fall to forage in preparation for winter. The National Zoo's bear seems to hear the call of the wild: He orients his pacing outward from the exhibit from May through July in what appears to be patrolling and mate-seeking behavior; then in late summer and fall, the time to forage in preparation for denning, the animal directs his pacing toward the area where the keeper approaches to feed. The bear's internal clock and instincts may be intact, but he cannot respond appropriately.

What Seidensticker and others see is that the zoo bear is not hopelessly detached from natural behaviors. Our captives are endowed with wild impulses and urges that must be freed from captive restraints.

Clouded Leopards

ELUSIVE IN THE WILD and enigmatic in captivity, the clouded leopard presents an urgent and dangerous problem for zoos. For these squat, arboreal cats, the unnatural zoo setting can be deadly. "For reasons we don't understand," says Portland's Jill Mellen, "there is high incidence of the males killing the females and it seems to be in association with courtship. The males are almost twice as big as the females."

This lethal activity appears confined to captivity, but studying these secretive, twilight hunters in the wild is difficult. In nature, a nonreceptive female could escape the much heavier male by scrambling up to the thinnest branches at the top of the tree that would not support the male. In the zoo, exhibit furniture is sturdily built and made to last. A terrified female cannot escape.

Biologically, clouded leopards possess characteristics of both big cats (little grooming activity, posture at rest) and small cats (they cannot roar). Little is known about their social behavior in the wild. In this unenlightened state, there is no doubt it will take us a long time to learn how to provide natural and stimulating environments for them in zoos.

All Animals Need Enrichment

THERE ARE PLENTY OF enrichment devices to go around for all sorts of animals. The Antwerp Zoo employs an air gun to disperse live crickets in the fennec fox enclosure. A simple mealworm dispenser (tubing with holes drilled into it and filled with mealworms, meal and sawdust) was suspended from the roof of an enclosure for meerkats (social members of the mongoose family) at the London Zoo, and digging and foraging behavior tripled for these exotic-looking, busy animals. Spending 37 percent of their time this way, they behave like wild meerkats. Shepherdson tells the story of a female kinkajou (a Central and South American member of the raccoon family with a prehensile tail) at the London Zoo who spent most of her time neurotically "chasing around in circles." Shepherdson hung apples from strings, and the kinkajou had to climb up and reach with her tail to secure the fruit. This simple idea cut her pacing down tenfold—from 60 percent of her time to just 6 percent. These enrichment tricks make the animals see their enclosure in a whole new way—even after the treats are gone.

For primates, the Bronx Zoo takes several approaches, according to primatologist Colleen McCann and her colleagues in a paper delivered at a national zoo conference. They try to keep the animals in "as spacious as possible naturalistic enclosures," occasionally alter elements of the environment, provide enrichment even in night cages the public doesn't see, create natural social groupings (more than 75 percent of various primates live in some sort of social grouping) and feed them in a way that encourages foraging.

The gelada baboons graze over two acres of boulder-strewn hillside, spending almost as much time feeding in this exhibit as they would in the wild. Every spring, the white-handed gibbons have a new environment to explore when they leave their indoor winter area for a naturalistic outdoor one. A couple of times a week, marmosets and tamarins are treated to mealworms. They also have gum arabic (a favored food item) painted along branches and vines. Lorises can capture live prey in the form of crickets. The huge baboon exhibit is filled with various grasses and seeds. For silvery marmosets, a feeder constructed of PVC pipe with holes drilled into it stimulated a 33.3 percent increase in activity.

Natural social groupings work themselves out. Slow lorises are housed individually, in breeding pairs or in mother-offspring groups; monogamous tamarins in breeding pairs; and the gelada baboons in three mixed-sex groups.

THERE HAVE BEEN plenty of harmless failures along the way as well. At the Los Angeles Zoo, keepers placed raisins and seeds in between the pages of books and magazines for the chimpanzees to slowly leaf and pick through. The smart apes simply shook the books out and scooped up the treats. Busch Gardens installed a run to exercise their cheetahs, who even then couldn't be coaxed beyond a brisk trot. And Providence's Tony Vecchio reports that when he hid treats throughout a baboon exhibit in another zoo, "they would race through as fast as they could, grabbing the food. You've got a whole troop of baboons and they are competing with each other for what they know is a very limited number of food items. I would spend more time hiding stuff for the baboons than they would finding it."

There have been a few more harmful ones. Tudge tells the story of chimps in an unnamed American zoo who were given a peanut puzzle. By poking their fingers through drilled holes, chimps could move the peanuts down to a drop-out hole. Dominant chimps loved it and their stereotypic behavior was reduced. Lower-ranking chimps never maneuvered themselves close enough to play with the puzzle and, perhaps in frustration, their stereotypic behavior worsened.

The Great Apes

GENETICALLY SPEAKING, DNA analysis reveals there is only a one to 2 percent difference between humans and great apes. Besides humans, only chimps and orangutans can identify themselves in a mirror. One of the things that we thought separated us was tool use; now, through Jane Goodall, we know better: Chimps, captive gorillas and orangutans all use tools. Physically, behaviorally and emotionally, they seem more and more like us all the time: Just watch young chimps tickling, giggling and chasing one another. They can be smart, social, altruistic, deceptive, aggressive and always complicated. In their furless, expressive faces, we see glimpses of ourselves. In captivity or the wild, they have startled researchers with unbelievable behaviors that provide a portal into their complex minds.

Great apes have been taught to use sign language, and many have coined phrases for things absent from their acquired vocabulary. They can link two or more old words together to name a new item. Chimpanzees have dubbed watermelon "drink fruit," a hot radish "hurt-cry food," Alka-Seltzer a "listen drink" and a Brazil nut "rock berry." An orangutan called contact lens solution "eye drink." Gorillas have used "white tiger" for zebra, "eye hat" for a mask and "bottle necklace" for the plastic rings holding a six-pack of soda together.

Jane Goodall has introduced us to a number of unforgettable simian characters. There was old Flo, the ragged-eared embodiment of motherhood. This doting, patient matriarch's death was marked by an obituary in the London *Sunday Times* and, unbelievably, by the death of her son, Flint, who became, Goodall believes, fatally depressed and lethargic at her passing. There was Mike, a low-ranking chimp who secured high status by cleverly and noisily rolling empty kerosene cans before him, clearing the path to alpha status. And Dian Fossey gave us a portrait of the gentle mountain gorilla. In *Gorillas in the Mist,* she tells of an old female, Coco, who "had a deeply wrinkled face, balding head and rump, graying muzzle, and flabby, hairless upper arms. She was also missing a number of teeth, causing her to gum her food rather than chew it." Coco's senses of hearing and sight were dulled and she had trouble keeping up with her group. But Fossey witnessed "remarkable displays of affection between Coco, Rafiki, Samson, and Peanuts." She describes this tender scene: One day, Fossey found the group spread out, with Coco trailing far behind the others. Rafiki called out and looked downhill. He and the others waited. Coco turned and moved in the direction of the call. "Once within sight of Rafiki, the elderly female moved directly to him, exchanged a greeting series of soft belch vocalizations until reaching his side. They looked directly into each other's face and embraced. She placed her arm over his back and he did likewise over hers. Both walked uphill in this fashion, murmuring together like contented conspirators."

Lucy, a home-raised chimpanzee who used sign language, demonstrated clearly that chimps can lie. Lucy had defecated on the living-room floor, and when researcher Roger Fouts asked whose mess it was, she signed "Sue's." Fouts told Lucy it was not Sue's and asked again, whom did it belong to? "Roger's," Lucy signed, before finally admitting she had done it and was sorry. Time and again, chimps have shown that they can mislead and lie if it is in their best interest. They clearly possess strong mental faculties and are even believed to play with imaginary toys. During a time when a home-raised chimp named Viki was using pull toys, she would sometimes appear to play with an invisible one, even going so far as to tangle the imaginary string.

But Lucy has also demonstrated how loving her species can be. Jane Goodall reports that if Lucy's surrogate mother was sick in bed, Lucy would "show tender protectiveness, bring her food, share her own food, or sit on the edge of the bed trying to comfort her." Goodall also cites Wolfgang Kohler, a psychologist-philosopher who studied a group of chimps established in the Canary Islands by the Prussian Academy of Sciences in 1912. He heard the cries of two chimps who had been accidentally locked out of their night quarters in a cold rainstorm. Kohler rushed over and opened the door to let them in. And even though the animals were shivering from the icy water, they took time, according to Kohler, before entering their dry, warm dens, to "put their arms round me, one round my body, the other round my knees, in a frenzy of joy."

Mothers have demonstrated great bravery to save infants, but there are also cases of heroism between unrelated chimps. Chimps cannot swim, and rescues of chimps by other chimps have been recorded at Lion Country Safaris in Florida. Washoe, the chimpanzee famous for being the first to use sign language, saved a three-year-old chimp named Cindy who was splashing helplessly in a moat. Washoe used one arm to hold on to a clump of grass and the other to pluck Cindy out of the water.

In the wild, chimps will clean the wounds of a relative, but in captivity, they will perform these tasks on nonrelatives as well. Captive chimps have cleaned wounds, have removed splinters and in one case even extracted a rotted tooth (a deciduous molar) to help a companion.

Adoption of orphaned chimps is not unheard of. At Gombe, in Tanzania, the female Pallas adopted the baby Skosha, who in turn adopted Pallas's baby Kristal at Pallas's death.

But chimps are not kind to all infants. In the wild, chimps hunt colobus monkeys, baboon babies and piglets. They are inefficient killers, however, and researchers at Gombe saw one member feeding on a colobus monkey who took forty-seven minutes to die.

The great apes are certainly not all alike: Gorillas are vegetarians, and chimps eat meat; gorillas are quite social, while orangs live independently of one another. But within this group we find a spectacular spectrum of behavior. They love and fight and, at least in the case of chimps, hunt and kill. They can be incredibly selfish or amazingly altruistic. They can communicate and understand. They are capable of deceit and can be adept at problem solving. They form emotional bonds, and some launch power coalitions. They even appear to be aware of the medicinal value of some plants. So how do we provide an enriched life in captivity?

One of the most important factors is to allow the social animals to form and maintain the kinds of groups in which they would live in the wild. More than 75 percent of various primates live in some kind of social grouping. Social interaction is arguably the most important item in attempting to enrich their lives. Forming new groups and allowing animals to interact can be dangerous business, but at this point, it is agreed that the benefits far outweigh the risks.

Goodall brings the wild to captive chimps through her institute's imaginative Chimpanzoo program. Sixteen zoos and 130 chimps participate in the organization, which compiles information for use in a national database and devises enrichment techniques for all zoos housing chimpanzees. Goodall herself designed the first "termite box" for chimpanzees in 1961, though at the time, zoos were not interested in using it.

Many years later, while at the London Zoo, David Shepherdson and his colleagues set up a simple puzzle feeder for groups of orangutans, chimps and gorillas. The feeder was constructed with a portion of plastic drainpipe, open at both ends. The animals could insert sticks through drilled holes in the pipe and push the food items to the open ends for retrieval. Aside from sleeping and resting, in the wild, these animals would spend a great deal of time foraging for food: gorillas, 45 percent; orangutans, 46 percent; chimpanzees, 53 percent. This activity doesn't just fill time, it is intellectually stimulating as well, since they must be discriminating in what they choose to eat (the world is full of toxic plants) and they may have to employ some ingenuity in tool use.

The puzzle feeder experiment results were positive, but not

overwhelming. All the animals spent time working the feeder. General activity increased for orangutans and chimps, and there was a slight reduction of regurgitation and reingestion for the gorillas. Shepherdson feels that because of variation among individuals and species, the puzzle feeder could be modified for improved use. The arboreal orangutans, for instance, worked the feeder while hanging on to the side of the enclosure. Their feeder could be placed even higher to stimulate this natural behavior. At the Bronx Zoo, whole fruits and hidden feed in the gorilla exhibit inspire them to scour their environment in typical foraging behavior.

Captive chimpanzees display some common behavioral problems—coprophagy, self-mutilation, repeated regurgitation and, even worse, intense aggression that can lead to severe wounds. Researchers from a chimpanzee colony kept by the University of Texas have furnished their captive animals with some imaginative enrichment devices, and they presented some of this information to an AAZPA regional conference in 1990. The first thing they did was change the feeding pattern, adding a monkey biscuit dispenser, spreading popcorn or sunflower seeds around, providing a finger-maze food dispenser several times a week with peanuts or popcorn, putting high-fiber foods that take time to process and eat on the morning menu. This increased the chimps' foraging and feeding time an incredible 500 percent, which in turn reduced aggression by 40 percent and abnormal behaviors by 64 percent.

Using videos to entertain these animals has had mixed and muddy results, but one thing is for sure: Tapes of other chimps fighting have proved most popular with the simian audience. Not surprisingly, singly housed chimps spent more time watching (74 percent of the time available) than socially housed animals who were separated out to watch the tapes (20 percent).

The group also began to serve the colony uprooted oak trees, which are replaced by fresh ones every six months. This device has elicited great interest from the chimps, who dine on parts of the tree, sit on it, run on it and play on it. Every new tree is met with great excitement, which dwindles slightly over time but never disappears. Even after five months, they continue to use it. The downside of this enrichment device is that there has been one escape "involving the use of a branch," and an increase in the number of corneal injuries, most likely caused by sticks scratching their eyes.

Once again, it appears that there is some danger, some risk, in the best enrichment devices. The stimulation, in this case, is worth the gamble.

Enriching Sex Lives

JILL MELLEN'S JOB at the Metro Washington Park Zoo in Portland, Oregon, is to understand breeding from the perspective of the animal. She wants to stimulate mating behavior naturally, without superovulating or electroejaculating. If the high-tech scientist can be called a sperm cowboy, then Mellen is the Venus de Mammal. Her science is the art of love. But if we possess the chemical solutions to breeding, why bother with the natural mating behavior?

"Because I think the animals are more than just their genes," Mellen says, "and that the behavior associated with reproduction and parental care is really important. Certainly, one of the things I'm real interested in is the ability of a hand-raised animal—raised in the nursery versus a maternally or parentally raised animal—to get along in a group, to be social and then to reproduce and care for offspring as adults themselves. And basically, if you raise them in the nursery, it's very likely they'll be pretty screwed up. So you could have a genetically very sound animal, but is that enough? That's not the animal; the animal is much more than that."

Mellen is trying to preserve behaviors we are probably still unaware of. Animals may see the world in ways we would never expect. Urine marking, which is important to a slow loris, might seem insignificant to us. Oliver Ryder in San Diego believes that gorillas who refuse to mate with one another may be recognizing racial differences that we do not detect by sight but may be able to track with sophisticated DNA fingerprinting. Artificial insemination has not worked with elephants: Perhaps there is a social component to mating that they require. Flamingos need to be kept in large groups in order to pair off, mate, lay eggs and rear young.

Mellen must be imaginative, insightful and flexible enough to see the surprising. She must size up all the environmental, genetic and social variables that could affect reproduction. In examining the enclosure, she looks at size, number of physical barriers, den sites, temperature, illumination, humidity and geographic location and distance from other animals. And for the animal itself, she considers the age, medical history, diet, group size, range in the wild, husbandry style, sex, relative inbreeding, origin and early rearing experiences.

Mellen has been intensively studying small exotic cats, such as African golden cats, bobcats, margays, ocelots, lynx, caracals and servals. These animals have a dismal record of breeding in captivity. In zoos, about half of all small cat pairings fail to produce offspring. So Mellen wanted to know what was different in the case of the successful animals. And she reports counterintuitive results.

"*The* most interesting factor that fell out that correlated with reproductive success was the amount of time the keeper spent interacting with the cats." Mellen discovered that a close relationship between keeper and cat was the most important element in breeding small cats successfully. Mellen watched how the keepers interacted with the cats, and rated them on a scale of one to five—a one for a keeper who never talked or touched cats to a five for those who treated them almost like pets. And she found that the more time a keeper spends with cats, the more likely they are to reproduce. "I absolutely would have predicted just the opposite," Mellen says, "because they're such solitary animals. But in a zoo situation, the keeper is an inevitable part of the cat's environment, and so of course I can rationalize it. The cat needs to feel comfortable with its caretaker."

It is especially surprising since it has been known for a long time that humans can hinder the reproduction of some animals. Zoo animals, especially those raised by humans, can come to see humans as conspecifics, or of the same species. They may be fixated or sexually attracted to human beings. In 1950, Hediger labeled this "zoomorphism." A drill at the San Diego Zoo finds human females—particularly blonds—sexually appealing, and the zoo capitalizes on this to collect semen samples.

Mellen is trying to measure and quantify the mystery of animal husbandry. In the zoo world, certain keepers are said to have the touch. These individuals understand the animals and are therefore treated differently by them. They possess secrets that are not easily articulated. Over and over, at zoos throughout the country, you hear of keepers or curators who've got it—John Lehnhardt with elephants, Melanie Bond with orangs at National Zoo and Charles Horton with gorillas in Atlanta. Young keepers must spend years with these people in an apprenticeship, a kind of initiation. But keepers are generally not paid well and there can be a high turnover in personnel. Mellen would like to quantify enough of this mystery to give new keepers an edge and the animals uniformly good care. And her field is catching on. Zoos are beginning to appreciate low-tech once again.

"This is *the* new thing that zoos are grabbing on to," Mellen says. "Right now, we don't know how to look at the animal's environment. We're better with the high tech; we're better at looking at the genetic components; we're better at the physiology. To figure out what is necessary in the animal's environment to make it reproduce, we don't know. I like to talk about the art and the science of animal management. And I very much respect the art of animal management because I've worked with some keepers who have this 'touch' that I don't know that they can even describe, but it's wonderful to watch. And I admire that very much, and I don't want to take away the art of animal management, but I want to add the science. I want to figure out how to measure what that person is doing so that I can transfer that information to another zoo without saying, OK, you have to follow in Gordon Noyes's footsteps for twelve years to learn everything he understands about bears. We're going to run out of time doing it that way.

"We're trying to develop a tool because we're really shooting in the dark here. We don't know how to do this. What Devra Kleiman [of the National Zoological Park] says is the reproductive physiologists can come in, they can anesthetize the cheetah, they can get blood hormone levels, they can electroejaculate males, they can come back and say, this is the reproductive profile of your animal. And what we're trying to do is see if we can do the same thing more from a behavioral management or environmental perspective. It's real new."

An MBA at the zoo is quite a different animal from what it is at Harvard. In zoo terminology, an MBA is a method of behavioral assessment, and two researchers at the National Zoo are working on a multizoo, multispecies investigation trying to figure out how to develop tools to look at animal management techniques. According to Mellen, this type of assessment was previously done by the "seat of the pants"—hit-or-miss science. Now there is a think tank convened to look scientifically at four species—maned wolf, great hornbill, cheetah and black rhino—that "don't breed well in captivity. We haven't a clue as to why and it drives us nuts."

Mellen says that some facilities have been successful with hornbills—"We're trying to measure aspects of management of these animals and use statistics to try to figure out what complex of variables correlates with successful animals and which correlate with unsuccessful animals."

Data sheets are being compiled noting early rearing experience—such factors as who were the animal's parents? Did it move from zoo to zoo? Whom did it grow up with? Was it alone? When was it removed from its parents? How many babies were in the litter? How many partners? Is the partner older or younger? What is its medical history? Has it been chronically ill? Whom does it live with? Who lives next door? Is the zoo in an urban area ("We have no idea if any of this matters")? What does their enclosure look like? How big is it? How complex is it? What's the light pattern? What do night areas look like?

One of the most important aspects of the research is the keeper questionnaire. "It's all in the keepers' heads," Mellen says, "and we're trying to get it out." Keepers are asked how they deal with the animals and what they provide in the way of enrichment, diet and behavior. They are asked how the animal responds to them and to others: Is it friendly? How does it respond to new situations? Whom do they like and whom do they not like? What kind of bond do you have?

Scientists are asking for personality profiles of the animals. That may have sounded anthropomorphic ten years ago, but it certainly doesn't anymore.

Risky Business

PREDATORS, PARASITES, drought, monsoon, conflict, disease, blistering heat, frigid cold. The wild is a perilous place. Even a simple cut, once infected, can turn deadly. It can dull an animal's senses, slow its step, separate it from its clan, push it out into the terrifying twilight. Standing alone, an injured zebra signals vulnerability under the African moon. Perhaps the zebra even releases chemical clues to its sad state—perfume to the wet nostrils of a hungry hyena.

Life in the wild is perpetual risk, a gamble of immense proportion. A person who loses half his friends and family members every year might be close to understanding danger on the operatic scale that the wildebeest faces.

A leopard is built for the kill, with camouflage coat, thick muscles, sharp teeth and eyes that transform night into day. But it must also be fit, powerful, disease resistant, cunning and quick. It must be physically nimble and mentally agile. A wild animal who reaches old age has been lucky.

Stress is a natural fact of life, and coping with stress is an evolutionary advantage. However, we have made life safe and stress-free for zoo animals. We have disinfected, dewormed, nutritionally balanced and deloused our captives like overprotective parents. And we have often created the biggest sissies in the animal kingdom— pampered, protected, pathetic. For these sheltered animals, even a slight shock can be fatal.

The zoo world recognizes this, but introducing risk is a significant challenge. How much stress should we place on the animals in our care? Isn't captivity enough? According to David Shepherdson, there is good risk and bad risk. In the wild, animals have appropriate behavioral responses to hazards. An impala can run and a baboon can race up a tree. An event triggers adrenaline output and they react appropriately. Their reflexes stay sharp. In captivity, there are stresses without relief, problems the animal is unable to control or solve. They cannot escape a bullying cagemate; often sensitive animals cannot hide from throngs of passing zoogoers.

So the zoo world wants to differentiate stress, adding a little of one kind and taking away the other—though certainly there are debates over what constitutes good stress. Some zoo people have actually talked about raising zoo animals' resistance to parasites by carefully infesting them. For some animals, such as cheetahs, competition among males may be an important factor in reproduction. Should we allow these precious predators to snarl and slash it out with one another for breeding rights? Zoologists believe that catching and killing live prey can also spark breeding behavior.

Chimpanzees used to be kept in pairs, yet now, despite the higher risk of infection and problems of aggression, we generally display them in larger, more natural groupings. Three groups of gelada baboons have learned to live with one another at the Bronx Zoo, although there were many anxious moments for the staff when two groups were initially introduced to the same exhibit.

Primatologist Colleen McCann has written: "Nevertheless, the benefits of housing primates in social groupings clearly outweigh most managerial difficulties." Gorilla exhibits are now being designed so that rival silverbacks can see one another and display aggressively without being able to do battle.

Patrolling territory is an integral part of life for spotted hyenas. Matriarchal clans scent-mark their turf by defecating and anal gland "pasting." They call out into the night to one another with eerie whoops and listen for the sounds of rival clans. Clashes are brutal and violent. They do not indulge in the bluff displays of some primates; clan conflict is often deadly business. Even if we could set up exhibits of rival hyenas, what zoo would allow such bloody battle?

In nature, predators chase and prey animals run for their lives. In zoos, predators lounge and prey animals peacefully graze. A lion could have a heart attack or break a leg while stalking an artificial game lure. To spook a gazelle inside an enclosure seems mean, unfair and dangerous. Part of the "outward bound" program for golden lion tamarins who might be returned to the wild is allowing them out loose on zoo property. They are taught the hard way that straying too far from the group can mean a cold, wet night spent entirely alone.

In these scenarios, we can recognize the inherent meaning of the word *risk*. In every case, a zoo animal could die. Shepherdson maintains in his writing: "Short periods of acute stress may not only be benign, they may be a necessity for normal behavioral and physiological development. Complete lack of stress in early life can reduce subsequent ability to cope with stress and may even lead to death through fatal shock syndrome." He maintains that a certain amount of hormonal arousal is necessary to set certain mechanisms of reproduction into motion. That may be why gorillas who have never attempted copulation suddenly become sexually active when relocated into an enriched environment.

But how far should we go? Even the experts aren't sure we are capable of great success. Shepherdson has written that for both practical and ethical reasons, we may not be able to provide the kind of realistic captive environment that would allow animals to learn the survival skills needed in the wild. "In these cases, and they may well be in the majority," he says, "we must rely on providing a captive environment that is at least sufficient to allow animals to retain the ability to learn and adapt to new environments."

Portrait of the Elephant as a Young Artist

RUBY IS AN eight-thousand-pound Asian elephant at the Phoenix Zoo whose paintings provide money for the institution and apparent contentment to the elephant herself. She chooses her colors with authority, and her vivid compositions sell for $1,000 each.

One of Ruby's works hangs in a private collection with a Robert Motherwell. And Ruby is not alone; the work of another Asian elephant—Siri—has garnered praise from renowned painter Willem de Kooning. As far back as 1957, the works of two chimpanzees were displayed at London's Institute of Contemporary Art. A gorilla, an orangutan and a capuchin monkey have also been known to produce art. And at Zoo Atlanta, Starlett O'Hara, a twelve-year-old African elephant, is producing works whose $35–$50 prices are much more affordable than Ruby's.

Ruby, however, has won the most fame. She was born in 1973, and as a bottle-fed baby was brought to the Phoenix Zoo. Despite the fact that elephants live in complex social worlds in the wild, Ruby lived alone for seven years. During that time, a succession of keepers passed through, and Ruby had no permanent family members—elephant or human—in her life. This kind of isolation was tough on her and she displayed some strange behaviors. She would use her own grain to lure ducks and geese close enough to stomp them to death and she would masturbate frequently with logs. She began to threaten keepers and treat them roughly.

But then life changed abruptly for Ruby. She was transformed. For a time, she had a more stable staff (though there have been shifts there recently) and two African elephants joined her. No one can measure precisely how much the painting sessions have altered Ruby's outlook, but it is clear that she enjoys them. One of her old keepers said that just mentioning the word *paint* causes Ruby to vocalize. And often, during the painting sessions, she would wiggle her ears, pat her cheeks, pull her nipples and raise her tail; she would also emit squeals, chirps, hums and rumbles—gestures and sounds, her trainers said, that indicate happiness. Today, Ruby has new keepers who work with her in a protected contact situation in which they never go in with her. They direct from behind the safety of barrier columns. But Ruby still paints.

The idea of an elephant painting isn't quite as crazy as it sounds. In the wild, elephants often use their trunks to draw in the dirt, and in captivity, they occasionally mark the ground with twigs or rocks. Ruby had always doodled in this way, but in June of 1987, when one of her keepers saw another elephant who had learned to paint, she was quickly provided with lessons and materials. Within a week, she mastered the basics.

Keepers give Ruby a canvas on an easel and several choices of brushes and jars of nontoxic acrylic paints in red, blue, yellow, green, orange, turquoise, magenta and purple. With her trunk, which contains fifty thousand separate muscles and can weigh as much as a man, Ruby delicately points to her selection of brush and color. She had used different-size sticks to doodle, so it was thought important to provide her with a variety of brushes. The brush is dipped in her color choice and handed over to her. She decides when to freshen the brush or switch color. She decides when the work is complete. When Ruby is finished, she either refuses to select another color or backs away from the work. You can lead an elephant to an easel, says her keeper Sheila Green, but you can't make her paint. She usually spends about ten minutes on each painting.

Over the years her oeuvre has evolved. The more recent ones are considered much more complex than her early work. According to a paper written by one of her trainers, Anita Schanberger, Ruby's early paintings were "composed of smears, but as the activity progressed, the paintings seemed to develop in composition with linear, triangular, and circular motions being noted." Ruby uses as much or as little of the canvas as she pleases and will not be swayed to change her area of concentration. She will also superimpose one mark on another using different colors. All of this may reveal compositional control and visual organization.

Whether elephants are colorblind or not is still being researched and debated, but Ruby does have preferences—red, blue and yellow. When keepers have tried to slip her a color she did not choose, she has refused it. They say Ruby leans toward brighter colors on sunny days and more muted tones on cloudy days. A bright color worn by a zoogoer will often appear in a work done that day. And in her well-known work "Fire Truck," the use of red and blue may have been inspired by emergency vehicles and personnel arriving at the zoo earlier in the day to rescue a man who had collapsed. Ruby had appeared to watch the event intently. When large construction vehicles worked nearby, Ruby went through a yellow phase. Experts point out that it could be the luminosity of colors she is reacting to rather than actually distinguishing color. We are not sure if Ruby sees color or not, but we do know from one examination that she is slightly farsighted.

Why Ruby paints, and why her two African companions show little interest, is not understood. The African elephants rarely participate, and when they do, they create monochromatic pictures without much pattern or organization. Not surprisingly, they never did as much stick marking in the dirt as Ruby had.

But we certainly cannot leap to any species stereotyping. Starlett, Atlanta's pachyderm Picasso, is African. Her keeper, Tom Walker, says that she revels in the attention she receives while painting. And in fact, Sheila Green also feels that the attention is more important to Ruby than the actual act of painting.

Many of us want to believe in the artistic expression of animals; we want a glimpse into their minds. But this is dangerous territory. Tony Vecchio doesn't care for the idea of painting elephants. He believes that it simply distorts the image of an elephant in the public's mind. Vecchio tells a story from the time he worked at the zoo in Atlanta. One day, an elephant there had written the word *Gary* in the sand. Gary was an elephant keeper. Vecchio says they all saw it clear as day, but he knows that anyone else who did not know that Gary was a keeper would have just seen scratches on the floor. The word *Gary* was written by their perceptions and imaginations, not by the elephant.

Schanberger wrote in her paper that Ruby will even ignore food in favor of painting. "Once the materials are sighted by the elephant she immediately approaches the easel and demonstrates the drawing behavior without any verbal instruction or direction. Trials in which food was placed next to the easel have resulted in the elephant completing a drawing prior to consuming the food." Ruby has also abandoned food in order to draw. What is clear is that this "abnormal" behavior has enriched the life of this particular zoo animal. And so the zoo has also experimented with other unusual enrichment methods.

Ruby's keepers also noticed her tapping stones on bars inside the barn and scraping across the grill of the drain in her yard. They constructed a giant, elephant-sized xylophone out of steel plates of various lengths with different tones. Ruby was interested. For the first few months, she really went at it, particularly when the other elephants weren't around. She would scrape rocks across the huge xylophone, or sometimes concentrate on a few plates. She often touched the keys with her trunk to feel the vibration after tapping. But Ruby's interest appears to have waned and she rarely bothers with it now.

Ruby has also participated in pachyderm soccer games. Clearly this and other captive activities are quite different from events in the wild. No matter how naturalistic we make some exhibits, we are still not re-creating nature. And in accepting this, we may find creative outlets that are not available in the wild, which isn't to say these activities are compensatory, or that an elephant is better off trading liberty for lithographs, but as long as the animal is in captivity, we shouldn't turn away from artificial means of enrichment. We shouldn't deny an activity to a creature because it doesn't look natural to the zoogoer.

At the London Zoo, chimpanzees had a burglar act in which they would undo several locks and bolts on various boxes to reach a food reward—grapes. These animals also participated in daily tea parties, which were described by James Fisher in *Zoos of the World* as "a valuable form of occupational therapy for the chimps." There are pictures of just such a tea party for young chimps and orangutans at the Bronx Zoo in 1911. Chimpanzees drove tiny motorcycles and Jeeps in shows at the St. Louis Zoo in the 1960s. And though the practice was ended, there are those, including Hediger, who have reported the glee of the simian participants. At a zoo in Stuttgart, Germany, a chimp used to feed the sea lions. But how about those shows that either capitalize on an animal's instincts or demonstrate tricks that are simply necessary to the animal's routine hygiene?

At the National Zoo, John Lehnhardt approves of the informal elephant shows that take place throughout the day. The five animals line up, hold their feet up, raise their trunks and back up for food rewards. The public enjoys watching the animals, but more important, it delivers discipline and stimulation to the elephants. They are not forced to stand on their heads or dance in tutus; all the behaviors are necessary to routine care and maintenance. An elephant's feet, too, require quite a bit of care in captivity. Calluses and nails, which would wear down naturally by walking in the wild, must be trimmed for zoo animals, and elephants must learn how to hold them out for their keepers. In the wild, elephants do, under certain circumstances, kneel or raise themselves onto their back legs.

Some sea lion shows capitalize on the animal's natural agility and the instincts they would use in catching fish with beach balls. Seals and sea lions are the only animals at the Central Park Zoo that perform. They leap and dive and wave and roll over for their bellies to be patted. Zoo officials say this routine permits keepers to approach the animals and inspect them.

Ultimately, Tony Vecchio may be right. Defining what exactly is demeaning to these animals, which routines distort the behavior of wild animals and what the animals get out of these man-made activities may be too murky. What crosses the line for one zoo director may not for another. Given the choice, animals may prefer excitement and engagement over a human notion of dignity. But perhaps the wisest path is to shun any activities that do not closely mimic those the animal would naturally perform in the wild.

Portrait of the Wild:
Naturalistic Enclosures

IN THE LATE nineteenth century, London zoogoers could throw food at huge bears kept in pits or hand some over to any bear clever enough to climb a center pole to reach the level of the visitors. Bear pits thrived in this century in American zoos, but they are mostly gone now because we have learned that the way animals are displayed affects popular perceptions. Bears in pits were considered clownish farm animals, leading a man to calmly climb down into the bear pit at the London Zoo in July of 1867 to recover his hat. The keeper saved him as he was being dragged away by the animals, who turned out to be more brute than barnyard. Today, most new exhibits place animals either at eye level or slightly elevated from the zoogoer. Studies show that animals viewed in naturalistic enclosures are described as active by zoogoers; those behind bars are seen as passive. Zoogoers walking into indoor facilities are hit by the smell of urine and feces. Unfairly, they may think these creatures are filthy.

We have, for the most part, stopped imposing our art and social order on zoo animals. Moorish buildings or Hindu temples for elephants, mosques for ostriches, African huts for hippos seem silly now. We no longer force the American nuclear family dynamic on chimps and gorillas, who are hardly monogamous and whose social structure defies our sense of morality. And we don't dress them up for tea parties.

We have stopped thinking of dirt as the true enemy of the mighty lion. Unfortunately, there are still plenty of public bathroom–style carnivore houses with tiled walls that can easily be cleaned (in the sixties, Philadelphia even had enclosures that flushed). But now, high-minded experts are toying with various "substrates" and understanding what makes basic sense: Animals probably like the feel of real mud—or grass or straw—under their toes. A paper delivered at the AAZPA conference of 1978 tells the story of a zoo-raised tiger released into a large, outdoor compound at the World Wildlife Safari in Winston, Oregon. The tiger "began stumbling and walking so erratically that it was thought to be ill. In fact," the paper explains, "the animal, born and raised on a flat concrete floor, was having great difficulty coping with a natural substrate having some variation in its terrain." The irony is that these sterile environments were probably unhealthy. The paper also noted: "Grossly inadequate and sterile captive environments—the typical 'naked cage'—not only result in behavioral defects, but also in physiological stress, which in turn can increase susceptibility to disease and parasites."

The ideas of Carl Hagenbeck, the visionary who concocted the first barless, naturalistic enclosures, largely ignored until the 1930s, have been unearthed—literally, in the case of the Detroit Zoo, whose renovation in the 1980s involved restoring plans originally laid out by Hagenbeck's family in the 1920s. Hagenbeck was the first to display animals outdoors, in natural settings without bars. His sightlines were calculated to intensify the illusion of species mixing together and the sensation of coming face-to-face with wild animals. He claimed to have calculated the leaping distance for each species in order to dig fail-safe moats. But moats can be a danger in and of themselves. In the Bronx Zoo, in 1951 a five-hundred-pound male gorilla named M'koko fell into a moat and drowned (despite the efforts of a gallant bird-keeper who dove in and hauled the huge gorilla onto dry land).

Science has finally caught up to the spirit of Hagenbeck and Hediger—two zoo pioneers who were ignored far too long.

The Wild Revolution

NORMALLY, THE fluctuations of the stock market wouldn't affect the life of a two-toed sloth, but in the 1980s, the flush national economy translated into lush zoo environments. According to *Newsweek,* a billion dollars was spent within that decade at 143 accredited American zoos. Across the country, zoos began to tear down old exhibits and design new, more realistic ones. The naturalistic movement was born . . . and though it had a silver spoon in its mouth, the results were mixed.

Atlanta built a $4.5 million rain forest. The Bronx completed the $9.5 million Jungleworld. Cincinnati's new red panda exhibit opened in 1985, filled with Chinese vegetation—Amur cork trees and Chinese wisteria. Sumatran tigers in San Diego were treated to a large outdoor exhibit containing hills, ledges and a waterfall. Seattle devised a Thai logging camp to keep its Asian elephants active.

In some ways, this business boom enhanced interest in zoo life. The Central Park Zoo went from what one former commissioner of parks described as "a Riker's Island for animals" to what almost everyone considers a bio-oasis. It took eight years from the start of planning to the grand opening, at a cost of $35–$40 million—under the smart management of the New York Zoological Society, and bankrolled in large part by the late Lila Acheson Wallace (founder, with her husband, of *Reader's Digest*). Though the number of animals at the zoo increased, from 155 to 450, most of the large animals—elephants, antelopes, big cats—were moved out of the five-and-a-half-acre facility and into bigger zoos. There are still polar bears and sea lions, but they have more space. The new 100,000-gallon sea lion pool is 30 percent larger than the old one. There are charismatic mammals on a smaller scale: red pandas, colobus monkeys, golden lion tamarins, Japanese macaques and river otters as well as birds, reptiles and amphibians such as penguins, puffins, toucans, caimans, turtles and poison-dart frogs. Dark, dank buildings were pulled down, and the new Central Park Zoo was organized into three areas: Tropic Zone, Temperate Territory and the Polar Circle (with animals from the Arctic and Antarctic regions). With elegant gardens and open, barless exhibits, the tiny zoo now seems spacious.

And zoo renovation didn't stop at the end of the decade. Since then, the Brookfield Zoo in Chicago has built Habitat Africa!, a series of naturalistic exhibits set on thirty-five acres for zebras, giraffes, wild dogs, hyraxes, ostriches and many other African animals. Jaguars and snow leopards explore a forest-edge environment at the Philadelphia Zoo. And a majestic pride of six lions can roam over one and a half acres at the Oakland Zoo.

The Woodland Park Zoological Gardens in Seattle won the 1993 AAZPA Exhibit award for its Tropical Rain Forest exhibit. Zoogoers are led on a two-and-a-half-acre journey through sights, sounds and smells of the rain forest. The structure took five years and $9.2 million to build. Now, working with a $31 million King

County bond issue (contingent on another $10 million from the private sector), the zoo is still reshaping itself.

Some basic patterns in animal display have altered as well. Many who grew up watching lions and tigers in side-by-side cages in the big cat house are surprised to learn that there are no tigers in Africa and there is only one place on earth where tigers and (Asian) lions may come into contact: the Gir Forest of India. Some zoos are organizing exhibits according to "zoogeography." Under this system, animals of the new world would be found close to each other—jaguars, tapirs and golden lion tamarins.

On my first trip to Africa, I was shocked to see elephants, cape buffalo and zebra in the same frame of my camera. Visiting postage-stamp-size zoos, we forget that each species does not live in a world unto itself. Now zoos are attempting to mix species wherever feasible. Giraffe, zebra and ostriches might be found together, or baboons, hyraxes and ibex.

Zoos have come a long way, but they still have a long way to go. While there are wonderful exhibits at the San Diego Zoo— bonobos (pygmy chimpanzees) lead an active outdoor life in their large enclosure; gorillas are surrounded not by bars but by the sounds of the jungle in their large outdoor area; and tigers romp in a hilly reserve that contains a waterfall—this world-famous zoo also has a huge complex of the old-fashioned cement-and-steel cages for primates. An African civet sits in a small, sunny, rocky enclosure, but the graphic tells us that it is a "nocturnal thicket dweller." Chinese wolves are displayed in a cement-floored cage. A press release from the zoo says, "Animals are no longer in the old confining enclosures. Call them captivating instead of captive." Zoo public relations, apparently, have advanced faster than the zoos themselves.

The San Diego Zoo maintains a vast collection—4,034 animals representing 820 species (that compares to 192 species in Portland, Oregon; 531 at the National Zoo in Washington, D.C. and 419 at Chicago's Brookfield Zoo). The climate is dry and warm. There are restaurants, concession stands and clean bathrooms throughout the complex. The zoo can be seen by foot, along moving stairways or from buses and aerial trams. And it is a spectacularly beautiful botanical as well as zoological garden. It's easy to see how the San Diego Zoo attracts 3.5 million people a year. But this increasingly sophisticated crowd is disturbed by antiquated enclosures sitting like garbage dumps next to the best in the zoo business.

In his book *Zoo Man,* Zoo Atlanta director Terry Maple says: "The San Diego Zoo has a huge, diverse collection of animals, and people can see a great variety in one place. But a huge collection has its downside. It's not possible to give every animal a wonderful living experience when you have so many and such variety. In general, zoos can do better if they devote themselves to creating the best facilities for fewer species, and that is what we have tried to do in Atlanta."

In fairness, zoos cannot be transformed overnight. Maple predicts it will take San Diego twenty-five years to become completely naturalistic. Parks in the process of updating can appear quite uneven. If a zoo knows it's going to spend a million dollars on a new primate area in a couple of years, it doesn't make financial sense to funnel a few thousand into small updates and repairs. Zoos, too, fail to inform the public about why certain enclosures remain the way they are. Perhaps they hope zoogoers won't think there's anything wrong with keeping a tiger in a bathroom or a gorilla on a simulated lunar surface.

Illusion

THERE IS NO DOUBT that many zoo exhibits look a lot better these days. But is the zoogoer simply being duped?

Take a good look at the exhibits in the zoo. We are often tricked into perceiving enclosures as verdant. Lush vegetation is planted close to where the zoogoer stands and again behind the animal's area. Our picture of the zebra or the giraffe is framed in green, but notice that there is only dirt and dust where the animal lives. If there is a tree or bush within the exhibit, squint a bit and most likely you will find electrical hot wires protecting it from the inhabitants.

Jungle scenes on walls of zoo cages have traditionally been painted for the benefit of a very visual species—the visitor. The only other mammals known to be fooled by artwork are giraffes. A giraffe at the National Zoo recently attempted to eat a leaf off a tall tree in a freshly painted scene. And at the Brookfield Zoo, giraffes licked painted acacia leaves off murals before the Habitat Africa! exhibit opened to the public.

So who is benefiting this time around from all the high-tech naturalism—zoogoers, or zoo animals, or both?

David Hancocks, director of the Arizona-Sonora Desert Museum, is quite frank. "The so-called greening of our zoos in recent years and the development of what we call 'habitat' exhibits have for the most part dealt only with principally cosmetic problems. We have prettified and merely covered up more fundamental issues." Rick Barongi, currently planning Disney's Animal Kingdom theme park in Orlando, Florida, says, "Landscaping is a big problem in zoos. Most of the time it's out there for window dressing—to just make an exhibit look good for the public. At Disney, we want to use landscaping to benefit the animal, providing shade or enrichment."

Hancocks and Barongi are willing to be more critical than most. When zoo directors speak to the press about new naturalistic exhibits, it is always about the animals' well-being. And clearly, the lives of some animals have been transformed—as evidenced by the fact that breeding successes are on the rise. However, in paper after paper delivered at meetings of zoo professionals, it is clear that exhibit redesign is aimed first and foremost at the zoogoer.

If the zoo enclosure is to be made more complex, we would argue for the use of natural materials, if only because zoo visitors are highly influenced by the aesthetics of an exhibit.   —AAZPA, 1978.

We wanted to mold an exhibit that would provide zoo
guests with an experience as natural as possible.
　　　　　　—AAZPA, REGIONAL PROCEEDINGS, 1987.

Most zoo exhibit evaluation contains a homocentric bias:
evaluating animal behavior in terms of how appealing that
behavior is to visitors, not in terms of how natural or normal that behavior is for the animal.
　　　　　　—AAZPA, REGIONAL PROCEEDINGS, 1990.

A good zoo exhibit is about people, animals and plants. . . .
After the designers, architects and contractors have gone, it
falls to the staff and particularly the keepers to perpetuate
the illusion.　　　　　　　　　　　—AAZPA, 1992.

In an article on zoo design in the December 1987 issue of *The
Atlantic Monthly,* famed zoo architect Grant Jones, of Seattle's Jones
and Jones, discussed his thoughts on the wonderful gorilla exhibit
he designed for the Woodland Park Zoo. Although he consulted
field biologists, and talks about making the animals feel secure, his
focus remained the zoogoer. He says he designed the exhibit from
the perspective of the viewer, asking himself, "In what sort of landscape would I want to behold gorillas? . . . I would want an experience that would take me back to a primordial depth myself. How
did I spend my day some millions of years ago, living in proximity
to this animal."

　Wanting to please the zoogoer is a legitimate goal. After all,
they are the customers, and more important, if zoos take seriously
their obligation to educate and inspire, then they must consider the
feelings of visitors in every aspect of the design. But making life
more interesting for the animals ensures activity, and active animals
delight zoogoers.

　John Seidensticker has written about the experience of helping
design a jaguar exhibit for "a well-known zoological park." What
the zoo wanted most was to create the classic picture of the jaguar

lying on a log, bathed in sunlight, with a tropical river as backdrop. Seidensticker reports that less than three hundred square feet was allotted and that the designers insisted to this expert on large car- nivores that the space was "adequate." Seidensticker predicted, based on previous studies, "that this exhibit, because of its small size, would and could only produce excessive stereotypic behaviors in the jaguar maintained in that space." This magnificent animal was given cramped quarters just to complete a postcard picture for the zoogoer. Such thinking can only backfire. Seidensticker, writ- ing with James Doherty of the Bronx, says, "Visitors, rather than being thrilled, inspired, and learning something about jaguars, would take home a negative message: a big cat in a beautiful but too small cage, and obviously not comfortable." Seidensticker and Doherty go on to make a tough observation: "It will come as no surprise to researchers who have been active in zoos that their find- ings frequently are only slowly or never implemented. . . . Diffi- culty in bringing new substantive findings into practice comes from no actual linkage between those who make the discoveries and those who care for the animals daily or design exhibits." Exhibits fail, these two respected zoomen say, when the characteristics of the animal are ignored. "Unfortunately," they write, "there are a multitude of examples of this shortcoming in most zoos."

Zoo design has changed from the days when it was obviously intended for the zoogoer; now the purpose isn't so obvious, it's much more subtle. The easiest and fastest way to test these charges is to look behind the scenes—at the night cages where the animals spend a good chunk of their time but where zoogoers never ven- ture. You won't find fiberglass trees here, no bubbling brooks, no potted palms with or without hard-to-see zap wires. If you're won- dering where all that cement and steel went, look no further. Han- cocks pointed out, in a paper delivered at the AZA Conference in 1995, "It is still the rule rather than the exception for most zoo ani- mals to spend the greater part of each day in concrete cubes or cages which mimic the conditions Hediger so eloquently argued against. Enter almost any service area in almost any zoo and you step back into the zoo conditions of 1950 and earlier."

A paper delivered in 1993 by members of the New York Zoological Society advocated for enrichment devices in holding areas
and pointed out that back here, away from zoogoers, such devices
don't have to be pretty, they just have to work. They're making the
point that animals need enrichment all the time and one must
worry about utility and not the aesthetics of these devices.

At the L.A. Zoo, keeper Rosemarie Weisz does what she can to
enrich the dungeonlike night area of the orangutans. She uses
brightly colored string in knotted puzzles for the animals to untan-
gle. She brings soft, clean T-shirts and other material for them to
play with and lie on. A bright shower curtain, which can be easily
cleaned, adds a dash of color. The zoo's Tiger Falls exhibit, which
opened in the summer of 1993, has a pretty waterfall and ponds,
installed at a cost of $276,000. But many keepers have complained
that the changes were made strictly for zoogoers. The nighttime
pens remained untouched and the actual size of the tiger exhibit
unchanged. At the Philadelphia Zoo, gorillas actually lost space in
the new primate house, according to John Sedgwick in *The Peaceable Kingdom.*

Providence's Tony Vecchio points to the old rhino exhibit at
the Pittsburgh Zoo as a perfect example. Designed by zoo architects, this enclosure followed classic naturalistic rules. Yet it was
constructed with a viewing area that did not allow the zoogoer to
gain perspective on the small space of the exhibit. Other problems
forced the zoo to cut in a second area, and from this one, Vecchio
says, it is clear that the rhino space is quite small. Vecchio, who
sometimes evaluates zoos for accreditation, adds, "I'm regularly seeing zoos that are actually giving them less space or the same
amount of space, just giving them different space."

And what of the illusion up front? Has anyone really been
"immersed" in a zoo exhibit and forgotten even momentarily they
are in a zoo in the middle of the city? News reporters and photog-
raphers who cover the opening of an exhibit appear to be the only
ones ever fooled by it. They film close-ups of the animals with a
blurred green background; they climb up to spots where zoogoers
are prohibited and film through the foliage. They record the back-

ground noise of jungle birds and whisper as though they're on safari. The rest of us never really go under the spell; we can see the exit sign while we wait our turn in big crowds at the glass viewing area; we hear passing traffic on the highway and we detect the very unjunglelike smells of hot dogs and popcorn.

The animals know the difference, too. A white rhino named Mandhala who had not bred in nine years at the San Diego Zoo was transferred to the Wild Animal Park and given ninety-three acres of roaming area. With space to mark a territory and twenty females to choose from, the rhino sired fifty-nine babies in thirteen years. Mandhala's efforts have helped push white rhinos off the endangered list.

In truth, though zoo animals are lethal to vegetation, in the wild, they use up a resource and move on; nature has time to recover. In captivity, there is no moving on. Animals concentrate all their energy on the same trees, bushes and plants; the same small plot of land. At the Brookfield Zoo, one troop of squirrel monkeys killed every bit of vegetation in their exhibit within three months. In Seattle, a gorilla pulled a ten-foot-tall hawthorn tree out of the ground, yanking the roots right up through the soil. Colobus monkeys at the Central Park Zoo have destroyed every plant not protected by hot wires. Zoos have engineered the solution—as *Zoo Life* magazine put it: "Using high technology to bring people back to nature." They have installed artificial vines, epoxy and fiberglass trees and gunite boulders and protective zap wires. Twenty years from now, zoogoers will look upon these exhibits the same way we look on murals today—as quaint, silly, decidedly false.

"When we provide trees, too often we resort to making them of cement and plastic," Hancocks argues, "deluding ourselves that these create a habitat. Indeed, it is not uncommon to see zoo exhibits built *entirely* of artificial concrete rockwork and referred to as a 'zoo habitat.' "

Terry Maple's solution is as simple as it is sensible. When gorillas in his beautiful outdoor exhibits at Zoo Atlanta began to yank, push and devour all the expensive vegetation ($20,000 worth in the first month), he ordered the furious and frustrated architect to just plant cheaper trees. Big, one-hundred-year-old hardwoods that provide shade for the animals are now hot-wired, but everything else is, as it should be, quite literally up for grabs. Maple says he is no fan of the "artificial stuff" and says that fake metal leaves used to fill out vegetation in an indoor rain forest pavilion at another zoo had cut the legs of staff members and no doubt the animals.

While even IBM has trouble keeping up with technology, local zoos seem unconcerned with the issue. In response to snowy, cold winters, many zoos have created massive, domed and skylit indoor rain forests. They are expensive to build, costly to maintain and exorbitant to heat to tropical temperatures in winter. The Bronx Zoo's Jungleworld cost $9.5 million; Pittsburgh's Tropical Forest, $8.8 million; Omaha's Lied Jungle, $15 million; and the shabbiest of all, Boston's African Tropical Rainforest, a whopping $26 million.

Worst of all, they crowd animals into spaces that are supposed to appear natural but almost always look like amateurish stage sets. Suburban malls simulate waterfalls better than most zoos. Somehow the deafening sound of water ricocheting off the walls of these cement palaces is intended to heighten the sensation of being lost in the wild. When I visited Brookfield's Tropic World, the African portion was closed for renovation. The Asian side was just so much mural painting on cement; ghostly, leafless pseudo trees; painted fake rocks; echoing voices and a few animals. A press release claims that Tropic World "engulfs visitors in the sights, sounds, and smells of the rain forests of South America, Asia, and Africa."

Deep within a dark cement building, the Minnesota Zoo has set up an indoor "Tropics Trail." Cinderblock walls, cement floors and tacky fake bamboo rails make up this "naturalistic" environment. Breathtaking Amur leopards are boxed into a small exhibit crowded with gunite rockwork. A color guidebook shows only close-up shots from this area. These are indoor rain forest exhibits at some of the country's best zoos.

Bronx's Jungleworld is in another league, though, as one curator there told me: "Most zoos just won't go the extra million." Here visitors walk along thick wooden planks inside wide open areas filled with sunlight and birdsong. Lush vegetation abounds inside exhibits and bursts out to walkways. Bronx has managed to imbue a sense of spaciousness and temperature; light and mist vary in different zones as one travels through the building. This indoor rain forest actually smells of sweet earth. And exhibits for white-cheeked gibbons, great Indian fruit bats and pied hornbills are large (though two black leopards, which were confiscated from would-be pet owners and foisted on the zoo when Jungleworld was nearly complete, are bunched into one small exhibit).

Boston's Franklin Park Zoo, which has just regained its accreditation with the AZA, is an example of the worst in indoor rain forests. Because of political battles and money trouble, the project was eleven years in the making and completed at a staggering cost. By the time it was finished, it was already outdated. The publicity department tells us how many acres the structure comprises, but that includes bathrooms, equipment areas, etc. The center habitat for the gorillas is a circle of gunite rock—a very unnatural surface in feel and aesthetic for these primates. The vegetation is carefully placed out of their reach. A deafening artificial waterfall drums all day long and side exhibits are just too small for the leopards or bongos (the largest forest antelope) or pygmy hippos they contain. After all that time and money, the nicest thing is to see the gorillas in mild weather released into an outdoor, totally natural, exhibit.

At Howletts, a private zoo in England owned by gambling magnate John Aspinall, the emphasis is on the enrichment of the animals. Huge football-arena-size cages filled with a deep litter of oat straw and dotted with ropes and platforms and tires and swings look nothing like the jungle and everything like a camp for adults, yet it provides these animals with constant activity. Aspinall tries to hold on to his keepers so they develop strong lifetime bonds with the animals. And these great creatures, who live in a "salad bowl" environment in the wild, are provided with more than two hundred types of food each year. Terry Maple says that even though Aspinall is unschooled, "most of his ideas about gorilla management are sound." The breeding success of these primates is legendary.

The great ape house at Chicago's Lincoln Park Zoo was built in 1976 and is filled with tall, glassed-in exhibits that look like shabby boiler rooms with cement floors strewn with food and thick metal ladders: "modern habitats," according to a press release. Yet Lincoln Park has had great success with gorilla reproduction—more than thirty-six births since 1970—and it houses the largest collection of lowland gorillas in the United States. I stood transfixed one summer afternoon by the antics of a huge silverback, Gino, tumbling and toying with a tiny three-year-old, Bahati. Though zoogoers on average spend only about a minute per exhibit, this scene kept about a hundred people glued in place shoulder to shoulder for almost half an hour. Gino hurled himself toward a mesh wall and mock-crashed to the floor as little Bahati leaped onto his massive stomach. They wrangled and pretended to bite each other like professional wrestlers on a Saturday TV show. They chased each other around the barren exhibit, sometimes the huge male pursuing the baby, often the other way around. Bahati placed her foot over a water fountain and sprayed the exhibit. She ate carrots when the male did and drank water when he did. Then the rolling, wrestling, chasing and grimacing continued. Finally, Gino was exhausted and sat with his back toward the crowd. Bahati climbed onto at him and two tiny fists appeared on either side of the great ape's waist as the two napped in this embrace.

The Best Architect: Nature

DALE TUTTLE, formerly of the Jacksonville Zoo in Florida, got a terrific idea for an elephant exhibit while leading a photo safari in Africa. Tuttle was canoeing his group down the Zambezi when a huge bull elephant mock-charged from a sandbar. The ledge of dirt beneath the animal gave way, and he plunged into the water, capsizing all three canoes. As Tuttle struggled underwater, he saw the elephant swim past and thought, "God, this would be neat if you could show zoogoers!"

His brush with raw nature resulted in plans, which were ultimately deemed too expensive, for an underwater viewing area in Jacksonville's $2.5 million elephant exhibit. Tuttle wanted to re-create this exciting moment by showing elephants doing something that is as natural to them as it is remarkable to us. Though zoos often lean toward flashy graphics or high-tech tricks, the true solution to creating timeless exhibits is to get as close to nature as possible. In the words of Isaac Bashevis Singer, "What Nature delivers to us is never stale. Because what Nature creates has eternity in it."

The wealthy San Diego Wild Animal Park, Zoo Atlanta and the low-budget Roger Williams Park Zoo in Rhode Island are great zoos savvy enough to let nature do much of the architectural work for them. The scene can be enhanced, plantings can be cleverly planned, but grass and trees and dirt are effortlessly "natural." An outdoor exhibit offers an animal choice: in the words of Heini Hediger, a pioneer of zoo biology, between "a breezy or a sheltered spot, a cool or a warm one, a sunny or a shady place, a damp or dry, a bright or dark one."

And it truly provides zoogoers with a glimpse of what they long for: animals behaving naturally. The simplest actions can mesmerize. On a sunny September day at Zoo Atlanta, I was among a large crowd transfixed by the sight of a tawny, lightly maned African lion facing our glass viewing area as he crouched at a man-made brook and lapped water. No one stirred. The silence was only broken when someone in the crowd mentioned that he cupped the water in a backward motion with his tongue, just like a housecat.

Nature has provided things that we overlook in our cages. We get into all kinds of trouble when we place a wild animal in a room. For example, lorises mark territory with urine. In captivity, where zoo cages are cleaned every day, lorises would have to drink gallons of water every day to re-mark their turf. Now we know enough to leave their claims alone. Rhinos may feel confused coming out into a clean yard in the morning after having patiently built a dung heap the day before. And sometimes we need to leave the animals themselves alone. In his pioneering book *Wild Animals in Captivity,* Heini Hediger stated, in 1950, that zoo animals sometimes need to withdraw "from the public gaze."

Natural zoo exhibits tend to provide hiding places for animals. And while many zoogoers may enjoy the look and feel of these areas, many others become exasperated by what appears to be an exhibit without animals on display. The red wolves at Roger Williams Park Zoo are often tucked away in their dens. Director Tony Vecchio says, "In the summer, the red wolves are in a hole underneath a log. If you know where to look, and you wait fifteen or twenty minutes, you might see one lift its head up and look around. That's all you're going to get when it hits ninety degrees." But Vecchio says hiding out comes naturally to many animals. "In the zoo business we try to find ways to make animals visible, but in the wild they're trying to make themselves invisible. . . . The safest reproductive strategy he can have is eat, mate and then get out of sight of predators." Since zoos provide food, that leaves a lot of time for hiding. If all captive animals were allowed to come out only briefly to eat and then dash back into a den, Vecchio says, "nobody would come to the zoo."

The Minnesota Zoo, which originally built a huge wooded exhibit for Siberian tigers, has had to give in to the complaints of zoogoers who cannot see the animals in the dense brush. The exhibit changed; brush was cut, fencing put up and raised walkways built, but the tigers still find a way to hide. On the warm August Sunday when I was there, a tail twitching from below a stand of trees in the distance was all I could see, despite circling back throughout the day. Perhaps as a strange concession, farther down the path, a small barred cage was erected next to a snack stand for a close view of a tiger. Telescopes in the lookout area seem a better compromise.

But Minnesota has also been quite creative in dealing with these opposed desires on the part of zoo animals and zoogoers. Their weasels enjoy a shift system. This gives animals time behind the scenes, and it also heightens the activity level in the display. Each hour, a new weasel is placed on exhibit and immediately begins to scent mark feverishly. Other animals are also rotated this way.

In Seattle, heated areas in the outdoor gorilla exhibit are close to the viewing section, thereby encouraging the animals—at least in winter—to be seen. As one zoo architect pointed out at an AAZPA conference in 1992, "Nature doesn't need enrichment."

Miami's climate allows the zoo to keep many animals outside, but it has been compared to a well-manicured golf course. At the National Zoo, a polar bear exhibit was built in the 1970s on the south side of a hill, catching the summer sun's most intense heat. But when the Louisville Zoo was to receive a panda on loan, they chose a gently sloping area, which contained two mature oak trees for protection against cold winds and a hillside that provided shade from the strong sun. The temperate and tranquil setting of the San Pasqual Valley gives the San Diego Wild Animal Park the feel of the African plain, but that feeling has been enhanced through extensive landscaping. There is illusion here, too—zoo land seems vast and limitless to the zoogoer, when, in fact, there are fences and boundaries.

Fences are needed not only to ensure animals stay in but to keep predators out. During my visit in December of 1993, a marauding mountain lion mauled a bongo (a beautiful, large forest-dwelling antelope). And despite miles of strong fencing, this was not the first or last time one of these wily and wild natives found its way in for the kill. And there are problems within as well as without.

Despite the park's size—twenty-one hundred acres—within two years of the opening, the animals had eaten and trampled the land bare. Fighting the browsing abilities of the animals and natural erosion, landscapers installed a complex irrigation system and hydroseeded large areas with grass—a continuing battle that costs about $5,500 an acre. But the landscaping design is planted firmly in knowledge about animal behavior. The park has considered the needs of the inhabitants in its careful layout.

Zebras happily roll in dust to repel insects, so plenty of patches are left grassless. Black-and-white-striped bachelor groups head for unwelcoming barren areas of the park when they want to be left alone. Foliage in these areas would make them lush and appealing to other animals, so the park doesn't tamper with them and the bachelors get their solitude.

Although zoo giraffes can grow accustomed to eating off the ground, at the San Diego Wild Animal Park their natural instincts are accommodated. Tall feeder poles serve the tall browsers. Tree stumps are left on the grounds as rubbing posts for rhinos. For the sitatunga (a fairly aquatic antelope), the stream provides water, and its banks are a good area in which to hide. And some of the eroded, rough terrain is left alone for mothers of various species who want uneven areas to hide their babies.

The park is working to breed the okapi—a shy and elusive forest animal that looks like a zebra but is actually a relative of the giraffe. These brown velvet ungulates with white-striped rumps and legs are found only in the humid Ituri Forest of Zaire. In captivity, there are four breeding groups—in San Diego (both the park and the zoo), Brookfield in Chicago and the Dallas Zoo. Not known to the Western world until 1901, okapis remain mysterious. It is not known how many survive in the wild, and their export is outlawed. Breeding programs are vital, and therefore the park wraps these delicate animals in a blanket of calm. Okapis in the breeding program are managed off exhibit in a shady and quiet paddock. Even here, any sudden noise spooks them.

Endangered bonobos—misleadingly called pygmy chimpanzees—have a lush two acres to themselves. These smart and sexual primates are a separate species from common chimpanzees (*pan paniscus* as opposed to *pan troglodytes*) and are genetically closer to human beings than to the other chimps. With their human faces and long black hair parted at the center of their foreheads, the bonobo group looks much like a family frolicking at a picnic.

Not surprisingly, the park maintains the best success rate for breeding a wide variety of hoofed animals, with a high—80 percent—survival rate for newborns. There are about 2,500 animals here, representing 260 species and subspecies such as cheetah, elephants (African and Asian), Grevy's zebra, plains zebra, giraffe,

Western lowland gorilla, rhino (Indian, Southern white, Northern white, black), waterbuck, eland, impala, wildebeest, springbok, gerenuk, addax, ground hornbill, Goliath heron, Arabian oryx, kangaroos, wallabies, koala, Sumatran tigers, Indian axis deer, domestic water buffalo, Indian gaur, Siberian ibex and Przewalski's wild horses (most commonly pronounced "Shevalski").

The San Diego Wild Animal Park transforms animal husbandry from science into poetry. A tapestry of earth and sky, plant and animal, woven with an artful, kind and wise hand, its threads spin away from illusion and toward reality.

Baboons in the Bronx

WHAT IS THE LESSON for the urban zoo? Unlike the San Diego Wild Animal Park, which has 2,100 acres at its disposal, the Bronx Zoo is much smaller. At 265 acres, though, it is still the largest urban zoo in the United States. Big and wealthy, the Bronx is also wise in its selection of animals and its design planning.

The gelada baboon exhibit is illustrative: active, natural and alive with flora and fauna. These land-dwelling baboons from Ethiopia are fascinating to watch. The males are huge and powerful, weighing as much as a hundred pounds and wearing impressive capes of hair draped over their shoulders. Both males and females have bare patches of light pink skin on their chests that turn an angry red when they are upset. At the other end, as the *Encyclopedia of Mammals* points out, the "rump of both sexes is also red and naked and rather fat."

One hot Saturday afternoon in August, under the rough-hewn logs of the African-inspired viewing area, I watched a large, visually striking male. His body and facial hair was a dark brown, except for a blond cape that cascaded from the top of his head down over his shoulders and back. His teeth were large and crooked and he blinked often, flashing light-colored eyelids. The bare patches on his chest were a brilliant red. As a female approached, he flipped his upper lip, exposing the pink lining. This gesture signaled that he was worried or uncertain. As she got closer to his rock perch, he threw himself down before her submissively. The two then scrambled onto the rock and she began to groom his inner thigh while he sat back and rested his head against the rocky wall, his head held high.

In the wild, these social animals live along the high mountains and grassy slopes of Ethiopia at elevations of more than ten thousand feet. They are shot and killed—up to fifteen a week—by encroaching farmers who consider these crop-raiding primates pests. Gelada baboons are now listed as a threatened species, and efforts to breed them in captivity have traditionally been unsuccessful. So, to New York, they were perfect candidates for a new exhibit. They are active, expressive and exotic-looking, and they have the most extensive baboon vocabulary of all, with more than twenty-five distinct calls. They are built for harsh weather conditions and therefore can be exhibited year-round. Though they are not endangered, their numbers are plummeting. The zoo is doing things the right way—mimicking the social and physical world of these complex animals. Slowly and cleverly, two distinct groups were established. These animals now belong to a group and interact with rivals. Also, because of the size of the enclosure, they graze a great deal of the time, as they would in the wild.

Because of political problems, the zoo was not allowed to trap baboons in a persecuted area and instead gathered twenty-five animals from several zoos—Cincinnati, Knoxville, Louisville, Baton Rouge, Zurich, Wuppertal, Stuttgart, Rio de Janeiro and Melbourne. Individuals were patiently introduced to one another, and two distinct groups were created and kept separate. Initially, hot wires divided the two-acre exhibit, so that the cohesive groups were aware of each other and learned to exist near one another. Within days, though, the hot wires came down and the two groups have maintained an appropriate distance from one another. And a young male has split off with four females to form a third group.

The design of the exhibit has allowed natural social relationships to develop, and for the grass to replenish itself, despite the punishment it takes from all these grazing baboons, along with their mixed-species exhibit mates—ibex, hyrax and African waterfowl. In the wild, geladas spend 45 to 65 percent of their time grazing, and the Bronx is proud to say that their baboons forage for about 40 percent of their waking hours. Dispersing corn and sunflower seeds as well as flakes of hay takes some pressure off the grass, but otherwise, the large area is holding its own with the help of an irrigation/sprinkler system. Keepers feed "monkey chow" to the baboons in their night quarters. Eight species of grass, including love grass, are thriving, as well as yucca, artemesia and other plants. The exhibit works for the experts who come here to study social behavior, group dynamics and reproduction of the gelada baboon. With its spacious, natural feel and busy atmosphere, it is also a hit with zoogoers.

Instead of seeing the needs of the animals in opposition to the desires of zoo visitors, the Bronx has made the two complementary. Maintaining three harems, for instance, is stimulating for the animals and at the same time ensures that one group or another will be near a viewing area for the zoogoers (free viewing through telescopes is also made available). Allowing these grazing animals ample opportunity to forage is the best enrichment possible, and presents an ever-changing show for the viewer.

This is a far cry from the tragedy of Monkey Hill at the London Zoo. In 1925, a hundred hamadryas baboons were thrown together on a thirty-three-by-twenty-meter island within the zoo. Six females turned up in what was intended to be a bachelor group, and with the overcrowding, sexual tension and breeding, by 1932, 92 percent of the females and 64 percent of the males were dead. Many zoos at the time, however, had thriving monkey islands with better-balanced social orders. Primates led socially dynamic lives in these pioneering exhibits. Most, however, did not have enough space for the natural progression of adolescents starting their own troops. The Bronx has clearly attempted to remedy this problem.

Unlike many zoo conference papers on exhibits that stress naturalism for the zoogoer, Bronx Zoo curator of animals James Doherty's presentation on the gelada exhibit for the 1993 AAZPA

Regional Proceedings, states in the conclusion, "The Baboon Reserve and the animal holding areas were designed to be spacious, labor efficient and most important to meet the needs of the animals." Another group from the New York Zoological Society also presented a paper; theirs began, "The care and well-being of primates in captivity is most effective when management and husbandry methods are primarily based on the natural history of the animal." Natural exhibits work at every level, and New York has capitalized on that.

Urban Oasis

THE ROGER WILLIAMS PARK ZOO in Providence, Rhode Island, has neither the acreage of the San Diego Wild Animal Park nor the financial clout of the Bronx Zoo. Yet, under the leadership of its progressive director Tony Vecchio, this tiny, small-budget zoo is something of a leader in the field. With only forty acres and a million dollars a year (plus varying capital improvement money), Roger Williams has transformed itself in a few short years into a zoo that is spacious, kind and dynamic.

The zoo houses fewer animals to give individuals more space. Cheetahs, bongos, red wolves and Roosevelt elk all roam and forage and hide. Three young African elephants are quite active in their enclosure and search for treats hidden in piles of hay, play with huge logs and even swim. Interestingly, there is nothing high-tech or fancy at this zoo. Most of the exhibits were designed and built by staff members, not expensive architects. An indoor small mammal exhibit (mongoose, naked mole rats, hyraxes) in the elephant building was renovated by one staffer for about $20,000— that's $70,000 less, Vecchio estimates, than if an outside firm were handling it. In the Tropical America exhibit, Vecchio himself installed the original misting device—a pinpricked garden hose snaked along a ceiling beam. The moss on these artificial trees may not be artistic, but Providence has charm and spirit at a bargain price.

In *Zoo Design: The Reality of Wild Illusion,* author Kenneth J. Polakowski outlines proper vegetation for various exhibits. For gorillas, the forest should not be dense, but the exhibit should have "large spreading trees" that have found deeper pockets of soil and "dominate" the scene. Cliffs should be "stained by weathering and fleshed green by mosses and ferns. . . . Here and there curtains of thin-stemmed Akebia and evergreen Clematis will veil the ancient rock faces." For tigers, he recommends "Dense canebrakes of *(Arundo donax), (Phragmites communis),* and giant knotweed will emerge from dark swamp pools. The afternoon light, filtered by the cane, will fall in spots and sparkling patterns among the pond lilies and duckweed, warming a great worn log lying across the water." For hippos, "The vegetation will be a mixture of coarse wetland grasses, sedges, and reeds bordering the stream."

Ultimately, in this century, we have begun to realize that the way we display animals truly affects the way people view them and how they treat them. Over and over, as I visited zoos, I witnessed people speaking reverentially and quietly before exhibits that were truly natural. Just as often, standing before old, barren cages, I saw zoogoers yell, throw food and make fun of the animals inside.

Ted Finlay crafted a master's thesis around studies he did in this area. He showed 267 participants slides of animals in different settings: in the wild, in "naturalistic enclosures" and in cages. According to an AAZPA paper from 1991, "Finlay concluded that animals viewed in traditional cages were rated less favorably than animals in either the wild or naturalistic cages. Zoo animals were seen as restricted, tame, and passive, whereas wild animals were characterized as free, wild, and active. Animals in naturalistic zoo settings received ratings similar to wild animals . . . if no barrier was visible."

The Cincinnati Zoo has developed a two-acre section that is as exciting for zoogoers as it is enriching for the animals. Before visitors enter the outdoor Jungle Trails, they are warned by staffers that others who have gone before them have never emerged out the exit. Entering through the rough-hewn portal, visitors are enveloped in a shroud of mist, immersed in natural-sound recordings of jungle birds and insects and surrounded by tropical plantings, a papyrus swamp and rushing streams. Following mud paths and swinging rope bridges, they observe animals from Asian and African tropical environments—bonobos, orangutans, storks, gibbons and lemurs in spacious and lush enclosures. This exhibit, which won a design award from the AZA in 1994, produces wide-eyed and reverential reactions from beginning to end.

At the Philadelphia Zoo, the sight of Abigail, a stunning Siberian tiger, pacing back and forth inside a dim, green-tiled building was all the more poignant after viewing tigers in the outdoor exhibit. Here, one huge striped cat lunged into the pool again and again, wrapping huge paws around a large plastic ball floating in the water. The tiger would fix a stare on the passing ball, dive in, sink it momentarily and then climb back out onto shore, often grimacing as if about to sneeze. Like a domestic cat watching tropical fish, this huge, wild animal would delicately stick out one paw and bat at the ever taunting ball. Again, the tiger would plunge in, to the crowd's delight.

One plastic ball and a pool of water bettered the life of one tiger and the experience of a hundred people.

2

ANIMAL MAGNETISM: WHY
WE ARE ATTRACTED TO ZOOS

Dangerous Seduction

A T THE SAN DIEGO ZOO, a visitor may find herself alone on the steep and shady path that leads down to the Tiger River exhibit. The vegetation on either side is dense and lush. The visitor is "immersed" in the exhibit, transported into a jungle in Asia. But this jungle is inhabited by tigers, and when a low growl is heard just beyond the next bend, the temptation is to run. The sensible tourist discovers other zoogoers pressing the display buttons of an interactive device that explains the tiger's vocabulary.

Across the country, at the Central Park Zoo, visitors stroll up to a glass panel on the side of a large pool and stop for a moment to gaze into the calm blue water. Suddenly, a beast as big as eight people swoops down, threatening to crash through the glass. The polar bears were so good at this game of "scare the zoogoer" that officials erected a barrier to soften the experience into a more tolerable one.

At the Brookfield Zoo in Chicago, snow leopards isolate certain children and go through the motions of stalking them—all behind safety glass.

Zoos may look very different today, but some Victorian impulses still thrive. We exhibit our mastery over the world with elaborate pavilions that bring the cycles of nature indoors. We thrill at approaching wild animals, near danger yet safely beyond reach. We order the natural world, putting lions in with lions, giraffes with giraffes—each wild animal safe and secure in its high-tech enclosure. We know chaos lurks inches away, and that's part of the zoo's appeal.

But who are "we"? Who goes to the zoo, and what does that person want from the experience? What makes us flock in such preposterous numbers through the gates of American zoos? About 120 million people visit accredited American zoos each year. According to a 1987 AAZPA study, 98 percent of adults in the United States and Canada have been to a zoo. One-third of the public has visited a zoo in the last year. Zoos themselves confront these questions and work constantly to pin down the answers. The Brookfield Zoo even employs John Scott Foster as a full-time zoogoer/zoo liaison. In this day of surveys and polls, we know a lot about zoogoers— who they are, what the makeup of their groupings is, how long they spend at each exhibit. The American Zoo and Aquarium Association compiled figures from forty visitor and attendance studies conducted by a cross-section of twenty zoos and aquariums across the country, and from that work we can conjure up the quintessential zoogoer: a married woman under thirty who is accompanied by a child or children. She has graduated from college, and her family income is $43,000. From several other zoo surveys, we know that she will breeze through the exhibits; she won't read many informational signs. And she will buy snacks and drinks.

According to the AZA study, zoogoers tend to have higher income and levels of education than average, with 38 percent having graduated from college and 12 percent having received a postgraduate degree. A full 75 percent of adult visitors are married. More than half of all visitors attend with children (children make up one-third of the zoogoing audience). The average party, excluding school groups, is three to four.

It is no surprise that we tend to visit zoos in the spring and summer—May, June, July and August. We stay for two to three hours and purchase drinks and food while there. Young families constitute a large portion of the zoogoing audience. The two biggest age segments are children six and under (25 percent), and young adults, eighteen to thirty (25 percent). Sixty percent of adult visitors are women.

We tend to spend one to three minutes per exhibit (just thirty seconds each for reptiles), according to work done in the early nineties by the National Zoo's curator of herpetology, Dale Marcellini.

Zoogoers are enthralled by active animals. "Almost any kind of animal activity doubles the holding power of the exhibit," according to seminal research conducted by Stephen Bitgood, Donald Patterson and Alene Benefield, and it doesn't matter if the activity is "the clowning of the primates or the slow, slithering movement of the snake." We are impressed by size. With all other variables constant, their survey revealed, "the larger the animal, the longer the viewing time." We also want to participate in exhibits. The researchers compared visitors' reactions to two different otter exhibits, one at the Arizona-Sonora Desert Museum, the other at San Diego. Both allowed underwater and den viewing, but visitors in Arizona were able to press a button that would light up the otter den. This simple device "appeared to generate much longer viewing times." Few things mesmerize the audience the way a baby does. At hippo, tapir and gorilla exhibits, researchers discovered that the presence of an infant "increased the viewing time of the visitors by at least 100 percent."

The study also found that people linger longer at exhibits in which they can clearly see animals. They tend to skip exhibits that are close to the exit, especially if they are tired. And they spend less time at an exhibit if other things are competing for their attention. Visitors are finicky about reading signs; big and simple illustrated ones garner the most attention. Brookfield's Foster says that if a sign competes with an animal, the animal will win. As people approach the elephant exhibit, for example, they are excited about seeing the actual animals, and few would postpone the pleasure to read a sign—even a well-designed one—first.

Our perceptions about various species affect which animals we visit. Zoogoers are attracted to animals that are considered dangerous or beautiful (although people often have the wrong impression of animals, believing hippos are harmless or some innocent snakes are lethal). In other work, Bitgood believes that novel animals— white tigers, koalas, pandas—attract more attention.

What do we want from the zoo? One study at the Metro Washington Park Zoo revealed the three most common reasons for disliking an exhibit: "inactivity, dislike of a particular species and poor visibility." Zoogoers want close and easy viewing of animals, and they want to see them in naturalistic enclosures. These two things are often in extreme conflict.

Our society has more disposable income than ever before, and our tastes have grown more sophisticated. Many of us have grown up watching wildlife films. We have seen Technicolor sunsets on the Serengeti; we have witnessed tiger hunting from silent stalk to fatal pounce; we have trekked via video to the most frigid and forlorn corners of Antarctica. So we are repulsed by the sight of noble lions trapped in cat houses, elephants in tutus or gorillas staring vacantly. According to a study conducted by the Roper Organization for Sea World in 1992 ("Public Attitudes Toward Aquariums, Animal Theme Parks, and Zoos"), nearly three-quarters of Americans say that "they have strong feelings about the way . . . animals are treated" in captivity. And yet we are also concerned about receiving enough bang for our buck. Many of us are impatient with naturalistic enclosures that permit animals to hide from us. Documentaries manage to bring us wild animals in the wild, and we never have to crane our necks, push our way through a crowd or wait more than a few seconds to watch spectacular behavior.

So when we walk into a zoo, we have high expectations. And yet this "sophisticated" public we refer to includes plenty of people who scream at the animals, toss food to them, climb over protective fencing and even assault the animals. Not surprisingly, according to a study conducted in 1984, teenagers are likely to be the culprits. Feeding animals at the zoo disrupts their diet, makes it impossible to track a particular animal's feeding record and can introduce disease to the animals—particularly to primates, who are susceptible to many human illnesses.

Even worse than throwing junk food into cages, some zoogoers take pleasure in harming the animals. While visiting the Bronx Zoo in 1993, I saw a small female gorilla recovering from a head wound she received from a zoogoer who had thrown a rock at her. Some of us have not evolved since the incident at the Philadelphia Zoo in 1874, when zoogoers poked a sloth to death with canes and umbrellas.

Zoogoers want to interact with animals. According to *Zoo Design: The Reality of Wild Illusions,* 47 percent expect to be able to "feed, pet or touch animals."

Going behind the scenes to write this book meant I was able to hold hands with an orangutan in L.A., climb into a cheetah exhibit in Providence, touch a meerkat and an okapi in San Diego and blow gently into an elephant's trunk in Washington. Those are experiences a great many zoogoers crave. Real, live animals are the edge the zoo has over TV.

The zoo is a noisy place, with a cacophony of roars, screeches, growls—not from the animals, but directed at them by visitors. Zoogoers exhibit a lot of disrespectful and primitive behavior, behavior that would not be tolerated at the opera or the ballet. Our impulses are different when we're at the zoo, and the atmosphere is different. But zoos need to better sate some of our impulses. Petting zoos should be for adults, too, because so many of us obviously want closer contact.

John Scott Foster says that as a biologist and a zoo employee, he revels a bit, as do his colleagues, in being able to do what the public cannot: get close to wild animals. But part of his job as liaison is to devise ways to make those contacts happen, always bearing in mind that only a few animals could handle some contact, and none would be able to withstand constant contact with their million or so visitors. For some zoos, that translates into a docent carrying a bald eagle or leading a llama out into the crowd.

We crave contact not only with animals but also with the humans who take care of them. When I spoke to the orangutan keeper outside the exhibit in Los Angeles, Rosemarie Weisz, a huge crowd formed within seconds, and everyone had a question. A walking, talking human being is better than signs, TV screens and interactive boards, any day.

Our rational views on animal welfare may have progressed over the last century, but our feelings, for better or worse, are quite atavistic. These raw emotions remain hidden from simple questionnaires; perhaps the joy or terror or awe we feel is an experience for which we can't find words. They are expressed physically—in a heartbeat, in eyes grown wide, in crackling and undecipherable messages racing along neural pathways.

Heart of Darkness:
Zoo Escapes and Attacks

NO ONE WILL EVER know what really happened. Only the killer and the victim had the story straight, and, as zooman Tom Dieckow says, "Neither one is talking."

Early Thursday morning, May 12, 1988, was like most others. Houston Zoo keeper Ricardo Tovar entered the tiger building. One big cat was in his cage inside the building. The other, Miguel, a 450-pound Siberian/Bengal mix, had spent the night outside in a fairly new natural habitat exhibit. Within the building, there are two separate doors on the way out to the exhibit, one in front of the other. Tovar opened and went through the first, a steel mesh door, and entered a narrow space in front of the second door, made of steel, with a small reinforced glass window at about chest level. This led directly to the outside enclosure.

Tovar made a mistake.

Despite rules against it, Tovar placed himself in a vulnerable position while alone in the building by walking up to the window—probably to check on the tiger's position. Because the yard is so large and the window so tiny (only about two and a half feet across), he most likely did not spot the cat and turned away. Just outside the window, Miguel, a large animal with a nasty reputation, spotted Tovar. The tiger lunged at the window, shattering the glass, and thrust his massive head and, it is believed, his right forepaw through. He pulled this full-grown man through the small opening, fracturing ribs and sending a rubber boot, watch and radio transmitter flying.

Tovar didn't stand a chance. His neck was broken. The fifty-nine-year-old veteran zookeeper was probably caught from behind, the cat biting into the base of his skull in the classic tiger death grip. From a second set of puncture wounds closer to the jugular, it is inferred that the cat had to release his grip momentarily because of his awkward position and perhaps because the radio transmitter, which Tovar normally wore on his belt, may have lodged in the small passage. Miguel may then have dragged Tovar out, using both paws on either side of the man's chest.

Another zoo worker came into the building at about 9:30. He saw the boot, the watch and Tovar's cap lying on the floor, surrounded by shards of glass. As he approached, the animal in the yard reared up, his ferocious face filling the window. An emergency call went out. Dieckow, a Marine veteran who had seen action in the Korean War, grabbed a shotgun and was surveying the scene within minutes.

From high up on the enclosure wall, Dieckow saw Tovar sprawled motionless below in the moat. About twenty-five feet away, the cat was relaxed, his back to the dead keeper. "We need to get out of this without anyone making a damn-fool mistake," Dieckow remembers thinking. He scanned the exhibit area to see if either the vet or zoo manager had yet arrived. When he looked back, he saw Miguel gently pick Tovar up by the head—"like a mother cat carrying a kitten"—and drag the body away. The powerful predator who had yanked his victim with such force through a small window moments ago now held him so carefully that the coroner would later report that no marks, no trace of a scratch, were left from this grip.

Dieckow didn't shoot. He felt certain that Tovar was already dead. Shooting at the animal would not change the situation, and if in fact Tovar was alive, he could be killed by a stray bullet. Others by now had taken positions around the area. Dieckow fired into the moat, driving the cat toward the building; another man on the rooftop finished the herding maneuver by spraying a fire extinguisher toward Miguel. The cat dashed into a tunnel that led to his night cage, where he was secured.

EMTs rushed in, only to confirm that Tovar indeed was beyond medical help.

A lapse of concentration or an error in judgment seems to be at the root of another killing by a tiger at the Miami Metro Zoo on Monday, June 6, 1994. According to the zoo, forty-five-year-old David Marshall, an experienced and respected keeper, began his shift at 7 A.M. by heading over to the zoo's Asian area. The tiger exhibit consists of a Cambodian temple replica (which contains night cages for five Bengal tigers) and a two-acre outdoor naturalistic habitat with a swimming pool and ficus and coconut trees. The tigers are rotated so that each enjoys some time out in the paddock.

Lucknow, a 350-pound white Bengal, had spent the night outdoors, and three tigers—young, playful and crowd-pleasing sisters—were scheduled to replace him during public hours. Early Monday morning, Marshall switched these three into a holding pen, in preparation for releasing them to the outdoor enclosure, and "locked down" the cage, according to spokesman Ron Magill. He then cleaned another cage for Lucknow and set out the cat's food. He raised the cage's guillotine door to the open position to receive the male.

Usually, the keeper lures the outdoor cat in, locks down and then heads out to the outdoor exhibit to clean up before releasing the next cat or cats. But for some reason, despite a sign that warned "Tiger on paddock," Marshall walked into the habitat without making sure that Lucknow had come in. The keeper didn't stand a chance. As evidenced by the pool of blood right at the gate, Lucknow pounced on Marshall immediately. Death, according to the Dade County Medical Examiner's report, was instantaneous. A tiger tends to attack from behind with the force of perhaps thirty men, quickly breaking the neck of its victim. In a new study, John Seidensticker has discovered exactly how they do it. Tigers employ a number of variations in attack, but with prey smaller than a buffalo, these cats sink their canines into the victim's neck, crushing the vertebrae.

Marshall, already dead, was dragged about twenty feet into the exhibit and bitten on the stomach, arms, chest and back. When fellow keepers couldn't raise him on the radio, they investigated, and found him lying facedown in the center of the exhibit; his white shirt was completely red with blood, and one of the cat's canines, which had snapped off during the attack, protruded up from where it was embedded in the man's jawbone.

We read of "maulings," we hear cats referred to as "man-eaters," but, surprisingly, tigers, capable of eating seventy-five pounds of meat in a sitting, do not attack out of hunger. They may devour human flesh in the wild, but in zoos, hunger does not motivate an attack. Just what does—territoriality or an instinctual response to quick movement—isn't known, according to tiger expert Ron Tilson of the Minnesota Zoo. What is known is that even zoo-raised tigers are efficient killers.

It is a vivid nightmare from our primitive past—lurid orange and black stripes, glinting white canines, jeweled eyes fixed in a deadly but impersonal stare. Human blood everywhere. The image rests fitfully on the dark forest floor of our deep unconscious. It rustles and moves menacingly forward into conscious thought when we hear of an event like this; our primordial past jumps into our sophisticated present.

Harold Kushner has written that zoos "remind us of our real place in the universe." Terry Maple, director of Zoo Atlanta, calls them cathedrals of wildlife. In fact, the zoo is a house of worship, a place of grandeur. We drink in the grace and beauty we see there, and it helps us find perspective in a confusing world. The raw beauty of nature proves that we are not the ultimate power; we do not control the cosmos. Standing before this dazzling array of creatures, we see that we are not the most powerful, the swiftest, the loveliest. We are relieved of the burden of false power and embraced by the mysterious.

Ralph Waldo Emerson has written of nature: "Its serene order is inviolable by us. It is, therefore, to us, the present expositor of the divine mind. It is a fixed point whereby we may measure our departure. As we degenerate, the contrast between us and our house is more evident. We are as much strangers in nature as we are aliens from God. We do not understand the notes of birds. The fox and the deer run away from us; the bear and tiger rend us. We do not know the uses of more than few plants, as corn and the apple, the potato and the vine. Is not the landscape, every glimpse of which hath grandeur, a face of him?"

The AZA claims it does not track the numbers of keepers killed or maimed by zoo animals. But a quick look around the annual zoo conference reveals a remarkable number of hands missing fingers (many lost to chimpanzees). And Tony Vecchio, zoo director in Providence, says that every keeper can tell you about a number of close calls. He himself vividly remembers one from 1979. Vecchio had spent the morning cleaning the primate cages and was to meet his partner back at the lion exhibit to clean the pool with him. Vecchio's partner was scheduled for some medical tests and had not had anything to eat or drink for at least twenty-four hours. The man, who certainly was lightheaded, had been running late and decided, shortly after starting the task and without telling Vecchio, that they should skip cleaning the pool. So he let the lions out of the holding facility and into the outdoor exhibit, then went to lunch. Because he wasn't thinking clearly, he did not follow safety procedures and left all the wrong signs up. When Vecchio arrived at the lion area, the exhibit door was unlocked, and the sign "Keeper on Exhibit" was posted. The barn was also unlocked with a "Keeper in Barn" sign up. "My mistake was, you should always check your animals to be 100 percent sure," Vecchio says, "but I didn't bother because I knew he was in there." The signs indicated what Vecchio had assumed—that his partner was in the exhibit, attending to the pool. "So I walked in the exhibit," Vecchio says, "and took about ten steps, and the male and the female lion were lying on the far side of the exhibit dead ahead of me, motionless. I didn't notice them until I was in the exhibit about a good ten steps. At that point, the female's head perked up—her ears went up and her eyes got about that big," Vecchio says, widening his eyes. "We both hesitated about a second and I headed for the door and she headed for me and we met at the door at about the same time. Fortunately, the door slammed into the barn, so that when she hit the door, it slammed closed behind me." The weight of the lioness held the door shut while Vecchio bolted it. "That was my closest call," Vecchio says. "I was very scared."

Zoo officials are never eager to discuss a killing or an escape, but zoo people often share these stories among themselves—like ghost stories told at summer camp.

A classic occurred at the Brookfield Zoo, outside Chicago, on July 17, 1969. A torrential rainstorm had filled the polar bear moat, and in the predawn darkness, seven massive bears, each capable of killing a five-hundred-pound seal with one swipe of its paw, swam to freedom. There were no visitors at that hour, but the zoo is filled with prey animals much more vulnerable than seals on the Arctic ice. However, these were the days when zoogoers fed the animals, and the bears headed directly for the snack stand. They ripped open the ice cream chest and cash register. And after gorging on chips, marshmallows and ice cream, they were herded back into their enclosure by a Volvo, a pickup truck and a few blasts from a shotgun.

Polar bears are considered the most likely to kill if given the chance. As one keeper says, the sound of polar bears in a nearby area is "your worst nightmare knocking." In March 1990, at the Cincinnati Zoo, keeper Laurie Stober touched that nightmare and lost her hand. An eight-hundred-pound polar bear named Icee managed to grab Stober's fingers as she stood close to the cage, offering a grape to the animal. The young keeper escaped with just a portion of her forearm. In a court battle between Stober and the zoo, a jury sided with the employee, awarding her $3.5 million in December 1994. Stober maintained, among other things, that the zoo had made the bear hostile by confining it in a small cage.

On the evening of May 19, 1987, shortly before the sky darkened at seven, but well after the 5 P.M. closing, three young boys decided to swim in the two-foot-deep polar bear moat at the Prospect Park Zoo in Brooklyn. According to reports, the boys had originally intended to swim in the seal tank, but on a dare entered the polar bear enclosure while the bears were sleeping. The three boys shed their clothes for a swim, and two of them actually climbed the high spiked fence barring the exhibit.

A woman who heard screams coming from the zoo called 911. Apparently, the bears, Teddy and Lucy, had been awakened by the boys. One bear lumbered out and merely looked at them, but the other raced down and dragged eleven-year-old Juan Perez back up to the den area, while the other boy who had also entered the enclosure, panicked and terrified, squeezed out between the bars of the fence. The two bears—each weighing more than nine hundred pounds and accustomed to eating twenty-seven pounds of food a day—tussled over the dead body.

Arriving police officers found the zoo gates locked and spent nearly twenty minutes waiting for zoo personnel. They spotted two partially clothed boys near the bear enclosure and shouted for them to wait, but the boys dashed away. Once inside, the officers saw the huge carnivores with the lifeless body. The boy's rib cage had been split open, and both legs were already eaten. Emergency Service officers were called in. Police statements say that because there was no way of knowing if there were other children hiding or trapped in the exhibit, they quickly decided to kill the bears. A full-scale barrage ensued—more than twenty blasts from 12-gauge shotguns and six bullets from a .38-caliber revolver—and killed both bears.

The *New York Times* reported that people asked what might provoke such an attack and stated that the bears had never attacked anyone before. A grave misunderstanding of animal behavior obviously exists. These huge carnivores are consummate hunters; there was nothing vicious about the attack to them. They had never attacked anyone before because no one had intruded into their territory before. Five years before, on September 26, 1982, a twelve-hundred-pound polar bear at the Central Park Zoo had already given us that insight. The animal quickly killed a twenty-nine-year-old man who had climbed into the bear's enclosure.

Big cats, like Miguel at the Houston Zoo, clearly do their share of the damage also. Two Siberian tigers at the Bronx Zoo mauled a twenty-four-year-old keeper in July 1985, in the zoo's only fatality ever. No one knows why, but at about 10 A.M., just before the Wild Asia exhibit was to open, keeper Robin Silverman and Barbara Burke, a volunteer trainee, unlocked two doors and entered the tigers' two-acre forested habitat, apparently without realizing the cats were nearby. Siberians are the largest subspecies of tiger and can weigh up to eight hundred pounds. The two tigers sprang from the dense vegetation. Burke managed to scramble up a sixteen-foot fence, but Silverman was attacked and killed by the two huge cats.

Even the most innocent-looking animals can be quite dangerous. It is said that hippos kill more people in Africa than any other animal. They are massive and territorial and have huge saberlike teeth. In July of 1988, a keeper at the St. Louis Zoo had his leg fractured and arm bitten by a mother hippo "defending" her newborn baby. And the panda Ling-Ling, the darling of the National Zoo, mauled her keeper just before Christmas in 1984. The fifty-two-year-old man survived the attack with deep wounds on his back, arms, neck, chest and leg.

Occasionally, zoo animals escape. Most often, their first impulse is to get back into the familiar surroundings of their cage, but not always. There is no doubt that a wild animal on the loose is dangerous, but interactions with zoogoers are sometimes comical rather than deadly.

At the San Diego Zoo, Malaysian sun bears managed to set themselves free four times in 1989 and 1990. During one outing, according to the *Los Angeles Times,* a one-hundred-pound male named Ringo climbed up to a patio area, and onlookers, thinking this was part of a show, tried to "cozy up to Ringo." In May 1994, Casey, a four-hundred-pound gorilla at the Como Zoo in St. Paul,

Minnesota, deftly scaled the fifteen-foot wall of his enclosure and walked leisurely around the perimeter. One woman, who was visiting the zoo with her daughter's kindergarten class, snapped a picture of the twelve-year-old Western lowland gorilla from six feet away before realizing something was wrong. A tranquilizer dart didn't knock the massive ape out, but did inspire him to return to his enclosure without incident.

But we are always reminded that zoo animals are not tame.

On the same day—September 28, 1992—gorillas at the Miami Metro Zoo and the Bronx Zoo broke loose from their enclosures and attacked keepers. At the Bronx, five-hundred-pound Kongo made his way into the zookeeper's corridor, biting two keepers; in Miami, two gorillas, Josephine and Jimmy, slipped out of an unlocked cage and attacked a keeper. Kongo was a twenty-seven-year-old who bit one keeper on the thigh and another on the shoulder. Both were treated at the Bronx Municipal Hospital and released. The huge silverback gorilla was tranquilized and dragged into his holding area after a standoff with the staff that lasted about fifteen minutes. Jimmy, a twenty-six-year-old silverback, bit keeper Kurt Mannchen on his leg and hand. Despite profuse bleeding from the deep puncture wounds, the hospitalized keeper recovered completely.

The gentle side of these giant vegetarians was captured on film at the Jersey Zoo, on one of Great Britain's Channel Islands. A five-year-old boy who had been boosted onto a wall overlooking the open-air gorilla habitat fell into the dry exhibit moat far below. The fall knocked the child unconscious, and a zoogoer videotaped the ensuing drama. What we see on the tape is amazing. Lying in the fetal position, his feet near a rusty puddle and his head resting against dry concrete, the boy attracts several gorillas. The 450-pound silverback crouches over the tiny child, and someone in the crowd above screams, "Oh, no!" The large male seems to keep the other gorillas away and gently caresses the boy's spine with the leathery knuckle of his index finger. After touching the boy, the gorilla sniffs his finger, glances around and sits. The boy begins to wake and stretch. The crowd yells, "Quiet!" and "Stay still!" but the boy rolls onto his stomach and lifts his head, looking in the direction of the gorillas. His cries send the silverback away, back toward the ape house. Two men drop down and haul the boy out using a rope. The gorilla surveys the scene from the entrance to his house.

The child sustained only minor injuries.

A 127-pound orangutan at the Kansas City Zoo unscrewed four big bolts from her cage to escape, sending zoogoers screaming in panic, in June 1990. Eighteen-year-old Cheyenne had been caged there for about seven years and tasted freedom for only about twenty minutes before a tranquilizer dart ended her adventure. No one was injured.

In fact, orangs are known as the Houdinis of the zoo world. They are dextrous, nimble, intelligent, powerful and patient. They pick locks. They unscrew bolts. They scale walls. Orangutans have decamped from exhibits in Omaha, San Diego, Tampa, Seattle and Washington, D.C. Although these apes are generally placid, any animal can become confused and aggressive outside its familiar habitat.

Nevertheless, the National Zoo is opening an exhibit called Think Tank, which will let these smart primates use computers and other tools. The zoo plans to transport the orangs from their living quarters to the learning station, five hundred feet away, by allowing them to climb on cables suspended forty-five feet above visitor walkways. Zoo experts across the country are chuckling over this plan. Everyone has seen what small birds passing overhead can drop. Now imagine what a high-flying, two-hundred-pound, fruit-eating primate can do to unsuspecting ground-dwelling humans. More seriously, many experts feel it will just be a matter of time before these animals find a vulnerability in the system or cooperate to lower a member down.

All zoo animals can be dangerous. A former keeper told me that the sound of a male zebra kicking a female "makes your teeth ache." And Sue Pressman, a former zoo health worker and current animal welfare lobbyist, recalls the trials of dealing with a cassowary—a large, flightless bird from New Guinea and northern Australia that has a naked electric blue neck and a sharp, bony "helmet" on its head. The animal is so nasty that Pressman describes it as "a cross between Big Bird and Freddy Krueger," who can "tear a hole in you from your lip to your pubic area." Pressman had one on the bed of a pickup truck in a crate one day, when it flew off the back. "We hit a metal grate in the road and wham! the box flew off the truck. It's the most amazing bird," Pressman says, laughing, "and now it's on the Southeast Expressway sitting in splinters. The bird was literally sitting on its duff." The animal was knocked silly, so Pressman and a colleague just tossed the cassowary back on the truck unrestrained and continued their trip.

The sex of the bird was unknown, and weeks later, a keeper was excited to tell Pressman that their lone cassowary had laid an egg. "Step on it," Pressman said. "Why?" the perplexed keeper asked, "we only have one cassowary, the egg can't possibly be fertilized." Thinking of how dangerous these birds are, Pressman deadpanned, "Let's not take any chances."

Elephant Handling:
A Deadly Game

THOUGH THE AMERICAN ZOO and Aquarium Association does not track keeper deaths, it does say that one zoo animal, surprisingly, is responsible for more than any other. It is not a big cat. Not a bear. Not a carnivore of any kind. It is, in fact, the much-adored elephant, which can kill quite deliberately, usually squashing the victim with its massive skull in what zoo insiders call a "headstand."

Just why elephants kill is unclear. But we do know that they are hierarchical and powerful—and because keepers at most zoos go into the enclosures with them, they also have opportunity. By most counts, about one elephant-keeper out of six hundred in zoos and private industry (circuses, roadside shows) in the United States and Canada will be killed by elephants each year. Using figures from the U.S. Bureau of Labor Statistics and the National Safety Council, John Lehnhardt, assistant curator of mammals at the National

Zoo, has calculated that elephant-keeping is statistically the most dangerous profession in the country—deadlier even than police work. And 1993 was a particularly bad year, with elephants killing three people (including two circus deaths) in the United States. In 1994, a circus elephant with a bad reputation felled her handler before being gunned down as she tore through the streets of Honolulu on a rampage. That brought the four-year total to nine elephant-related human deaths. Contact between people and elephants is tricky business; in India, Asian elephants take the lives of about 150 people a year.

These animals are so large that we might be led to believe that some of these deaths have been accidental. But one need only watch the adults around a baby elephant to understand just how aware they are of their own bulk and how nimble they can be. An elephant's boneless trunk is 6 feet long, weighs 180 pounds and contains as many as 100,000 muscles. With it, the elephant can deftly pick up a coin or brutally knock a person out. Even their relatively tiny tails pack the punch of a baseball bat. An African elephant can stand 13 feet tall and weigh in at 14,000 pounds—and because of its cushioned feet, that same elephant can walk up behind a person as silently as a cat. When elephants harm someone, it is intentional.

When I visited the National Zoo in Washington, John Lehnhardt asked me if I wanted to go in with the elephants. Despite all the gory stories I had read, nothing could deter me. We walked through the shady and dark elephant building out to a sunny and dusty enclosure bordered by a moat and visitor walkways.

The four elephants were excited to see John, but I was novel. Simultaneously, all trunks wheeled around and danced like charmer's snakes. One elephant stepped forward, and John blew gently into her trunk and then massaged her tongue with his hand, simulating wild elephant greetings. She brought her trunk within an inch of my mouth. The gray tube hovered before my face, taking me in in the elephant way. I reached out and held the surprisingly rough, bristly and well-muscled trunk. "Hellooo down there!" I called into it as the keepers rolled their eyes. Then I whispered what I thought she was trying to figure out. "Pasta salad, that's what I had for lunch. Pasta salad."

What the elephant wanted to know and what she found out about me is a mystery, though I suspect she did understand that I wasn't afraid. And further, I suspect she figured out much more about me than I did about her in those few minutes we shared. "It's amazing," Lehnhardt says, starting to laugh, "they could probably tell you incredible things about yourself that you wouldn't want other people to know about! They know if you're pregnant, if you're having your period, if you've had sex in the last five days, they'll tell you everything. They know it because they are so tuned in to our hormones and the smells that we give off." Scientists may still be grappling with tests to determine when an elephant is ovulating, but elephants seem to have perfected their tests on humans. This is only based on anecdotal evidence from elephant-keepers who have seen changes in elephants' attitudes according to the keepers' cycle, being much more curious around a pregnant human, for instance.

Such stories about elephants from the experts who study them, both in captivity and the wild, give the impression that elephants are wise beyond expectation. And on the day that I entered this almost mystical realm of the elephant at the National Zoo, I caught only a glimpse of why that is.

Most of us know very little about the complex world of these creatures. Before we can hope to sort out the many obstacles to the management of captive elephants, we have to understand the nature of their world in the wild. Free elephants must maneuver two kinds of terrains: not just the land with its ever-shifting resources but a complicated social landscape.

Understanding Elephants

Daphne Sheldrick has devoted her life to saving the lives of baby elephants who have been orphaned by poachers in Kenya. Her husband was the chief park warden at Tsavo National Park;

now widowed, she makes her home outside Nairobi National Park. She has lived among these great creatures and calls them quite definitively "human animals." Given the evidence, her claim seems reasonable.

Elephants use their trunks and tusks to lift sick or injured companions. They can bring food to incapacitated elephants. They help each other during labor and in the rearing of young. They will on occasion adopt an abandoned baby (this was recorded on film by Derek and Beverly Joubert). When attacked, elephants often run toward one another instead of away. They frequently stand vigil over the dead and will even bury a fresh carcass. When confronted with the bleached bones of a fallen comrade, elephants will touch, caress and lift the remains. They concentrate most of their attention on the skull and tusks, and many biologists who study them say they appear to have some awareness of death.

At birth, most animals' brains are 90 percent developed—leaving them 10 percent with which to learn new things. Humans, however, are quite different from other animals; our brains are only 27 percent developed at birth. Remarkably, that figure is a close 35 percent for elephants. Both species have plenty of learning space to grow into.

Elephant babies often suck their trunks as humans would a thumb. The young animals even have trouble with this ungainly piece of equipment, and often trip over it. Elephant mothers care for their young into their teens. "Elephants have comparable lifespans to ours," Sheldrick says. "They have similarly long development. They have strong emotions; they have a sense of death; they have loves, loyalties and they have many human traits—they can be competitive, jealous and disobedient."

The babies Sheldrick cares for have been traumatized. Usually they have witnessed the bloody death and dismemberment of their entire family at the hands of poachers. Once in Sheldrick's safe haven, they will often refuse to eat and wake night after night screaming. One six-month-old baby became completely attached to Sheldrick. When the surrogate mother spent two weeks away to attend a wedding, the baby "died of a broken heart," refusing nourishment and withering away. Sheldrick's partner in the elephant-raising business is a thirty-five-year-old named Eleanor—herself an elephant. After the age of three, baby elephants are handed over to Eleanor at Tsavo National Park for reintroduction to the wild. Eleanor, who was also an orphan nurtured by Sheldrick, raises them to maturity. Although Eleanor is given these babies, she has also rescued one male herself.

Eleanor saves her tiny charges when they struggle in quicksandlike mud, protects them from lions and teaches them how to survive. Friends of mine who have met Eleanor say she has been known to pull ivory bracelets off the arms of visiting tourists. It is plausible, given the animals' behavior around the remains of other dead elephants, but what is really remarkable about Eleanor, according to Sheldrick, is that "she is a typical matriarch."

GREAT BULK WAS AN evolutionary adaptation that freed elephants to do what ruminants could not: eat a wide variety of plants and not just the softer parts. Elephants could harvest what other herbivores could not reach or digest. Asian elephants have adapted to thick forest, and African elephants to the open savanna (though there are forest-dwelling elephants in Africa).

African elephants *(Loxodonta africana)* and Asian elephants *(Elephas maximus)* are not subspecies of elephant but two completely separate species. Africans are much larger, with bulls weighing up to 14,000 pounds and standing 13 feet tall (the largest bull in recorded history, who was killed in Angola in 1955, weighed 22,050 pounds; his remains are at the Smithsonian Institute). Asian males reach about 10,000 pounds and stand 11 feet tall. Asians have smaller ears and rounded backs, and usually only the males have tusks. The ears of the African elephant resemble a map of Africa. Both male and female Africans have tusks. Africans have one less nail on each foot (four on the front and three in back), but one more vertebra than the Asian. All elephants stand on tiptoe, with a fatty, spongy layer of tissue encasing and cushioning the toe bones. All elephants have four molars in their mouths at a time (each weighing 4 pounds) to grind down the enormous amount of food they consume. And each elephant will wear out six sets of these teeth over a long lifespan, the last set coming in at about age forty-five. The trunk is actually an elongated nose and upper lip combined. Asians have a single "finger" at the tip of their trunks; Africans have two.

There are many stories in the scientific literature about the cleverness of elephants and their extraordinary social bonds. Working elephants in India are set free at night to forage (elephants sleep a total of only four or five hours a day). Bells are strung around their necks so they can be quickly located at daybreak and rounded up. Since they are punished if they pull the bells off, these elephants stuff them with mud for silence and longer freedom.

Derek and Beverly Joubert have captured incredible elephant behavior on film. In *Reflections on Elephants,* for National Geographic, the Jouberts recorded the adoption of a baby elephant. The abandoned calf paces in the shallows of a watering hole and frantically cries out into the night. He is too young to understand the value of silence on the savanna. Hyenas hear his pitiful wails and move in, but suddenly a group of elephants splashes into the spotlight, water darkening their legs and patches on their bodies. The predators retreat. The group sniffs at the baby and leaves. The hyenas are back. Now the group returns to sweep the infant into their ranks.

Elephants in captivity have fewer opportunities to display altruism because so much of their life is supervised and monitored by zoo staff. And yet they, too, demonstrate the kind of caring their wild cousins are known for. Lehnhardt can tick off case after case of such behavior in zoo elephants. In Calgary, Lehnhardt says, one elephant became violently ill, possibly with Western equine encephalitis, just weeks after the birth of her calf. Her brain swelled and she lost control of her bodily functions. She often could not stand. Every time Kamala fell to the ground, another female, Swarna, would race over and, with exhausting effort, lift her sick comrade to her feet. "Finally," Lehnhardt says, "she got so tired of doing that, that she lifted her up and pushed her up against the wall and then stood and held her up with her body for twelve hours. Clearly an altruistic act." As a new mother, Kamala began a nervous pacing behavior and would not allow her infant to nurse. The staff initially blocked her path to keep her still, but soon relinquished the duties to Swarna who would hem "the mother elephant in so the crying baby could suckle."

Lehnhardt also tells the tale of a car wash that was installed at the Calgary Zoo so that three "little Sri Lankan" elephants could drink or play in water whenever they pleased. The device was set up so that an elephant pulling the chain at the doorway would activate the shower. Two of the elephants learned how to pull the chain and took baths all the time. "The third didn't have a clue," says Lehnhardt. For seven years, he says, Swarna would walk over to this doorway and signal that she wanted it activated. One of the other elephants would pull the chain for her, refraining from drinking themselves. After years of this behavior, the clueless elephant went to investigate a new piece of white tape she saw on the chain. She reached up, caught her trunk in the metal loop, turned the shower on by accident and from that moment forward pulled it all the time herself.

The basic elephant family unit consists of a matriarch, her female relatives and immature offspring of both sexes. Mature males wander alone or join loose bachelor groups. Elephants can live to be seventy, and it is the wisdom of the aged matriarch that can save groups of elephants during disasters such as drought.

In the wild, elephants amble over vast ranges and are able to communicate with a network of related animals using infrasound, which is too low for the human ear to detect. Infrasound isn't easily blocked by trees or rocks; it rolls around objects and can travel for miles. It explains the coordinated and choreographed movements of different elephant groups that puzzled researchers for years. These great beasts develop a social pecking order as they grow and use their communication system to avoid or join up with other groups. Related groups will meet on the savanna with excited trumpeting, trunk embraces and the free flow of fluid from the temporal glands on either side of their head—a pachyderm party.

There is no need for conflict: dominance and order have long been established.

That is not as true for males during a mysterious and still little-understood period called musth. About once a year, depending on how well fed and healthy they are, males enter a strange hormonal state, lasting a few weeks to a few months, that makes them lethal to humans and other elephants alike. Musth males are tanked up on testosterone and tend to become brutally aggressive, impervious to pain and impossibly unpredictable. Large, healthy and fearless, these are the males that will most likely mate with females in estrus. An elephant's sperm count remains the same. "What changes in musth," says Lehnhardt, "is an elephant's ability to compete for the opportunity to breed. He becomes more aggressive and potentially moves himself higher on the hierarchy of male elephants in the area when he is in musth and the other elephants are not. Elephant musth may be staggered so that elephants don't have to compete with other bulls that are too tough for them."

A musth male is a sight to behold. His temporal glands are swollen and leak profusely. His penis is engorged and dribbles urine constantly, turning the penis sheath a greenish-white color and staining his back legs. He is restless and on the move, ready for trouble. In her book *Echo of the Elephants,* elephant researcher Cynthia Moss describes running into one of these males: "When he arrived upwind of us his smell almost knocked us sideways. It was a pungent, sharp, somewhat musky scent which I had grown rather partial to." She once witnessed two big bulls in musth spar with each other over a ten-and-a-half-hour period. Her coresearchers would not go near one particular male when he was in musth. Bad Bull "will go as far as 200 metres [650 feet] out of his way to threaten and charge us. We always . . . give him a wide berth."

To a receptive female, a musth male is a creature of beauty, but to an Indian mahout or an American zookeeper, he is a deadly force of nature. It is small wonder that most zoos will not keep male elephants and are fearful of breeding, since it may very well produce a male calf. Out of a population of 375 Asian and 225 African elephants in North America, fewer than 50 are Asian males, and of those, fewer than 15 are fit for breeding. And that, of course, poses a breeding problem for a species whose numbers have been drastically reduced and is in desperate need of help. In 1930, it was estimated that there were 5 to 10 million elephants in Africa; by 1989, that figure was reduced to 600,000 by poaching and habitat loss. The Asian elephant is endangered because logging and farming have wiped out huge ranges. There are only 25,000 to 40,000 alive today. Dale Tuttle, AZA species coordinator for elephants and executive director of the Jacksonville Zoo, pointed out in a paper delivered at the 1994 zoo conference that "It is estimated that the Indian Moghul, Jehangir, possessed over 40,000 elephants in his kingdom in the early part of the sixteenth century. A number that nearly equals that of the Asian elephants left in the wild today." For both species of elephant, an incalculable amount of genetic diversity, "culture" and experience has been lost forever. If zoos are to create a breeding program for elephants, they must establish a safe and humane way to deal with them.

Tuttle warned at the conference, "Without major advances in successful reproduction, we could lose all breeding potential in as little as eighteen years when all of our females have passed the twenty-five-year mark." Tuttle went on to say, "We are in need of facilities that can handle at least five to six elephants and, preferably, can handle young bulls prior to entering their breeding years. Several regional breeding centers would also be of great use. These would need to be capable of holding up to a dozen elephants in a breeding environment with the presence of at least two bulls."

We can only guess at the intelligence of a wild elephant, the emotions they may experience. What goes on inside that massive skull? What secrets beat within that huge heart? We must consider just how desolate we have made life for captive elephants. We remove them from a rich and varied landscape. We stunt their range from hundreds of miles to a few square feet. And most important of all, we sever ties that may be counted in the hundreds in the wild and allow them only the company of humans or very often just one other elephant. When we warp the world of an elephant, we pay the consequences.

How to Handle an Elephant

IN THE WILD, elephants walk supreme. In the zoo world, elephant-keepers walk supreme. They are the cocky top guns, the peak of the zookeeping hierarchy.

These keepers must maintain a psychological edge. Too often, however, they resort to a physical one. Today, the best physical edge is a protective barrier, but routinely in the past—and to an unknown extent now—it has been brute force. That means chaining an elephant, beating it while it is defenseless and then rewarding its submission with a banana.

It's hard to imagine condoning that regimen today, but Saul Kitchener, director of the San Francisco Zoological Gardens, told *Newsweek* in 1988: "How do you get a 10,000-pound elephant's attention? Hit him, that's how." The article centered on two events. Earlier that year, Dunda, an African female elephant, had been transferred from the San Diego Zoo to its Wild Animal Park, where her former keepers charged that she was beaten with sticks. Zoo officials were unabashed. "Dunda is 100 percent better than she was at the zoo," spokesman Jeff Jouett told *Newsweek*. "The ends seem to justify the means." Allegations of similar treatment at the San Francisco Zoo in October 1988 were dismissed by a panel of elephant experts.

The radical animal rights group People for the Ethical Treatment of Animals (PETA) has a videotape of a young, screaming elephant in Asia being "broken," as well as footage of a number of beefy men in tank tops unloading elephants from a Ringling trailer. The handlers use bull hooks not only to tear at the animals' tender ears but also to bludgeon them. It's not just animal rights groups that find fault, however; some of the top elephant experts in the country are critical of a great deal of elephant handling.

There are two things elephants are not now getting in captivity. One is intense social contact with many other elephants, the other is sufficient exercise—an elephant in the wild may walk twenty miles a day (though they are capable of fifty)—to keep their feet and nails trimmed, which is important in guarding against life-threatening infections. Treating one of these infections, says Portland's Jay Haight, is like treating "the entire Seattle Seahawks team all at once." Keepers join elephants to boost the social contact and to have easy access to their feet, which need constant attention in captivity.

IN THE WILD, elephant groups are slow to change. In zoos, keepers, many of them low-paid, come and go in a constantly changing lineup. It takes time to know an elephant and gain its trust. And many keepers don't have that time.

In August of 1994, the network news carried horrifying footage of a twenty-one-year-old circus elephant named Tyke rampaging through the streets of Honolulu. The female African elephant was cut down in a hail of bullets (eighty-seven of them hitting their mark), but not until she had killed her experienced and well-respected trainer, thirty-seven-year-old Allen Campbell. It was said that a groom (a low-paying, human pooper-scooper position) spooked Tyke by walking behind her, though in elephant circles this was an animal with a very bad reputation.

CharLee Torre, twenty-five and an elephant-keeper at the Lowry Park Zoo in Tampa, Florida, was killed by Tillie, a four-ton Asian elephant, in the summer of 1993. Two months earlier, Tillie had pushed Torre, but officials at the zoo had decided the incident was not sinister. On July 30, Tillie grabbed Torre with her trunk, threw the woman to the ground and stomped on her. Torre crawled away but died a short time later. She had been on the job for six months.

John Lehnhardt has a similar story, though he is alive to tell the tale. His incident occurred at the Calgary Zoo in 1980. Lehnhardt was "brand new," just a few weeks into his job. A young male elephant, who was six or seven at the time, was showing signs of aggression, but Lehnhardt says he was a novice with bulls and didn't recognize them. "It wouldn't happen to me now," he says. The day of the incident, he noticed the young elephant behaving strangely: "He would run, spin real quick on a dime, drop to his knees and drive what would be tusks, if he had any, into the ground." Late in the day, Lehnhardt participated in a zoo demonstration, chaining the elephants up for the night, with another zoo worker explaining to the crowd why they did this ("Now I feel the need to explain why chaining is not necessary to people," Lehnhardt says). As they were lining the animals up, the elephant reached out and touched Lehnhardt's hair, and the narrator made a joke about his shampoo. "I turned and looked at the narrator," Lehnhardt says, "and that's when he attacked me." The elephant made the same tusking motion he had practiced all day long, but this time Lehnhardt was underneath him. Lehnhardt recalls a surreal thought he had at the time. The night before, he had watched the Robert Redford movie *Brubaker,* in which a man's neck is broken. Lying beneath the massive elephant, Lehnhardt heard a crack that sounded just like the one in the movie. Lehnhardt got up and finished his work. Years later the old fracture was detected on an X-ray.

Jay Haight has worked at the Metro Washington Park Zoo since 1976. He knows elephants. I talked to him one cold, rainy Portland afternoon in the elephant building. Haight is a straight talker, no-nonsense. Without hesitation, he says Torre's minimal training was "a recipe for disaster."

Lehnhardt differs with Haight on a number of philosophical issues, but the two men come down squarely on the same side on the question of so many keeper deaths. "I believe 100 percent that every single situation was predictable and could have been avoided. Every single one," Lehnhardt says. People are not trained or experienced enough, and neither are the elephants, he maintains. He clearly finds the "beat-up approach" repugnant, wasteful and ultimately unsuccessful.

Haight has little respect for the "elephant hot dogs," the keepers who play rough with their animals. The traditional method, Haight says, was to break them with brutality and force. "There are two things you can *make* an elephant do," Haight says, "run away or kill you. But you can *get* an elephant to do a number of amazing things."

Lehnhardt says elephants kill "because they can." Meaning they kill because they are given the motivation or are allowed to develop behaviors that lead to aggression. "If we allowed the baby [elephant at the National Zoo] to push and shove us it would escalate to the point where it injured us. Baby elephants can sock another elephant and nothing happens, but if 8,000 pounds socks 125 pounds, we're in serious trouble. They often kill intentionally, but often they are just knocking people around." Males are supposed to spend their lives pushing and shoving, and certainly musth can provoke an attack out of the blue.

And some kill clearly for retribution. Lehnhardt believes that controlling an elephant does not mean dominating it. That physical approach infuriates Lehnhardt: If you beat an elephant, you shouldn't be surprised when the payback comes. But the payback may not arrive until the next handler or the one after that. What really surprises Lehnhardt is how few elephants do retaliate. Only 3 percent of the elephants in North America have been involved in human fatalities. Haight believes elephants have an innate "sense of fairness," and Lehnhardt calls them a "forgiving" species.

Haight and Lehnhardt have plenty to say about one of the hottest topics in the elephant world: the use of protected contact, in which keepers are shielded by some sort of barrier when dealing with the animals. Haight did not invite me to go in with the elephants, and when I reached for a trunk snaking toward me through bars, on that rainy day in Portland, I was quickly told to back off. Haight is not afraid of elephants even though he's been knocked around. His zoo, however, employs protected contact, and Haight is a believer.

"Certain animals will always be fine," Haight says. "Rosy [a Portland elephant who died in 1993], if she were in Thailand, she'd be in the village taking care of the kids. I've never seen her make an aggressive move. But she's kind of an exception." Yet, Haight says, one time they chained Rosy up so they could give her baby a shot, and "Rosy rears up, snaps both chains and comes charging down on us. She gingerly reaches in, pushes us aside and brings the baby back with her."

Despite the great care and respect Haight pays to them, he maintains a wry sense of humor. "Elephants have three neurons," he explains: "eating, shitting and panic." He says, "We have Disney to thank" for moments like the one in which he caught a zoogoer holding her baby over a railing for the huge male, Packy.

Portland has created one of the largest and most successful breeding programs for Asian elephants in the world. The first elephant born in captivity in the Western Hemisphere after a barren forty-four years was Packy in 1962. Since that time, Portland has produced twenty-five babies. The elephant barn here covers one and a half acres and contains a remote-controlled hydraulic restraint chute called the crush because of its movable walls. The crush is located in a passageway to the yard, and the animals pass through it every day on their way in or out of the barn. They are not always restrained in it, but they are habituated to the mechanism and remain quite calm while in its cold embrace. If the animal needs medical attention, he or she is instructed to halt in the chute and the sides glide in close (without actually "crushing" the elephant).

Packy is given a wide berth by those who know him. On the day I visited, the massive, twelve-foot-tall, fourteen-thousand-pound elephant was stopped in the crush. The wide, strategically placed spaces between the bars allow keepers to touch the animal without allowing Packy the maneuverability to do harm. Haight is comfortable with the setup, but says completely confined or protected contact is a mistake. He likes more flexibility. Many elephant experts feel that situations may arise—a medical crisis, for instance—in which the keepers will have to go in with the animal. If a keeper's entering is not routine, his or her sudden presence could alarm the animal. If the keeper had been doing that on an occasional basis all along, the animal would feel at ease. Haight believes that protected contact is not *the* solution, but that zoos need to admit to some serious mistakes in elephant handling, and they need to pay staff enough to keep them working with the elephants for a long time.

Lehnhardt says he would use protected contact with any male elephant over the age of seven or eight, and with any elephant he believed would be a risk. But as much as possible, he says, the key to success is hiring keepers with a great deal of sensitivity and working closely with the animals to develop a strong relationship. This process takes time and commitment and money, so some critics charge that zoos are misusing protected contact as an inexpensive safety shortcut.

Lehnhardt doesn't take shortcuts. In fact, he knows and trusts his elephants so much that he allows one—Shanti, the young mother—to have contact with the public. The elephant always instigates the encounters herself. When she indicates a desire to reach out to the public, Lehnhardt supervises a spontaneous meeting. When delighted little girls wrap their arms around Shanti's trunk, Lehnhardt says, the elephant "hums and sways back and forth. She's loving it, and these people walk away with an incredible experience they're not going to forget. And they're going to care about elephants." Lehnhardt says he has confidence in Shanti and her training, but he would never force or even nudge her toward these encounters. It is always Shanti's choice.

The perfect exhibit, Lehnhardt says, would have plenty of space, but even more important is what one does with that space. Providing the appropriate social context is "where zoos in North America have failed most dramatically," Lehnhardt says. Social context for females is having other females around and raising young. "We should be headed toward a minimum of five animals per exhibit and a variety of age groups—multigenerational, youngsters, preads, teenagers, mixing with adults and learning," Lehnhardt says.

In addition, there should be water to play and splash in, mud to roll in, sand to throw on their backs; the elephants should be able to scratch and rub themselves against rocks and trees and have items they can move around. They should have access to a lot of browse (tree limbs, food sources that are also activity-oriented). And Lehnhardt would include in his ideal exhibit a lot of human interaction.

Then, add to this perfect facility a few bulls (and the equipment necessary to keep them), so you can periodically move one in with the females for mating. Let them interact normally, Lehnhardt says, and breed naturally. Let males push and shove and fight as they would in the wild. Set up three chunks of forest and rotate their use so these massive animals can play, forage and push trees over.

The Jacksonville Zoo in Florida is incorporating some of the elements of this fantasy today. "If you are going to keep the animal, then keep it right," former executive director Dale Tuttle has written. Jacksonville is spending $2.5 million on a facility that is large enough to hold twenty-four elephants. The plan includes a huge indoor facility with various heat zones from which the animals can choose; a restraining chute; two display yards of more than an acre each, plus other smaller yards; half an acre of swimmable water; termite mounds for rubbing; and a fake baobab tree that will disperse food.

Building the right world for elephants in captivity is wildly expensive. But after spending the bulk of his professional life around these animals, John Lehnhardt thinks they are worth it. "My first experience with an elephant was at the Brookfield Zoo when I was a child," Lehnhardt says. "I used to visit my cousin, and we'd walk over and see Ziggy the elephant chained up. He was a male elephant chained from 1941 to 1979 in the corner. I always remember that image from when I was ten, eleven, twelve years old." Years later, Lehnhardt went to work at Lincoln Park Zoo. He was supposed to work with the lions, but through some bureaucratic hiccup, he was switched on that very first day to the elephant house. He discovered his first elephant, and says, "It was just instantaneous . . . love. And that's what it's always been since."

Within his working life, Lehnhardt has seen a dramatic shift in the philosophy of captive elephant management. As assistant curator of mammals at one of the country's top zoos, he can ban the kind of cruel practices he has witnessed. Lehnhardt's mix of compassion and scientific reason stands as a beacon of hope for the future of zoos.

Yet the image of a powerful elephant chained and dominated by man—the image that so bothered Lehnhardt as a boy and a young adult—stands as a metaphor for the history of zoos. The desire to capture and tame nature herself has driven the story of zoos throughout much of recorded time.

3

ALL THE KINGS' ZOOS

IT IS QUITE SHOCKING to learn that animals were tried and hanged in Victorian England for offenses such as bestiality. That women of tribal societies, throughout time and around the planet, have suckled the orphaned infants of wild creatures. That tigers are ranched in China today so that their organs may be used in traditional medicine. Or that great Roman ornithologists often ate the objects of their study.

We can learn a great deal about a culture from these stories. Mahatma Gandhi once said that we can judge the greatness of a nation by the way it treats animals. And indeed, this issue does tell us the world about the way a society views nature, God or gods, and its place in the cosmos. The zoo, loosely defined as a place to keep exotics in captivity, is an ancient notion. And if we trace time through the pits and cages and exalted temples used to display animals, we discover more about the fickle soul of man than about the steady behavior of beasts.

Since about 3000 B.C., with the development of urban centers and ruling classes, humans have maintained dangerous and exotic animals in captivity. We may not have used the word *zoo* until the middle of the nineteenth century, but we have had them, nonetheless, for millennia. We have worshiped animals and held them sacred. We have slaughtered them and pitted them against one another. We have used animals for entertainment and scientific research. They have been sources of national pride and, particularly in wartime, sources of food. The famous and infamous from the history of humankind show up in the story of zoos—Aristotle, Alexander the Great, Charlemagne, Marco Polo, Kublai Khan, Christopher Columbus, Louis XIV, William Randolph Hearst, Theodore Roosevelt.

The technology of animal capture, transportation and husbandry has evolved over time. But one thing that has not changed is our basic awe of nature. The sight of a lunging lion or bristling bear brings the raw edge of fear raking across our psyches today, just as it did in our primitive past.

Whether it is Nero sharing supper with a pet tigress, the Prince of Orange cuddling his orangutan or a modern-day zoogoer whispering to a shy deer, we instinctively grasp this basic relationship. We have sought to appease the power of nature, to seduce it, fight it, control it and revel in it.

Throughout history, the most powerful kings, queens, pharaohs and philosophers have created zoological gardens. Ships heavy with gems, jewels and spices still made room for wild cargo—lions or monkeys or parrots. The value of these animals was given great weight. Display of a stately giraffe or a fierce tiger said little or nothing about the animal itself or its home environment, but it spoke volumes about its possessor. Ownership of such an animal was potent proof of wealth, stature, daring and mastery of nature itself.

But these are not just tales from faraway lands and a time long ago. The distant urges at work in the early fifteenth century, when China opened trade with Africa in order to secure a giraffe, seem close at hand today in the circles of diplomacy, international intrigue and the many millions of dollars that swirl around the giant panda.

Zoos Before the Enlightenment

THE FAINT TRACES OF the earliest zoos are impossible to verify, but within the royal estate of Great King Shulgia (2094–2047 B.C.) in Mesopotamia, during the third dynasty of Ur, we find what historians claim is typical of the earliest zoos. Much is known about the mechanics of the city through clay tablets. Much is recorded about the purchase of domestic animals, but beyond the fact that there were lions, there are only guesses at what else this animal park, seven miles outside the divine city of Nippur, contained and how the animals were kept.

We find the true start of zoos more than a thousand years before the birth of Christ in ancient Egypt, according to the preeminent zoo historian Gustave Loisel. We know that the ancient Egyptians protected certain exotic animals such as lions, baboons, bulls, snakes, hippos and crocodiles that were considered holy, and that pharaohs and Ptolemies sought out strange creatures through expeditions and then built parks for them. After death, many of these animals were embalmed. In *Animals and Men,* Herman Dembeck asserts that "it is a virtual certainty that every pharaoh had a menagerie in his palace park, reserved for himself, his court, and foreign diplomats."

Gathering beasts was not limited to men, however. Queen Hatshepsut, of the eighteenth dynasty, launched the first recorded animal collecting expedition around 1490 B.C. Along with myrrh, gold, ebony and ivory, her crew packed aboard five ships leopards (or perhaps cheetahs), greyhounds, exotic birds and monkeys from the shores of "The Land of Punt"—what is probably present-day Somalia. Her zoo held a number of domesticated animals and an elegant giraffe, probably the first ever seen in Egypt—a damaged relief of this animal still exists. These stunning creatures have caused a sensation throughout zoo history: A live giraffe would not be seen in France until the Pasha of Egypt sent one as a gift in 1826; they reached Vienna in 1828 and the United States in 1837.

By 1250 B.C., Ramses II had several giraffes in his menagerie, along with ostriches, antelopes, monkeys and cheetahs. It is said that his favorite lion, Antam-nekt, accompanied him even into battle. The animal kingdom was respected and worshiped in varied and complex ways. Imagine the spectacle of hundreds of wild beasts surging forward in a huge royal processional, a tidal wave of hooves and manes and trunks, spots and stripes, bright banners and glinting gold. Though these animals were not kept for the public's pleasure, crowds were allowed in to watch the lions being fed live prey at the Temple of the Sun in Metropolis and to feed meats and cakes to the sacred crocodiles of Lake Moeris.

Keeping wild animals was not a fetish particular to the ancient Egyptians. Around 1100 B.C., during the Zhou dynasty, King Wen, who was idolized as one of the greatest rulers of antiquity, set up a scientific zoo called the Garden of Intelligence or, according to some translations of "ling you," a "divine park." The details, of course, are sketchy, but we do know that this 900–1,500-acre walled preserve about halfway between Beijing and Nanjing was considered a sacred place; that it was created 800 years before the Great Wall; and that it housed all kinds of deer, antelope, goats, birds (including pheasants) and fish. Though it very likely may have been used as a hunting park, Chinese historian Sarah Queen observes that "It is important to note that animals were also believed to facilitate communication between the human and spiritual realms."

The royal families of ancient Assyria collected animals. Semiramis, a courtesan in the ninth century B.C., was fascinated by leopards; her son, Ninus, by lions. The last important king of Assyria, Ashurbanipal, also kept lions and is depicted on reliefs fighting them. It would seem that some lions were coddled as pets and others were raised in parks for fighting. But the oldest known zoo in the Assyrian Empire was that of Assur-uballit I (1365–1330 B.C.), who imported exotics from Egypt.

By the fourth century B.C., animal collections formed a part of the fabric of ancient Greece, probably found in most urban centers. Again, they were used to display power and wealth, but the ancient Greeks were also interested in nature as a science. In a society with a love of wisdom and respect for scholars, the study of animals became a discipline. Aristotle, student of Plato and teacher of Alexander, was raised in a world where young intellectuals were shown these collections, which probably included monkeys and talking parrots, as part of their education.

Alexander the Great brought all sorts of creatures back from his military conquests (elephants) and was given others as gifts (a tiger), some of which his teacher Aristotle probably used to study and write about in his zoological encyclopedia, *History of Animals,* which catalogs about three hundred species of vertebrates. Although Alexander is often credited with establishing the world's first public zoo, it is one of his generals, Ptolemy I, whom he installed as king of Egypt, who built the zoo in Alexandria.

A wonderful zoo was founded where two cultures met. Here, in Alexandria, the Egyptian facility with animal husbandry met the Greek passion for the study of zoology. One of the few things we know about this early zoo is that it contained a Bactrian camel (two humps), a gift from another general, Seleucus I (king of Syria and Babylon). Under Ptolemy II (285–246 B.C.), this zoo grew into the most fantastic the world had known.

We do not have clear records of the zoo's inventory, but we do know that all the animals were displayed in a parade to celebrate the Feast of Dionysus. It took all day for the procession to march by the stadium. Ostriches were harnessed; tree limbs laden with exotic birds were carried aloft; cage upon cage of peacocks, pheasants and parrots were presented. Yoked in teams of four, ninety-six elephants pulled twenty-four chariots. Goats, wild asses, thousands of hounds, hundreds of sheep and various oxen and oryxes were included. According to James Fisher, in *Zoos of the World,* "The people of Alexandria with a taste for 'more exciting' animals were not disappointed. The procession included 24 lions, 14 leopards, 16 'pantheroi' (probably cheetahs), six pairs of one-humped camels, a 'white bear,' a giraffe, a gigantic snake said to be 45 feet long (most likely a python of something over 30 feet), and, wonder of wonders, a rhinoceros." The white bear was probably not a polar bear but rather a pale brown bear. The rhino probably came from the Sudan, but Fisher points out that capturing and shipping such a magnificently powerful beast must have been a spectacular feat. It is estimated that this collection surpassed that of any modern zoo.

The glory of the Greek menagerie shined in size and scope, science and sophistication, but in the amphitheaters of ancient Rome, the business of collecting exotic creatures rounds a brutal and bloody turn. Early in the ancient Roman Empire, wealthy families, like those in so many other societies, maintained small menageries and aviaries. Marcus Terentius Varro (116–27 B.C.) owned one of the best-known collections. Varro was fascinated by birds and, along with domestic poultry, he raised pigeons, guineafowl, peafowl and songbirds. Like most of his contemporaries, Varro admired birds but also often ate them. By 186 B.C., we begin to see wild animals imported for games. Marcus Fulvius Nobilitor supplied the lions and leopards for the earliest event recorded. Rome's expansion into north Africa provided fresh animals from that continent. Officials gained popularity from the public by staging ever-more bizarre and savage games that involved humans and animals. In 29 B.C., following a victory over the troops of Antony and Cleopatra, Octavius, known to history as Caesar Augustus, established a zoo that rivaled that of the Ptolemies. Many of the inhabitants of his zoo, thousands in fact, waited in the wings until it was their turn to enter the arena. Hippos, rhinos, tigers, cheetahs, bears and elephants were slaughtered. (In discussing the elephant's role in battle, Wilfrid Blunt notes in *The Ark in the Park,* "Elephants, in spite of their intelligence in other ways, were never very reliable battle-animals, having a regrettable lack of ability to differentiate between friend and foe— a defect which sometimes led them to score an 'own goal.' ")

The great naturalist Pliny the Elder, who died during the volcano eruption in Pompeii in A.D. 79, represented the humane and studious attitude not shared by the throngs who packed arenas every day for bloody spectacles. In his examination of the natural world, Pliny asserted that hippos walk backward out of the water to confuse predators.

Nero, the emperor best known for his cruelty, sent horsemen into battle against hundreds of bears and lions. His pet tiger Phoebe dined with him and, according to anecdote, occasionally dined on unpopular guests. (This often-told story is, of course, questionable, since tigers do not attack on command.) Trajan was so giddy with his Dacian victory in A.D. 106 that he held games over four months during which ten thousand gladiators and eleven thousand animals were killed. (Jeremy Cherfas points out in *Zoo 2000* that that figure breaks down to one hundred animals killed per day.) The Coliseum was occasionally transformed into a lake so that hippos, seals and crocodiles could be hunted and killed by gladiators in boats.

Menageries existed simply as bullpens, warming up the beasts to be farmed for slaughter. For centuries, these killing fields stretched far beyond Rome, into every corner of the empire. The governors of Roman colonies gathered animals as tribute to Rome and for their own games. The Nile provided hippos; lions arrived from Mesopotamia, tigers from Persia and bears from Asia. While acting as governor of Cilicia in Asia Minor, Cicero was pestered by letters from a friendly magistrate back in Rome. The magistrate was desperate to receive leopards from Cicero for some official games. After several letters, Cicero finally responded that there was, in fact, "an extraordinary scarcity of the beasts." Considering the relentless hunting that went on, that may very well have been true.

Constantine, the first Christian emperor of the Roman Empire, put an end to these games, but by the sixth century, Justinian, who married the daughter of a bear-keeper, brought them back. They continued to flourish well past the fall of Rome and into the twelfth century. Even through the Dark Ages, wild animal collections survived, maintaining their allure across political and cultural upheaval, but now, these collections were scaled down, held by royal families or on the grounds of monasteries.

An animal lover, Charlemagne received what was said to be the first elephant, "Aboul-Abas," ever to be seen in France from Harun ar-Rashid (the caliph of Baghdad and a hero of the *Thousand and One Nights*). This first emperor of the Holy Roman Empire is also said to have received a tame lion from the pope and bears and another lion from the emir of Cairo. In the eighth century, he owned three menageries, the best known near his palace in Aachen.

Zoos clearly had diminished over time, but with Frederick II (1194–1250), king of Sicily and emperor of the Holy Roman Empire in the thirteenth century, the notion of the menagerie expanded once again. He was a naturalist, ornithologist and author with huge collections in Palermo and elsewhere. And when he traveled, he packed up hyenas, cheetahs, camels, lions, monkeys and elephants to accompany him. He even had a giraffe, which he received in a trade for a polar bear from the sultan of Egypt. Though he, in fact, discovered many things about animal behavior—for example, that the lead crane, flying in a V formation, changes places during flight—he is best remembered for the grand procession of animals he arranged at Worms (in Germany) to celebrate his marriage in 1235 to Elizabeth, sister of Henry III. Elephants, cheetahs, monkeys, panthers and camels participated in the wedding.

Henry III moved the menagerie of his grandfather (Henry I), which included camels, lions, leopards and lynx, from its place in Woodstock to the Tower of London. Henry also received an elephant, the first ever seen in England, from his brother-in-law, Louis IX of France. His collection would eventually include a polar bear, which was allegedly brought daily to the Thames on a leash so it could fish. The fishing arrangement was struck for reasons of economy. Henry decreed that London itself should pay for the bear's food. The sheriff and the bear-keeper concocted the frugal plan for this daily expedition. The keeper allegedly had to wade into the water with the bear, a notion that modern bear biologists would scoff at.

The royal collection with its expensive upkeep had nearly faded away until 1445, when Margaret of Anjou, wife of Henry VI, received a lion as a wedding gift. Her interest in animals sparked a rejuvenation and renovation of the royal collection. The animals remained in the tower even after the royal family moved out. The public was allowed in at three half-pence a head, and visitors who brought a pet dog or cat for the lions' supper were not charged admission. Generations later, the animals of this collection would be moved to Regent's Park for its opening in 1828.

Marco Polo, the Italian explorer of the thirteenth and fourteenth centuries, visited Kublai Khan's marble and stone summer palace in Shangdu in inner Mongolia, which Coleridge made famous as Xanadu in his poem "Kubla Khan." Here, according to various versions, he saw panthers, leopards, lynx, rhinoceroses, bears, boar, deer, horses, camels, civets, porcupines and elephants kept in a sixteen-mile walled preserve. The Mongol chieftain is said to have carried a leopard or (more probably) a cheetah with him on horseback as he galloped about the park. At another Chinese palace, he observed lions and tigers wandering loose. Polo describes the tigers as lions "with longitudinal stripes of black, orange, and white."

Exotic creatures affected policy and trade between nations. In 1417, Emperor Cheng Tzu, of the Yung-lo period of the Ming dynasty, opened up trade with Africa because of a giraffe. Giraffes were unknown in China until a group of sailors saw one in Bengal in 1414. The animal looked to them like a *qilin,* a mythical beast of good luck that resembled a unicorn, with the body of a deer and the tail of an ox. And, in fact, upon hearing the similar-sounding Somali word for the animal—*girin*—the sailors were convinced they had stumbled upon the fabled creature whose presence was thought to be highly auspicious. Two giraffes were eventually given to the emperor, opening trade between China and Melindi on Africa's east coast.

And in 1487, Lorenzo de' Medici and a giraffe became entangled in international intrigue. According to one version, he brokered the release of the brother of the sultan of Egypt, who was being held in France, with the promise of several exotic gifts, especially a giraffe to Louis XI's daughter (it was never delivered). His menagerie in Florence was visited by poets and painters; Leonardo da Vinci drew monkeys, bats and snakes in a zoo in Milan. Leo X, a Medici who became pope, set up a menagerie at the Vatican with bears from Hungary, monkeys, leopards and lions. King Manuel I of Portugal sent him an Asian elephant and a snow leopard. Cardinal Hippolyte, yet another Medici, created a menagerie of exotic human beings—Africans, Moors, Tartars and Turks.

Columbus rates an entry in zoo history for bringing macaws from the West Indies and parrots back to the gardens of Ferdinand and Isabella. And in the New World, the Old World discovered one of the most fantastic zoos yet seen. In 1519, Spanish explorer Hernando Cortés entered the Aztec capital of Tenochtitlán. Past the stunning architecture, beyond the aviaries throbbing with the spectacular plumage of exotic birds, behind Montezuma's palace was a huge zoo. Bronze bars secured pumas and jaguars, sloths, monkeys and armadillos. It is sometimes reported that Cortés saw lions and tigers here also, but these were probably mountain lions and jaguars—it is very doubtful any African and Asian animals had made their way to Mexico. Nearly three hundred keepers cared for ponds full of ducks, tanks of fish and enclosures filled with snakes and another three hundred for the rest of the animals. It is said that five hundred turkeys a day were thrown to captive eagles and hawks. Another area displayed deformed humans. There was apparently one plains bison that the Spaniards were told had come from "the land toward night."

When Cortés attacked the city in 1521, many of the city's 300,000 survived for a time by eating the animals from the menagerie. But then the entire city was leveled by the conquerors.

Across barriers of distance, geography, time and culture, we have kept exotic animals, in worlds as different as ancient Egypt and Rome, Mexico and China. From the beginning of civilization itself, the only thing stunting the growth of exotic animal collections was geography. And with the rise of the shipping trade, that barrier would fall.

A Zoo in Every Port

MENAGERIES WERE taking a quantum leap forward as explorers pushed open shipping routes and trade brought unprecedented wealth. The shipping trade funneled the money and the means to bring exotic animals back to Europe. Immense menageries appeared wherever ports thrived as rich merchants in the early Renaissance beefed up their private stock.

King Manuel I of Portugal had Brazilian monkeys, macaws, gray parrots, baboons, elephants, a rhino and trained cheetahs in his royal park. He bought and sold exotics and for a short time controlled the market on certain animals such as monkeys and parrots. In the Bavarian city of Augsburg, a wealthy merchant family, the Fuggers, established a large animal park. Wild animals were unloaded in Genoa, Pisa and Venice. And merchant ships in Antwerp and Rotterdam brought in animals from all over the world. In the seventeenth and eighteenth centuries the success of the East India and West India companies carried a vast array of beasts to Amsterdam.

The Prince of Orange (who had a pet orangutan) maintained many menageries. The one at his royal residence at Loo, near the Hague, was increased in the next century and was described by Loisel as "the most interesting in Europe from the point of view of the naturalist." At his death in 1605, Akbar, the great mogul of India, had in his collection five thousand elephants and one thousand camels. He ruled most of what is now India and Afghanistan. His zoos seem quite modern by today's standards: all were open to the public; no baiting was allowed; many animals were allowed to roam freely; and the animals were cared for by a well-trained staff of medical specialists. Despite all this, Akbar could not entice his stable of one thousand cheetahs to breed, a problem even modern zoos are still tackling. In Akbar's lifetime, only one litter of cheetahs was born, and though that may seem like a dismal record, another litter of captive cheetahs would not be produced until 1956, at the Philadelphia Zoo.

With Louis XIV and Versailles we stumble across another possible first in the history of zoos. In 1665, the king built a spectacular palace with gardens and a menagerie. This was the first time in the Western world that flora and fauna were exhibited in close proximity. The animal enclosures radiated out from an octagonal courtyard and pavilion, and plants and bushes and trees surrounded them. Because so many foreign dignitaries were entertained at Versailles, the zoological garden was seen by many and imitated in other countries. Eventually, Louis lost interest in his beautiful menagerie, the gardens became overgrown and the animals that died were not replaced. It enjoyed one rebirth when Louis's daughter-in-law Adelaide, princess of Savoy, became enchanted with it, but with her death, the park was once again barely maintained.

In 1752, the Holy Roman Emperor Francis I created an imperial menagerie for his wife, Maria Theresa, queen of Hungary and Bohemia and archduchess of Austria near the Palace of Schonbrunn. Set in a beautiful garden, the queen would eat breakfast at a center pavilion from which she could watch camels, elephants and zebras. She also acquired a rhino, Cape hartebeest and birds such as the American trumpeter, scarlet ibis, eclectus parrot from Papua and the macaw. In 1765, Francis I's son, Joseph II, opened the zoo to the public. (It is now the oldest zoo in existence.)

Back in Versailles, in October of 1789, following the French Revolution, a mob came to the Menagerie du Parc to liberate the animals. The crowd wanted the animals set free so that others could catch them and eat them, outraged that these animals grew fat while the people starved. Once the zoo director explained how dangerous the lion and rhino were, and that some of the creatures would eat the crowd rather than vice versa, the revolutionaries decided to "liberate" only the more edible captives. The remains of the collection ended up at the Jardin des Plantes. And this inaugurated what is considered the scientific age of zoos.

The Jardin had been founded in 1635 as a living laboratory for doctors and scientists studying the medicinal qualities of herbs. By the time the royal menagerie in Versailles was looted, the Jardin in Paris was considered a national natural history treasure. Many were opposed to the notion of the animals from Versailles and other collections trampling their botanical garden, introducing disease and relegating the park to public spectacle. Though famed French naturalist George-Louis Leclerc de Buffon had earlier suggested combining plants and animals for the study of natural history, in 1782 the Jardin's director, Bernardin de Saint-Pierre, was steadfast in his opposition to the idea—until some powerful people applied pressure. In 1793, when the Versailles animals (including a lion, the lion's pet dog and the now extinct quagga) arrived, the Jardin was already loaded with animals from menageries, and had recently banned traveling circuses and animal shows that had been confiscated by the police. By 1798, it had received twenty-six trained bears, leopards and monkeys from within Paris; thirty-six animals from the duke of Orleans's estate; two Asian elephants from Holland and much more. However motley the collection, however popular with the people of Paris and however unwilling they were originally, the men who ran the park insisted that it be viewed and treated as a scientific laboratory. Chemistry, physiology, zoology and even philosophy were studied there by such well-known scientists as Jean-Baptiste de Monet de Lamarck, Georges Cuvier (comparative anatomy) and Pierre-André Latreille.

The awe that giraffes inspire is illustrated by the mania surrounding the first one shipped to France. A beautiful female left Alexandria in 1826 aboard an Italian brigantine, with her every comfort cared for. She had a room cushioned with straw, an ocean view from a shaded window, a Muslim medal around her neck to keep her safe, three Sudanese keepers and three cows to provide twenty-five liters of milk a day. She wintered in Marseilles, rejecting many of the meals adoringly presented to her, consuming mostly milk and a maize-and-barley porridge. Life was a whirl of formal parties and, in nicer weather, elaborate parades with her retinue of three cows reassuringly at her side. A poncho and hood were sewn for her five-hundred mile journey to Paris. It took two months for this elegant ungulate to make the trip on foot and all along the way, crowds lined the streets, dazzled by her exotic beauty. King Charles himself fed the regal animal rose petals from his hand. Hundreds of Parisians came to see her and a cottage industry of giraffe goods grew—giraffe soaps, cake molds, paperweights, toys, ointments, wallpaper, parasols and toothpick holders among them. Later, in 1870, when the Prussian army besieged Paris, many of the zoo animals were once again consumed.

The Jardin des Plantes became such a respected scientific institution that it inspired a group of British men to create something similar at home.

The Class Menagerie

DURING THE MID-1820s, Sir Stamford Raffles, founder of the colony of Singapore, distinguished and industrious colonial administrator and avid naturalist, returned to England and embarked on a mission to invent a zoo that would, from its inception, be a scientific endeavor. In his travels, Raffles had discovered some new species of flora and fauna for the West—one flower, the largest and perhaps most aromatic (smelling like rotted flesh) in the world, was named for him, *Rafflesia arnoldi*. He also built a small menagerie for himself, which included a tapir and a clouded leopard—but all were lost at sea when his ship burned. Raffles was able to put together a new collection before he set sail for England three months later.

In her book *The Animal Estate: The English and Other Creatures in the Victorian Age,* Harriet Ritvo makes the case that it was certainly no coincidence that this empire-builder would be the one to establish a national zoo for England. Ritvo says, "Raffles's activities as a naturalist echoed his concerns as a colonial administrator: he made discoveries, imposed order, and carried off whatever seemed particularly valuable or interesting. The maintenance and study of captive wild animals, simultaneous emblems of human mastery over the natural world and of English dominion over remote territories, offered an especially vivid rhetorical means of reenacting and extending the work of the empire, and Raffles intended to continue his colonial pursuits in this figurative form after returning to the center of English power and enterprise." Whatever his empire-building impulses, Raffles was also a remarkable man, devoted to scientific inquiry. Clearly, though, the Victorian Age brought zoos once again sharply into focus as symbols of power and colonialism, and it is the London Zoo that gave birth to our modern concept of zoos.

Raffles enlisted society's elite and made plain that this was not an idle venture into the common world of entertainment. The prospectus for a Zoological Society of London emphasized that the society would "offer a collection of living animals such as never yet existed in ancient or modern times" and that the animals would be "brought from every part of the globe to be applied either to some useful purpose, or as objects of scientific research, not of vulgar admiration." From its inception, this zoo was to be set far apart from those in other countries and it was to be set apart from the traveling circuses and commercial menageries that were thriving in England at the time, such as the famous Exeter Change Menagerie, where animals were packed into small cages in a commercial building in London. Admission was graduated at many of these establishments, based on the visitor's class—gentlemen, tradesmen and working people.

Since Raffles was only interested in gentlemen (not until 1827 were "ladies" admitted as members), his list of collaborators was dazzling, including pioneer chemist Sir Humphry Davy (inventor of the miners' safety lamp), botanist Sir Joseph Banks (who had accompanied Captain James Cook on his first voyage and had arranged the surveying voyage of HMS *Bounty* under Captain Bligh), eminent entomologist William Kirby and noted naturalist Thomas Horsfield. The government provided five acres—today it is thirty-six acres—in Regent's Park, and in 1828 the Zoological Gardens was opened to members and their guests. By this time, however, Raffles had died of a stroke—or apoplexy, as it was called then—at the age of forty-five. There were two hundred animals, which included or soon would include a giraffe from King George (he had received it from Mohammed Ali, of Egypt); a brown bear from the marquess of Hertford; a pine marten from the marchioness of Londonderry; American bison, red fox and silver fox given by Hudson's Bay Company; and many of the remaining animals from the royal menagerie at the Tower of London.

It obviously wasn't entirely a scientific enterprise. In May of 1842, Queen Victoria visited the zoo and wrote of her visit, "The Orang Outang is too wonderful preparing and drinking his tea, doing everything by word of command. He is frightful & painfully and disagreeably human." Clearly then, the zoo was a smash hit. Despite being restricted to members and their guests, attendance in 1830 was 224,745. By 1834, written permission to enter the park was not too difficult to obtain—they were even changing hands in pubs. By 1846, as the novelty had worn off and attendance figures fell, the society saved itself by opening admission up to anyone with the fee. Because of crude economics, and not an egalitarian impulse, "strangers" no longer needed written vouchers from members; now a shilling would get them in. In this manner, the London Zoo avoided the fate of other elitist parks. According to Ritvo, the Leeds Zoological and Botanical Gardens, which opened in 1840 to "the higher classes of society," was bankrupt by 1848. But Regent Park's decision to educate the public paid off. Between 1848 and 1854, hundreds of thousands of new zoogoers poured through the gates at a penny a person. In fact, in 1868, the word *zoo* was popularized by a Great Vance song, with the modern-sounding line, "Walking in the zoo is an OK thing to do."

Zoos sprang up in Dublin, Berlin, Frankfurt, Antwerp and Rotterdam. It was the industrial age when humans began to feel they could control everything, even nature. It was the Victorian Age, a time of empire building. And these two great impulses came together quite neatly at the zoo.

Private menageries still existed, and one that earns a place of honor in zoo lore was that of Britain's eleventh duke of Bedford. In his three-thousand-acre Woburn Park, a single species of deer was saved from extinction. Named for the French Jesuit missionary

Père Armand David, Père David's deer is a large relative of the red deer, with a long, tufted tail and splayed hooves.

Once widespread in China, the deer was driven to extinction in the wild by hunters and, later, during the Boxer Rebellion in 1900, the last remaining specimens in the emperor's care in Beijing were killed. Fortunately, the duke, an aristocrat, had taken some into captivity, and the versatile deer did quite well at his estate. The duke's breeding program was simple: Those that survived the harsh winters bred. Père David's deer is also fortunate in that its genetic makeup allowed it to pass through this population bottleneck with no side effects. Now Père David's deer can be found in captivity all over the world. In fact, the deer is so abundant that it is farmed in New Zealand for venison. So much for success.

The captive breeding of this deer was not a well-managed, scientific program. Nature took its course and the deer sorted out their own breeding program. Fortunately, the deer's hardy genes could sustain the trial.

There are still private menageries to this day, though the more famous ones have not contributed much to science: Tito's island of Brioni, off the coast of Istria in the northern Adriatic, included a modern hotel for his guests and a private zoo.

William Randolph Hearst built the world's largest private zoo on his 250,000-acre San Simeon estate. Signs along the 5-mile drive from the gate to the castle warned, "Always drive slowly—animals have the right-of-way." Winston Churchill allegedly was delayed on the road for more than an hour by a stubborn giraffe.

America, however, was slow in joining the wave of new zoos, but once it lapped our shores, the momentum was impossible to stop. Traditionally, zoos or menageries have sprung up in cities—places with large populations, places far removed from nature and rural agriculture and places of cultural achievement with a wealthy class. Early Americans concentrated on surviving in a new frontier, fighting for independence and struggling to establish communities. Colonial America was a rural place with few large towns. Not until after the Civil War, during a period of growth for the country and a shift from agriculture to industrialization, was there money, time and energy for zoos.

That doesn't mean there was no curiosity about wildlife among the settlers. Occasionally someone would display a bear at a tavern, and by 1720, sea captains were bringing exotic animals to big ports like New York and Boston. By 1768, Americans had seen a lion, a polar bear and a leopard in shows. In 1789, a tiger, orangutan, sloth, baboon, buffalo and reptiles were put on display in New York. Traveling shows and menageries were flourishing here by 1813, bringing in the country's first zebra (1805), rhino (1826), giraffe (1837) and hippo (1850).

After the Civil War, the stage was set for creating real zoological gardens. The natural sciences were growing in stature, becoming professionalized and specialized. When this independent, maverick country began to establish its own zoos, it turned an apprentice's eye toward Europe. American parks were born and began to flourish during a rather stagnant time in the evolution of zoos. The people who started the first zoos here most often went to Europe for ideas on collections, architecture and animal care. As U.S. zoo historian Vernon N. Kisling Jr. has written, "Americans were still impressed and influenced by European science, technology, and culture. At the same time, they had strong nationalistic feelings and they wanted to surpass these European endeavors." From the late 1800s on, Americans arduously imitated the great European zoos—that meant, to a great extent, postage-stamp collections (one of each) and buildings that were ornate on the outside and easy to clean on the inside.

The Natural

ONE OF THE MOST startling changes in the concept of zoos was hatched by the son of a fishmonger and started in a flat potato field outside Hamburg, Germany. Carl Hagenbeck, an animal supplier and showman, opened the first zoo without bars in 1907.

Willie B.—an impressive silverback—was once called "the loneliest gorilla in the world." He spent his solitary days in a cage built like a cement bunker. Today, Willie B. enjoys a lush outdoor habitat and the companionship of other gorillas at Zoo Atlanta. *(J. Sebo)*

Kudzu, Willie B.'s offspring, is a healthy symbol of Willie B.'s dramatic change of environment. *(J. Sebo)*

The new bear exhibit on the Northern Trail in the Woodland Park Zoo in Seattle is by far the best in the country. It has impressed zoo professionals with its physical and "psychological" space. Even Fannie the arthritic Kodiak bear *(right)* was inspired, before her death, to behave like a wild bear, preparing a daybed for herself out of vegetation. The environment is a stimulating playground for the two young grizzlies, Denali and Keema. *(Karen Anderson)*

Deep snow inspired stalking and playing behavior in the young, heavily furred snow leopard on the day I visited the Bronx Zoo. Biologists can track these magnificent animals for years without catching a glimpse of them. *(Hugh Breslin)*

Dr. Terry Maple, director of Zoo Atlanta and a primate expert who worked hard to transform this zoo from one of the worst into one of the best. *(J. Sebo)*

Dr. David Shepherdson, enrichment expert at the Metro Washington Park Zoo in Portland, Oregon. "Active animals are psychologically healthy and more likely to be able to reproduce and integrate into a social group," he says. *(Michael Durham)*

The 2,100-acre San Diego Wild Animal Park transforms animal husbandry from science into poetry. The vast expanse gives animals plenty of room, but zoogoers can get closer to the animals on special tours.

Cincinnati Zoo's Jungle Trails rain forest exhibit is one of the best "immersion" exhibits, surrounding the animals (such as this orangutan and gibbon) and zoogoers with the sights, smells and sounds of the natural world.

John Lehnhardt, assistant curator of mammals at the National Zoo, with Kumari, a beloved baby elephant who did not survive. Providing appropriate social context for these animals is "where zoos in North America have failed most dramatically," Lehnhardt says. *(Jessie Cohen)*

Jay Haight massages Tamba's tongue to simulate an elephant greeting. Haight says, "There are two things you can *make* an elephant do— run away or kill you. But you can *get* an elephant to do a number of amazing things." *(Michael Durham)*

Hagenbeck's father had dabbled in showing animals, but encouraged his son to establish himself in the more lucrative fishing business. Hagenbeck, however, became an animal supplier just in time for the "zoo boom," which took place, according to Emily Hahn in *Animal Gardens,* as "cities all over Europe were trying to catch up with London's Zoological Gardens." By the time he reached his twenties, Hagenbeck was the top animal dealer—for a time, the exclusive supplier to Barnum. In twenty years, Hagenbeck reputedly imported one thousand lions, four hundred tigers, more than seven hundred leopards, eight hundred hyenas, three hundred elephants, forty-three rhinos, tens of thousands of monkeys and six hundred antelope.

During one emergency, Hagenbeck had to personally take over a shipment of animals stuck in Suez when his hunter became ill. Hagenbeck oversaw elephants, giraffes, antelopes, ostriches and sixty massive cages filled with rhinos, lions, panthers, cheetahs, hyenas, monkeys and birds. A hundred goats had to be packed up as well to provide meat and milk. Hagenbeck got the whole shipment to Europe, where he made offloading stops in Vienna, Dresden and Berlin. The number of animals that must have died in capture, forced marches and transport is incalculable.

But the demand didn't last forever and Hagenbeck moved quickly into an even stranger business: exhibiting exotic-looking humans. He imported a group of Lapps complete with skis and reindeer; Eskimos who paddled around in kayaks; Somalis; Buddhist priests; and finally the grand Ceylonese tour in 1884, which included sixty-seven people, twenty-five elephants and many cattle. (The New York Zoological Society also displayed a human being in 1906. Ota Benga, a twenty-three-year-old African Pygmy, was on exhibit with chimps until a group of black clergy protested. Eventually, he would take his own life with a revolver at the age of thirty-three.)

By 1893, Hagenbeck had moved on to trained animal acts, and he won international fame at the Columbian Exposition in Chicago with a lion riding a horse and a tiger riding an elephant. Hagenbeck then pioneered a gentle method of animal training, but after supplying animals to everyone else's zoo, and after amassing something of a fortune (particularly off the human exhibits), he decided he wanted his very own zoo.

He bought a potato field in 1900 and set about implementing his own unique vision, hiring engineers, architects and sculptors. He used moats, hedges, artificial rocks and winding walkways to produce a zoo that had no bars and fabricated the illusion that predators and prey were side by side—or that there was no barrier between humans and dangerous animals. According to Emily Hahn, Thomas Edison was a victim of this sleight of land. In 1911, while visiting the zoo, Edison rounded a corner and came face-to-face with a deadly African lion a few feet away. The inventor, who originated the proverb "Genius is one percent inspiration and 99 percent perspiration," sweated out this optical illusion.

Exploiting sightlines, Hagenbeck built prospects from which lions apparently coexisted with zebras. He mixed species and sculpted breathtaking panoramas of flora and fauna. His zoo, with moats and mountains, trees and meadows, was much larger than others. And for the first time, animals were displayed not taxonomically—all the world's big cats under one roof—but zoogeographically—African animals together.

The magical and whimsical sculptures—huge trumpeting elephant heads, massive polar bears and lions—of the front gate, called "monstrously ornate" by Jeremy Cherfas, leave no doubt about the realm a visitor is about to enter.

The crowds loved what Hagenbeck had accomplished, but other zoos dismissed him and his ideas for the most part until the 1930s. Many believed that the moats placed the animals too far from the visitors. Yet slowly the idea caught on, and by the 1960s just about every zoo in the United States had at least one "naturalistic" enclosure. In fact, the Hagenbeck family did some design work for the Detroit Zoo in the 1920s, work that was altered over the years. In 1982, while struggling once again to renovate the zoo, photos taken of the Hagenbeck designs were uncovered and much of the renovation was merely the restoration of the original scheme.

There is some debate about Hagenbeck's motivation and

vision: Was he trying to exhibit animals in the most realistic and naturalistic environment possible, or was he merely painting a pretty picture with little regard to authenticity? He did bring animals and zoogoers into the fresh air and the more natural outdoors. Hagenbeck himself wrote: "I desired above all things, to give the animals the maximum of liberty. I wished to exhibit them not as captives, confined within narrow spaces, and looked at between bars, but as free to wander from place to place within as large limits as possible," and "I desired to refute the prevailing notion that luxurious and expensive houses with complicated heating apparatus were necessary for keeping wild animals alive and healthy."

In fact, this was a fairly new notion. Emily Hahn writes: "Until 1902, no lion, no tiger, parrot or monkey in Regent's Park was permitted fresh oxygen, and when one quickly died, as such animals usually did, it was assumed that somehow in spite of all precautions it had been subjected to a fatal draft."

Unfortunately, Hagenbeck is not treated with any reverence in the zoo community. Although he introduced the great outdoors to animal exhibitry, he did not crash through any boundaries with the hard-to-maintain animals—intelligent primates and bears. While Hagenbeck's vision was more illusion than science, many of his ideas still influence zoos today.

The Turn of the Century and Beyond

THE BRONX, New York, is well known—some would say infamous—for many things. But few realize that this East Coast urban center is in good part responsible for the return of bison to their majestic home on Western plains.

About 50 million bison roamed the West before the Civil War, but there were fewer than a thousand left at the beginning of the century. They were slaughtered by the millions—some to feed the westward-moving population, others simply to keep them from the Native Americans who needed them to survive.

It was the conservation-minded and freshly minted New York Zoological Society that bullheadedly worked to bring these animals back. Perceiving its role in a way no other zoo ever had, the New York zoo launched a pivotal moment in the world of zoos. This was not only a scientific endeavor but a moral one as well. The men who spearheaded this zoo were men of action as well as naturalists. Their aims were at once lofty and level-headed. And that can be seen in the earliest accounts of the bison mission.

The Society's editor and photographer, Elwin R. Sanborn, bore witness to the long trek of redemption. From his writing about the 1907 journey, we see that it was as spiritually significant as it was comical in appearance. Two long horse cars left the station in the Bronx carrying fifteen bison and a cadre of well-dressed city slickers who were insured under accident policies taken out with Grand Central Station.

Sanborn wrote in the Society's *Bulletin:* "It was a bit awe-inspiring . . . to realize that in the midst of this vast station with its multitudes of people, its coughing, booming trains, in the center of the greatest city of the new world, were fifteen helpless animals, whose ancestors had been all but exterminated by the very civilization which was now handing back to the prairies this helpless band, a tiny remnant born and raised 2,000 miles from their native land."

This herd was established at Wichita Forest Reserve in Oklahoma. More Bronx-bred bison made their way to Montana in 1908 and South Dakota and Nebraska in 1913. There are now about 100,000 bison alive and well in North American reserves.

THE NEW YORK Zoological Society stood alone as a leader in conservation then, and its legacy continues today: It is still by far the leader of all American zoos in conservation, spending more money on field research than even the World Wildlife Fund.

Through conservation and progressive policies, the Society has distanced itself from other zoos, yet in many ways it represents in the extreme the three great elements that came together to ignite

The Modern Ark

this country's zoo boom: healthy, growing cities, available cash and nascent concern for wildlife.

Urbanization in the late 1800s supplied an enormous audience. Industrialization furnished that audience with the time and money to visit. It also provided some with a rather extraordinary amount of money. In the words of Russell Baker, "Brand-new millionaires shot up like weeds, and since there were no taxes to speak of, there was nothing to do with those millions but spend them." And spend they did. Names like Carnegie, Mellon, Scripps, Rockefeller, Chrysler and Dodge litter the history sections of zoo guides.

The progress that made so many rich, however, had taken its toll on the landscape. Within a single lifetime, Americans saw ranches and towns where there were once great shaggy seas of bison. Pronghorn numbers plunged from 40 to 50 million in 1850 to 13,000 by 1920. Our wealthy society was waking up to the treasure that was being stolen out from under us. Thoreau's "Walking" was published in 1862. The Audubon Society was established in 1886 and the Sierra Club in 1890.

New York's story may be the most important in the history of American zoos, but it is not the earliest.

THE ISSUE OF THE first American zoo is a matter of some debate. The Philadelphia Zoo is considered the oldest in this country—their zoological society was formed and its charter approved in 1859. However, the Civil War intervened and the Philadelphia Zoo didn't actually open until 1874. In between, the Central Park Zoo opened between 1861 and 1862 and the Lincoln Park Zoo in Chicago in 1868. But these zoos are considered to be nothing more than simple menageries. By contrast, the Philadelphia Zoo was a well-planned, scientific and civic undertaking. Housed in the arsenal, the Central Park Zoo held a black bear, a pair of Kerry cows, Virginia deer, monkeys, raccoons, foxes, opossums, ducks, swans and other birds—pets and cast-off carnival animals. The Lincoln Park Zoo began humbly with two pairs of mute swans from Cen-

149

tral Park, but by 1872 it included peacocks, prairie dogs, deer, elk, wolves, eagles and a bear. It bought a bear cub in 1874 for $10 and, in 1889, an elephant from the circus.

Markedly different, modeled after its London counterpart, the Philadelphia Zoo was built in Fairmount Park, around the last tract of land owned by John Penn, grandson of William Penn (the state's Quaker founder who once owned the entire state of Pennsylvania). The city, home to Ben Franklin, had strong scientific leanings (the first American scientific society, the first botanical garden and the second museum of natural history). In the zoo's first year, 200,000 people paid 25 cents each (10 cents for children) to see 6 giraffes, kangaroos, lions, a tiger, zebras, a rhinoceros, an elephant, a pair of chimps named Adam and Eve—282 animals on exhibit as well as 674 birds and 8 reptiles. President Grant donated two curassows (birds from Central and South America) and Brigham Young, the Mormon leader, handed over two black bears.

The founders pledged that "the scientific purposes of the Society shall be carefully guarded," but the zoogoers weren't exactly sophisticated. Within a few weeks of the opening, a sloth had been poked to death by canes and umbrellas. And though the zoo boasted the phenomenal attendance of 677,630 in 1876, during the U.S. Centennial Exhibition in Fairmount Park, that number was only a fraction of the 9,910,966 people drawn by the Centennial itself.

The zoo-building trend gained momentum. The Roger Williams Park Zoo opened in 1872, Cincinnati in 1873, Buffalo in 1875, Ross Park (New York) in 1875, Baltimore in 1876, Cleveland in 1882 and Dallas in 1888. Then, in 1889, the National Zoo backed into existence, evolving from a collection of animals gathered to serve as models and specimens for taxidermists.

In 1887, the Smithsonian's Museum of Natural History created a department of living animals under the direction of William T. Hornaday, a naturalist and taxidermist. Animals were kept so that taxidermists could view their habits and movements to create more naturalistic stuffed animals in more lifelike poses. There is some question over whether or not this collection became a trial zoo on purpose or whether people just heard about it. In any event, it wasn't just taxidermists coming to see the specimens, people from all over Washington poured in, and as the number of animals increased, a full-time keeper had to be hired. More and more animals and people crowded into the little makeshift menagerie, and soon Hornaday and others were lobbying for a real zoo with a charter, land and permanent structures. (Another great zoo figure, Abraham D. Bartlett, superintendent of the London Zoo from 1859 until his death in 1897, had also started out as a taxidermist, gaining fame over time and even stuffing the queen's departed pets.) In two sessions, over 1888 and 1889, Congress decided the zoo would receive half its money from the federal government and half from the financially strapped District of Columbia. Congress was so stingy with the zoo, that, early on, a special statute had to be passed to secure the $38 needed for the zookeepers' rubber boots. Nevertheless, famed landscape architect Frederick Law Olmsted was commissioned to design the garden, situated on 175 acres in Rock Creek Park. Although his plan was never fully realized, the zoo eventually laid out a path that closely follows Olmsted's original vision.

Despite the money and personnel problems, the National Zoo opened on April 30, 1891, with a healthy surplus of animals. In fact, it was often overrun with living gifts and had to turn down an offer of eighteen American bison from Buffalo Bill Cody. Elephants were donated by a circus. Alexander Graham Bell offered Mandarin ducks. A golden eagle came from President Grover Cleveland, and in 1904, the zoo received a lion that was a gift to Teddy Roosevelt from the Abyssinian king. Hornaday, meanwhile, after traveling through the American West, had become a great believer in conservation, and he envisioned a huge center where endangered species, such as the bison, could thrive. Disappointed over several issues (he was not chosen as the zoo's director), Hornaday resigned in 1890 before the zoo was unveiled—a pivotal event in the course of zoo history.

Washington's loss was New York's spectacular gain. In 1899, the New York Zoological Park was established through great effort by lawyer Madison Grant and paleontologist Henry Fairfield Osborn and under the directorship of Hornaday (who had been selling real estate for six years in Buffalo). Hornaday had for some time been publishing scientific tracts, such as "The Extermination of the American Bison," while in Washington. The marriage of conservation-minded founders with a conservation-minded director was nothing short of magic.

The zoo tapped into the vast wealth available in New York City—Andrew Carnegie, John D. Rockefeller, Cornelius and William Vanderbilt, Levi P. Morton, John L. Cadwalader, William E. Dodge, J. Pierpont Morgan, Charles T. Barney and William C. Whitney were among the contributors. Hornaday's salary started at twice what he would have received from Washington, and the zoo he helped create was soon the envy of every other park.

The zoo's advertised aims were to advance the study of zoology, to educate the public and to preserve the animals of North America. The country finally had a zoo that clearly dedicated itself to research and conservation. This is the institution that ushered in the modern American zoo.

The conservation ideals came from its founding members—Theodore Roosevelt and the other wealthy big-game hunters in the Boone and Crockett Club, who had become concerned with the spectacular slaughter of American wildlife. They drew up a charter, coerced New York to provide a site and raised money. While few European zoos of the time were more than 30 acres, the area in the South Bronx Park designated for the New York Zoological Park was 265. The progressive founders kept much of the heavy forest, hills, meadows, waterways and boulders of the park intact. Large spaces were set aside for breeding animals, such as bison.

And the more zoos that were created, the more New York stood alone. Nuremberg was established in 1912, Munich in 1928 and Zurich in 1929. Worldwide, there were about 120 zoos in 1920; 309 in 1959; and 883 in 1978. Zoo numbers were growing, but zoos themselves were not changing. Despite advances in other sciences, the brutal way animals were captured, the unenlightened way they were kept and the rare veterinary care they received continued.

Many modern zoos throughout the world did not have staff veterinarians until the middle of the twentieth century. A small group of zoo vets began meeting informally in 1946 and established the American Association of Zoo Veterinarians in 1960. New York once again led the pack by opening the office of the country's first full-time zoo veterinarian—William Reid Blair—in 1902.

The whole spirit of the New York zoo was different. What Hornaday knew at the beginning of this century is still not entirely embraced by other zoos, but it must be if they are to survive into the next. In the Society's Annual Report of 1913, Hornaday wrote:

"The cause of wild life protection by the Zoological Society has been placed in the front rank of importance among the objects of the Society. The serious conditions that now surround the wild birds and mammals of our country, and the world at large, actually relegate to third place some of the zoological causes that twenty years ago were of paramount importance. Strange as it may seem, ours is the only Zoological Society in existence that regards the saving of wild species from extinction as a duty decidedly paramount to the comfortable and unruffled study of anatomy and habits of those species."

Indeed, according to an article about the National Zoo by Jake Page in *Smithsonian* (July 1989): "Captive breeding of native endangered species—Hornaday's original dream—went by the board as the zoo sought donated animals to please local crowds, by way of proving its worth" to Congress and the District of Columbia. Page goes on to say that the man who led the zoo starting in 1925, William Mann, "wanted rarities, first."

Acquisition was the main priority for many zoos for years to come. The Brookfield Zoo outside Chicago was the first to exhibit Emperor penguins (bought from Admiral Richard Byrd) in 1935, a giant panda in 1937 and Indian rhinos in 1948.

Out in the sunshine of San Diego, the emphasis was on attractive settings and moated exhibits. Though in 1927, through a gift from newspaper heiress Ellen Browning Scripps, the zoo founded a hospital and research institute.

In New York, the zoological society had everything going for it. The zoo had business barons bankrolling it. Political heavies batting for it. And the zoo had a unique and sometimes swashbuckling staff exploring the world of animals and getting the public excited about its work.

In the first five years of the zoo, New York City provided $425,000 and private donors another $250,000. The big-name private donors who had helped to launch the zoo continued to give. In 1914, Andrew Carnegie was tapped for another $100,000 in the name of conservation. Margaret Olivia Sage established a fund that reached $600,000. And the twenties brought in more money from the likes of John D. Rockefeller Jr. and Edward S. Harkness.

Political influence was just as important in lobbying for the legal protection of animals: the Alaskan Game Act of 1902, McLean-Weeks Migratory Bird Law in 1913 and the Migratory Bird Law Conservation Act passed in 1929.

The zoo had an ally at the top—after all, Theodore Roosevelt had been instrumental in the zoo's start. In 1908, Hornaday wrote this letter to naturalist Henry Elliot in an exchange about the catastrophic drop in the fur seal population of the Bering Sea:

"Now let me give you some sound advice. Take the matter up directly with the President. If you can make an impression upon him, the thing is done out of hand. . . . The President is interested in all animal life; he is a thorough naturalist, and if you can convince him that Canada is now right to join in an agreement to prevent the extinction of the fur-seal herd, he may simply direct that the necessary action be taken. I have now appealed to the President three different times on matters which were utterly hedged in elsewhere. In each case, he took a friendly interest, and the thing that I desired was done."

It's no surprise that Roosevelt, the robust adventurer and naturalist (of course, his interest in wildlife was quite often lethal), would cross paths with Charles William Beebe, the zoo's curator of birds.

Beebe was a star. Scientist, explorer and philosopher, he was more likely found far under the sea in a Jules Verne–like contraption called the bathysphere or in the steaming jungles of South America than behind his desk. Beebe's far-flung and romantic exploits were not always appreciated by Hornaday, but they were by the public. Beebe wrote twenty-four books in his career, many of them quite popular.

In *Saving Wildlife: A Century of Conservation,* we see black-and-white photographs of Roosevelt and his wife sitting around the dinner table of Beebe's field station in Venezuela in 1916. Beebe atop the bathysphere that would take him a record 3,028 feet below the surface. Beebe surveying the Himalayas. Beebe in China. In Burma.

Conservation was already considered smart and morally right, but Beebe helped make it sexy. He had no trouble finding backers for adventures in the Galapagos and Bermuda. NBC radio broadcast Beebe's bathysphere observations to millions via cable and phone hookups.

But Beebe was also a serious scientist and a gifted writer. His thoughts on conservation are still quoted today:

"Let us beware of needlessly destroying even one of the lives—so sublimely crowning the ages upon ages of evolving; and let us put forth all our efforts to save a threatened species from extinction; to give hearty aid to the last few individuals pitifully struggling to avoid absolute annihilation.

"The beauty and genius of a work of art may be reconceived, though its first material expression be destroyed; a vanished harmony may yet again inspire the composer; but when the last individual of a race of living beings breathes no more, another heaven and another earth must pass before such a one can be again."

At the very moment this poetic plea for the protection of wildlife went out, many zoo collectors were slashing, burning and shooting their way through the world's wild places.

Romance and Death

MORE ANIMALS DIED at most zoos than were born there. Keeping a well-stocked zoo meant capture and importation. And there were many animal suppliers available to do the job, but many zoo directors would commission collecting trips for themselves on a grand scale. In the mid-1920s, William Mann, director of the National Zoo, persuaded Walter Chrysler to sponsor an African expedition. Chrysler's $50,000 paid for six months of travel and yielded a thousand animals, including a purple-faced monkey, giraffes and a leopard. Animal suppliers and zoo directors burned, shot, dug and noosed their way through South American jungles, African savannas and Asian forests. And though there were many glamorous and colorful tales from these wildlife adventurers, many simply set up shop in foreign ports, paying the natives for the specimens they brought in.

One of the most famous of these suppliers was Frank Buck, who allegedly battled man-eating tigers, venomous cobras and powerful rhinos—all without creasing his khakis or smudging his blindingly white shirts. Buck starred in a series of films about his work and wrote a swashbuckling book of adventure called *Bring 'Em Back Alive,* published in 1930, that might have more aptly been titled, "Kill Most of Them along the Way." Countless adult animals were slaughtered so that offspring could be collected, and more died from harsh conditions and stress during travel. For every animal reaching a U.S. zoo, scores of others perished in the process. Throughout his career, Buck delivered (according to his own estimates) 39 elephants, 60 tigers, 62 leopards, 52 orangutans, 5,000 monkeys, 40 kangaroos and wallabies, 40 bears, 100 snakes—all in all, 10,000 mammals and 100,000 birds. The number of animals who didn't make it is incalculable.

The enlightened Carl Hagenbeck was single-handedly responsible for the deaths of thousands of animals during his animal-dealing days. As he observes in his book, *Beasts and Men,* "The demand for wild beasts was continually growing, Zoological Gardens were springing up on all sides, and public interest in exotic animals was stimulated by the circuses and travelling menageries, which were now becoming numerous both in Europe and in America." Circus owner P. T. Barnum bought exclusively from Hagenbeck after the German dealer told him about racing elephants and "the use of ostriches as saddle animals." Hagenbeck says capturing a rhino or an elephant is tricky and that young specimens "cannot as a rule be secured without first killing the old ones." The adult elephants would usually be disabled by having their Achilles tendons slashed. "If the blows have been delivered with sufficient skill and force, the arteries of the hind legs have been cut, and the elephant bleeds slowly but almost painlessly to death. If there is a gun at hand, his sufferings are more quickly terminated." If this animal were defending a baby, clearly the "his" would be a "her." To capture baby giraffes, herds were chased on horseback until the young fell behind. Despite herds of goats supplying fresh milk during transport, Hagenbeck says, "even with this precaution a large number of the captives die soon after they have been made prisoners, and scarcely half of them arrive safely in Europe." For hippos: "The young, of course, are alone selected; and the harpoons are hurled so as to inflict as small a wound as possible. With constant attention this will probably soon heal up. Although this mode of harpooning calls for much skill and experience, no less than three-quarters of the hippopotami formerly brought to Europe used to be caught in this fashion." Sometimes pits were dug, though very often the hippo would either die during the fall, or be discovered by a lion before the trappers could arrive. Baboons were lured into large traps and then "With the forked ends they catch the baboon's neck, and pin him to the ground. When all the baboons have been thus secured the upper part of the cage is removed, and the creatures are firmly bound. First their jaws are muzzled with strong cord, made of palm-strips; then hands and feet are tied; and lastly to make assurance doubly sure, the animal's whole body is wrapped up in cloth, so that the captive has the appearance of a great smoked sausage!" Often the old ones were shot. He also describes a zebra hunt, with two thousand soldiers encircling a herd. "When they are thus securely penned in, a barbarous spectacle takes place. A thousand soldiers attack the zebras with long whips, and thrash them for hours, until they are thoroughly exhausted, and their spirit tamed."

Trips to Siberia for wild sheep, ibex, tigers and wild asses were just as deadly. Hagenbeck estimated that "half the animals usually die in transit." He glumly recounts one particular expedition during which "More than sixty of the animals were captured, but lived only a short time. In the course of the journey home every one of them died from diarrhoea."

Hagenbeck tells the story of the largest shipment of African animals he ever handled. His collector, Lorenzo Cassanova, became gravely ill at the end of an expedition in 1870, and Hagenbeck had to meet him in Suez to take over. Hagenbeck writes of the moment he reached the Suez Hotel: "I shall never forget the sight which the courtyard presented. Elephants, giraffes, antelopes and buffalo were tethered to the palms; sixteen great ostriches were strolling about loose; and in addition there were no fewer than sixty large cages containing a rhinoceros, lions, panthers, cheetahs, hyaenas, jackals, civets, caracals, monkeys, and many other kinds of birds." And all these animals needed to be fed along the way. "Besides the hay, bread, and sundry other vegetable foods which were needed for the elephants and other herbivores, we also took along with us about a hundred nanny-goats in order to provide the young giraffes and other baby animals with milk. When these goats were no longer able to supply us with milk they were slaughtered and given to the young carnivores to devour." The trip to Alexandria was a trial with a railway truck catching fire and the escape and recapture of the ostriches. Also, Hagenbeck notes, "the poor creatures were so closely packed together that it was impossible to feed them. . . . The whole of the next day was occupied in feeding and in general attendance upon my unfortunate beasts, which had suffered considerably from their long train journey." They were met in Alexandria by another of Hagenbeck's animal caravans. The two groups included, according to Hagenbeck, five elephants, fourteen giraffes, four

Nubian buffaloes, a rhinoceros, antelopes and gazelles, wart-hogs, aardvarks, seven young lions, eight panthers and cheetahs, thirty hyenas and twenty-six ostriches. Cassanova died here, and the next day, Hagenbeck supervised the animals being loaded onto a steamer. "It will be readily believed that I suffered no little anxiety when I saw my valuable animals, cumbrous elephants and long-legged giraffes, hanging from the crane betwixt sky and sea. However, at last they were all safely deposited on deck. . . ."

Hagenbeck depicts one animal caravan, which included hippos, forced to cross the desert: "However carefully we organise our expedition, it is inevitable that many of our captives should succumb before we reach our journey's end. The terrible heat kills even those animals whose natural home is in the country. The powerful male baboons are very liable to sunstroke, which kills them in half an hour; and any weak point in their constitution is sure to become aggravated during the journey. Whether this is due to the terror and strain which they underwent at their capture, or to being confined in cramped cages, I cannot say. But the fact remains that not more than half of them arrive safely at their destination, despite our utmost care." In the early days of natural history, a collecting tour meant shooting an animal and bringing back the hide. But progress—bringing animals back alive—was not necessarily more humane. With zoo expeditions, many animals had to be killed to capture just one.

Animal welfare lobbyist Sue Pressman, who worked at the San Diego Zoo in the late 1960s, reports that "lots of baby gorillas came over with buckshot still in them." An indication of how they were wrested from their kin.

Transportation was another problem. "If enough specimens die en route, the collector finds himself 'in the soup,' " wrote Frank Buck. Dealer A. A. Lecomte attempted to bring back the first zoo collection from the Falkland Islands in 1868. He started out with at least eighty-four animals, lost seventy before he reached Uruguay and docked in London with only eight.

Quite often these animals would arrive at the zoo only to die within a few days. Exhaustion and stress killed many, but diet was another culprit. At the turn of the century, it was all but impossible to keep a gorilla alive in captivity. Part of the problem was the totally inappropriate menu devised for these vegetarians. According to Wilfrid Blunt's *The Ark in the Park: The Zoo in the Nineteenth Century,* "The daily ration at one zoo consisted of two sausages and a pint of beer in the morning, followed later in the day by cheese sandwiches, boiled potatoes and mutton, and more beer."

The effect of this husbandry is made clear in a passage about gorillas in the fifty-cent *Popular Official Guide,* of the New York Zoological Park, by William T. Hornaday, from January 1921: "It is very rarely seen in captivity. The only specimen which up to 1911 had reached America alive lived but five days after its arrival. Despite the fact that these creatures seldom live in captivity longer than a few months, they are always being sought by zoological gardens. The agents of the New York Zoological Society are constantly on the watch for an opportunity to procure and send hither a good specimen of this wonderful creature; and whenever one arrives, all persons interested are advised to see it *immediately,*— before it dies of sullenness, lack of exercise, and indigestion." Not surprisingly, the first birth of a lowland gorilla in captivity would come much later—in December of 1956 at the Columbus Zoo in Ohio.

There was some good news for many zoos during the Depression: The Works Progress Administration (WPA) appropriated more than $800,000 for the National Zoo. Using that and other money, the zoo gained a new elephant house, small mammal house and an addition for the Bird House.

During World War II, any progress ground to a halt as resources were diverted to the war effort. All over Europe, zoos were ruined by neglect and destroyed in battle. Zoos in Warsaw, Rotterdam, Belgrade and Nuremberg sustained heavy damage. Hagenbeck's zoo was destroyed by fire in July of 1943 and just about all the animals killed—some shot by keepers to save them from burning to death. A mule, an emu and a handful of flamingos were the only inhabitants of the Duisburg Zoo to survive air raids. Although the Berlin Zoo stood through one battle in 1943 with casualties (human and animal), it was reduced to ninety-one animals after a second battle that same year (there had been several thousand animals in 1939).

After the war there was a slow recovery process. But almost all of the zoos seriously affected by the war were rebuilt.

THE RARE Mammal House at the Philadelphia Zoo, built in 1965, typified the "progress" in zoo architecture of the time—bathroom tiles are laid down on the floor and entire cages can be flushed like toilets.

Nevertheless, the sixties ushered in an era of change. Nature programs on television, such as "Wild Kingdom," sparked a grassroots interest in wildlife and conservation. Zoos began to realize that captive breeding was not only morally superior to collecting, it was becoming cheaper.

Advances in field biology, veterinary medicine and animal behavior restored the patina of cutting-edge science to zoos, just as they had in the days of Aristotle in Greece and later, Raffles in London. Jane Goodall was studying chimpanzees under the wing of Louis Leakey. Zoo veterinarians were developing better tranquilizers and immobilizing techniques and keeping meticulous records. Other biologists were comparing the behavior of animals in captivity to those in the wild.

In 1972, the American Association of Zoological Parks and Aquariums (AAZPA) was incorporated. This group, which oversees accreditation for North American zoos, had been around since 1924 but had previously been part of various park organizations. In 1976, a code of ethics was adopted, which demands that, among other things, zoos do not sell animals to hunting ranches. Today, there are 149 accredited zoos in this country. But it is estimated there are in total 1,400 licensed zoos and animal parks.

Accreditation teams from member zoos visit applicants to scrutinize everything from the care of animals to financial stability, ethics, education, services, science and conservation. Accredited zoos—most big-name, big-city zoos are accredited—are reviewed every five years by the association, which, in 1994, shortened its unwieldy name to the American Zoo and Aquarium Association, or the AZA.

Despite the murderous collecting trips and even two world wars, the story of zoos progressed in a straight and perhaps even predictable line. The true benchmarks of zoo history can be counted on one hand: the creation of the earliest zoos, the marriage of husbandry and science in Alexandria, the scientific perspective of the Jardin des Plantes, the scholarly purpose of the London Zoo and its popularity with the paying public, Hagenbeck's development of naturalistic exhibits. These milestones are clear, but the next great shift in zoo history would begin quietly, with a simple genetic study.

Sharing Secrets

IN THE late 1960s and 1970s there was some talk among geneticists about problems associated with inbreeding. Nate Flesness raised the issue in a paper presented in 1977 about breeding the endangered Przewalski's horse. The present population of these animals is based on only thirteen founders and many are severely inbred, resulting in some infertility and a nervous disorder that affects coordination. After the Endangered Species Act was passed in 1973, zoos were forced to think about becoming (re)producers. No longer allowed to reach into the wild to restock inventories, they had to make captive breeding work. Released in 1979, an eye-opening study by Katherine Ralls and Kristin Brugger and Jonathan Ballou of the National Zoo revealed just how dangerous inbreeding of zoo animals is, connecting high juvenile mortality rates to inbreeding.

The original study was based on research with sixteen species of hoofed animal. In fifteen of the sixteen, babies were more likely to live past six months if the parents were unrelated. A later study, which included forty-four types of mammals, resulted in the same conclusions. Other factors, such as birth season or order and management, were ruled out. In fact, with Dorcas gazelles, animals born to unrelated parents had better survival rates even if they had to endure the trauma of capture and transportation. The gazelles born to related parents had died of all kinds of medical problems and infections. For the scimitar-horned oryx, noninbred babies had only a 5.4 percent mortality rate within the first year. For inbred oryxes, an astounding 100 percent died within a year of birth.

With inbreeding, hidden deleterious elements of heredity stand a greater chance of being expressed. We have known for a long time from the work of Gregor Mendel about the dangers of recessive alleles. These allow people to be "carriers" of medical problems without actually having the problem themselves. Inbreeding increases the chance of these matching bad alleles meeting up and being expressed in offspring. And infertility is a problem often associated with inbreeding.

Some species, such as Père David's deer, appear to have little or no harmful genetic material lurking in their systems. Inbreeding this species produced no problems, but that simply is not the case for most other animals. Ralls's study caused a stir, but it was perhaps only a catalyst for change in a community that was already boiling over with new ideas for saving species. Almost simultaneously, a group of scientists associated with AAZPA decided it was time for shared learning and scientific cooperation among the country's zoos in order to tackle the overwhelming threat to so many species in the wild. SSPs, or Species Survival Plans, were conceived by AAZPA in 1981.

Previously, zoos that maintained vigorous and healthy species had jealously guarded their secret formulas. Other zoos were seen as competitors. In *Zoo 2000,* by Jeremy Cherfas, Gary Clarke, former director of the Topeka Zoo, tells the story of buying a robust and randy Przewalski horse stallion, famed for his proven fertility, from a West German zoo. Rolf enthusiastically mated with all the mares at the Topeka Zoo, but no young resulted. A later examination revealed that the stallion had received a vasectomy before his transportation. Zoo competition had prevented a fresh new strain of genetic material from entering the American population of these still endangered animals.

But those days of secrets and deceit would hopefully end. The wake-up call went out: Zoos now saw their animals as part of a larger gene pool. There was suddenly the notion that zoos were fighting on the same side of a war and that cooperation would directly benefit everyone. SSPs linked zoos together in an effort to produce healthier, more viable offspring for endangered species. And by 1989, there were fifty species in the program. But the transition wasn't easy. For a struggling zoo to give up its star attraction—a virile young gorilla or a fertile female rhino—requires tremendous commitment and often a sacrifice of enormous financial consequence. Participating zoos receive and send animals in a loan program that was initially eyed with some suspicion and is now quite popular, though clearly not always without rancor, even today.

Such population blueprints are being drawn for about 130 species including the cheetah, African wild dog, the giant panda, okapi, Bali mynah and Partula snail. SSPs puzzle out the best breeding methods for captive animals such as the Puerto Rican crested toad. Breeding is triggered for these amphibians by specific climatic conditions, and biologists are working to simulate dry spells followed by torrential rains so that toads in Toronto will be as productive as those in the Guanica region of Puerto Rico.

4

THE FUTURE IN THE FREEZER

Scientific Sex

HERDS OF ELEPHANTS, countless rhinos, cheetahs, tigers and gorillas exist today in a state of suspended animation, thousands of the most precious species riding on a timeless plane into a mysterious future. They do not eat or drink. They are not aging. They are safe from disease. And each requires no more space than a plastic drinking straw.

With this technology, Noah's task would have been much different, for today's ark floats on a sea of liquid nitrogen at minus 196 degrees centigrade in small rooms in San Diego, Cincinnati, Washington and a few other more recent banks. Tissue, sperm, eggs and embryos of the world's most endangered species are gathered protectively in cryogenics freezers. It is a cost- and space-effective insurance plan for the future and a crucial and almost bottomless reservoir of genetic diversity.

Zoos have clearly marshaled their forces and taken a quantum leap into the Space Age since the inbreeding studies of the late seventies and early eighties. We are cracking the codes of life—but slowly and with some false starts. We are discovering the microscopic secrets of reproduction. We've pushed animals to the brink of extinction, and now we have some of the technical know-how to commence construction on a bridge back.

But there are two problems: Our building blocks may not be as solid as originally thought, and because of a burst of expansion, the structure may be a little quirky and off-kilter. The progress in genetic research has been stunning, but there is no overarching philosophical blueprint; in fact, funding has dictated the direction of reproductive research, and consequently fissures and strains and stresses are revealing themselves. There are questions about which species will be saved and, just as important, which will not. How should rescue be accomplished—for example, removing at-risk remnant populations from the wild—and what are the rules? There is the dilemma of whether to save all subspecies of a particular animal (there are probably four for the tiger) or to telescope them frugally into one species. We must ask what to do with the surplus animals, the extras who require food and space and medical attention but do not contribute desirable genetic material to the meticulously detailed Species Survival Plan. Then add in politics, greed and ego, which manipulate the picture. And finally, just what are we saving—wild animals and wild places, or are we breeding everything in an unnatural selection that propagates the fat, stupid and lazy along with the fit, cunning and alert? And since we're talking about returning these animals to the wild, we must evaluate what we are doing to conserve the wild. Are the eyes of the zoo community narrowly focused on the lens of a microscope or are there enough talented researchers looking well past the petri dish to chart not just a suitable pairing of egg and sperm but an intelligent course for the future?

These questions must be answered. Zoos hold the key for the futures of many animals, but all the zoos in all the world could fit into an area the size of Brooklyn, New York. And for many species, such as the Siberian tiger, the captive population (seven to eight hundred) is greater than that in the wild (three hundred). According to various estimates, between 20 and 50 percent of the planet's biological diversity will be lost before we see this century out. Something like two thousand species of vertebrates alone will require captive breeding to pull through. And yet our tiny zoo community has the capacity to save only about nine hundred species.

Consequently, this community is working feverishly.

In 1980, AAZPA declared conservation its highest priority, and in 1981, the Species Survival Plan was born. Each SSP assists zoos across the continent to cooperate in saving an individual species. There were 7 SSP programs that first year; today there are 80 plans representing 130 species. Asian and African lions; black, white, greater one-horned Asian and Sumatran rhinos; snow leopards; lowland gorillas; tree kangaroos; tigers; maned wolves; Grevy's zebras; bonobos; elephants; orangutans; red pandas; cheetahs; condors; Bali mynahs; Humbolt penguins; white-naped cranes; Chinese alligators; Puerto Rican crested toads and Partula snails are among those who have deck chairs on this ark.

Using a technology originally designed to help paraplegic men father children, zoologists cause bull elephants to ejaculate while in captivity, and the zoologists gather as much varied sperm as possible in the wild with a rectal probe that emits electrical stimulation. Biologists separate sperm from semen and dunk the material in a biological antifreeze. They superovulate female bongos with hormones to make use of countless eggs that never would have entered the population. A sleeping tiger is implanted with an embryo produced by the egg and sperm of two other tigers, which were joined in a petri dish. A zebra embryo is carried successfully to term by a domestic horse—a trend that could allow endangered species to be gestated inside more common ones. Healthy sperm gathered from a dead bonobo five years ago is still viable today, and there is hope for the future of eggs collected while still warm from a Sumatran rhino just moments after her death. The Brookfield Zoo employs a cytogenetic analyzer to sort chromosomes, which allows them to sex more easily such birds as the Humboldt penguin and to help distinguish closely related subspecies of the South American spider monkey (only a few of the 375 spider monkeys in U.S. zoos are of known species and subspecies).

Geneticists employ computer models to track changes over generations in zoo populations. Computer databases holding family trees and DNA fingerprinting prevent inbreeding. The once difficult task of determining the sex of bird species is now a quick and simple procedure with fiber optics. The black-footed ferret, Père David's deer, Arabian oryx, California condor and Asian wild horse were all saved from extinction by captive breeding programs. And all this data can be shared among the world's zoos through a computer data base called ISIS (International Species Information System). SSPs cooperate with EEP (the European equivalent) and the ASMP (Australasian Species Management Program). And there are TAGS (Taxon Advisory Groups), which oversee whole groups of related species—cats, apes, lizards. It all sounds like science fiction, but some of this so-called futuristic technology has been around for a long time. The first successful embryo transfer was accomplished in England in 1890 at Cambridge University when Walter Heape surgically implanted the embryo of one rabbit into another.

In 1981, a rare and endangered gaur calf (the largest kind of cattle) was born to a very common—but suddenly famous—domestic Holstein cow named Flossie through embryo transfer at the Bronx Zoo. And in 1983 and 1984, the reproduction machine went into high gear with a baby boom of breakthroughs. At the Louisville Zoo, a zebra was born to a domestic horse. In Cincinnati, a baby bongo was born to a much more common eland mother. In what is now a legendary zoo story, the embryo flew over half the country—from San Diego to Cincinnati—in a commercial airline, nestled in test tubes taped in the armpit of Dr. Betsy Dresser, former director of research in Cincinnati and now senior vice president of the Audubon Institute and Audubon Park and Zoo in New Orleans.

"At that point we were using what we call fresh embryos, and so we knew we didn't have a lot of time," Dresser said in her office at the Cincinnati Zoo. "We didn't know how much time in culture, if you will, or in a test tube, these bongo embryos would last, but we weren't going to take any chances. And at that time, too, in 1983, there weren't a lot of reliable incubators or warm carrying cases. Yes, you could carry cold, but not warm, and so we were afraid of an incubator failure as we were coming across the country. So we collected the embryos in the morning and we had the eland hormonally synchronized for transfer that afternoon back here, which meant we had to collect, jump on a plane, get back here, make the transfers as quick as possible. And so the most reliable thing is body temperature. And there are several parts on your body," Dresser begins to laugh, "that reliably hold . . . well, among the most reliable is in your mouth or rectally, but we weren't going to do that! Another is the armpit." The five bongo embryos, worth an estimated $60,000 each, were taped in containers under Dresser's arm. "We wish the rest of the people on the plane knew there was a herd of bongos in there." Dresser also remembers with some amusement that the media, which met them on their return to Cincinnati, concentrated their lenses on Dresser's carrying cases, not knowing where the embryos really were.

Though it has turned into a funny story, the scientific achievement is not lost on Dresser all these years later. "That I was there when that calf hit the ground," Dresser says, "was one of the most exciting things in the whole world." The bongo calf, born to an eland, was quite healthy and has since grown and produced two calves of her own.

At the London Zoo, two baby marmosets were born after having been frozen as embryos. Weeks later, the Cincinnati Zoo announced the birth of a baby eland appropriately named Frosty. Like the marmosets, this also was from a thawed embryo, but it had been frozen for quite some time—a year and a half—before being implanted, which meant that these embryos had been harvested and frozen long before the London Zoo's marmosets ever dipped their germ plasm in nitrogen.

Many of these animals were closely related to domestic animals, and formed the bridge between domestic and wild animals for researchers to cross over. For each species there is a complicated puzzle of hormone cycles and storage temperatures and methods for sperm, eggs and embryos. There are great differences among species and even where there have been breakthrough births, scientists have often failed to repeat them. National news magazines and network news programs announce the births, and the public believes that the reproduction mystery for another species has now been clearly mapped. But it simply isn't so. Werner P. Heuschele, director of research at the Center for Reproduction of Endangered Species (CRES), says some people in the field "oversell technology. Oh, yes, we have transferred embryos of bongos into common eland and had it give birth to live offspring . . ." He pauses, then adds, ". . . once." It's understandable, says Heuschele, because researchers want to arouse excitement about what they do.

Though so much is unknown, researchers claim the culprit is cash. Oliver Ryder in San Diego says that if the president made tiger breeding the nation's number-one priority, we would be implanting test-tube tigers in the wombs of wild ones in no time. Betsy Dresser agrees. Why have we had a ten-year dry spell? "There's a somewhat complicated answer to the question," Dresser says, "but I can boil it down to just one word and that's funding." In fact, Dresser's research center is a shimmering altar to technology, all sparkling floors and walls of electronic equipment, surgical theaters, test tubes and microscopes. But it is almost a ghost town: all that sophisticated equipment and very few working human beings. Dresser's bongo work was abandoned when cash ran out on that project, but flowed in for work on big cats. Some are critical of media attention-grabbing breakthroughs, but if they help attract funding, Dresser says, then you have money to take all the little, less glamorous steps in research work. Dresser, in fact, went back to work on bongos, receiving funding to implant bongo embryos into wild eland in Africa. But there is much to be done: Science does not have bongo reproduction down pat. Breakthroughs are not always easy to repeat. "The weakest link in most all species—bongo, eland, cats, rhino, whatever," Dresser explains, "is the hormonal synchrony of the surrogate mothers. There are a lot of questions. And so what happens is that sometimes through trial and error, you hit that synchrony."

Sometimes it's almost through sheer luck, and the researchers aren't sure why it worked. Then, even if they do puzzle out the chemistry and timing in one species, it is rarely applicable for another. "We had the little gaur born to the Holstein, after we did the eland/bongo work," Dresser says. "Well, we tried a lot of similar things with the gaur mothers to get those embryos and it wasn't working. You see the same thing in cats. You can do something with the Indian Desert cat that you do to a jungle cat or a leopard cat and the differences are so obvious that you just think, 'Whoa! We're back to square one.' "

Terry Maple, director of Zoo Atlanta, says, "Any zoo that sits around and tells you that the strength of zoos is the SSP is blowing smoke. We're going to save animals by being great educators and awareness-builders and great fund-raisers and building essentially an ethic or an attitude about animals in the people who visit us and participate in zoos that will eventually allow us to save the wild. We just flat out aren't going to save these animals in zoos, and I think everyone's finally coming around to understanding that."

There are plenty of problems we don't read about in the newspaper. The endangered Przewalski's horse simply will not superovulate, a trait shared by all equine species. Embryos won't freeze properly in the pig family. There has not been one successful birth through artificial insemination of an elephant. Only one gorilla baby has been born as a result of artificial insemination, though in October 1995, in Cincinnati, a test-tube gorilla was born, which is a first. Two tiger cubs survive—one from artificial insemination and another from embryo transfer—but despite more then thirty other attempts, the feat has not been repeated. One of these test-tube tigers is kept in a tiny tiled cage at Omaha's Henry Doorly Zoo—living out his miraculous existence padding around a barren cell.

While the formula for freezing sperm and embryos has been worked out for several species, we have not figured things out for eggs in just about any animal. "Where egg freezing would really help an endangered species," Dresser says, "is when you have necropsies or animals that die unexpectedly. But what happens is that when they die, hormonally, they might not be just right at the point where the egg is any good. So what we're doing is looking at maturation of eggs in culture . . . you can collect all the eggs you want, but if they're not what we call mature, and ready to be fertilized, they don't mean a thing."

Dresser started the work that resulted in the birth of the world's first test-tube gorilla. Part of the problem with artificial insemination in these valuable animals is that zoos were reluctant to experiment with "invasive" procedures with them. If a female was producing naturally, zoo directors wouldn't monkey around with them in the lab. Consequently, Dresser says, for years the only gorillas in reproduction experiments were proven nonbreeders. Today, reproductively sound females are available. The project started from square one.

"The real unknown, always in this kind of work, is that you don't know much about the females," Dresser says. "And their cycles are so darn important because you can inseminate all you want, you can transfer embryos all you want, if it's the wrong time of the cycle, or if hormonally those females are not in synchrony with where the sperm is or where this embryo is, then you don't get any pregnancies." The most reliable way to track cycling is through blood tests, but these tests must be conducted on an almost daily basis, a difficult feat when working with many species like gorillas and rhinos. Dresser is hoping to finesse a reliable assay for urine testing of gorillas' cycles. In fact, it is not very surprising that gorilla urine assays are quite similar to those of humans; gorillas have menstrual cycles with vaginal bleeding quite like ours; and infertility drugs developed for humans have some potential for other primates. In fact, Dresser reports that several women have approached her to volunteer, as members of a related but common species, to carry one of these endangered animals to term. Dresser says she is not taking them up on it.

Recent advances in human fertility technology are already benefiting these great apes. Egg collection, which used to be done laparoscopically, can now be accomplished vaginally with the help of ultrasound. A simple needle puncture through the vagina will allow an egg to be aspirated.

Sperm collection, too, is a problem. "You know they always used to make the joke of being built like a gorilla." Dresser laughs. "Well, let me tell you, they have very small little testicles and the electro-ejaculation response is not great." Sperm counts are low, motility is low. That might be normal for the species, or electroejaculation could be to blame. Researchers are trying to teach these animals to masturbate or use an artificial vagina. The problem, Dresser says, is that, unfortunately, the sample often "hits the floor and it's either contaminated or the sperm go through cold shock, so you really don't get good sperm." It shouldn't be surprising to most zoogoers, who have seen this behavior so often at zoos, that there has been more progress with chimps in this area than gorillas.

Rhinos are another reproduction mystery. There has never been a successful birth from artificial insemination or embryo transfer, and for most species of rhino, natural reproduction, except with white rhinos, has also been a problem. "Nobody's ever inseminated successfully," Dresser says, "and nobody's even seen a rhino embryo. I have rhino eggs frozen here because animals will die and we collect the eggs. Now, I can't even tell you they're mature eggs, it's just that what I've done is frozen them, frozen the DNA, in the event that who knows in the future? Maybe you'll be able to inject DNA into an egg and start fertilization." Even worse, Dresser says, is that we are at sea when it comes to ovulation cycles. There are guesses, but "nobody can agree on what the cycle is. So that to me says a lot more work needs to be done, and yet there's no funding for it."

And though the SSP has helped cheetahs greatly, there is a firestorm of controversy about managing these animals and lingering questions about research. A cheetah is simply not a cow, and learning about reproduction, artificial insemination, superovulation, embryo transfer and just plain natural reproduction in wild animals has been cryptic.

The "frozen zoo" that we have read so much about "is in its infancy," says Dresser. "We have probably—and I think I can safely say this—the largest embryo bank in the world right here. And it only represents nine species of exotic animals. These are species [gaur, oryx, bongo, eland, etc.] that we know we can freeze and thaw. There are lots of embryo banks and, let me tell you, there are tons of sperm banks, but nobody knows the viability of these cells. Yes, they're frozen, and when they're thawed out, some of the sperm move, but sperm also have to be matured in order to fertilize." Though Dresser has more than nine species represented, because she is not sure of their viability, she will not claim them.

The thrust of these programs is propagation, but general health is just as important. Researchers coordinate information on what the animal eats, how much space it needs, what its normal social group is, how it advertises for and chooses mates in the wild, what its family tree is, how fit its genes are, what its normal behavior is and what diseases it is susceptible to. Detailed records are kept of the genetic backgrounds of available animals in what is known as a studbook. The SSP decides not only which individuals will mate with which but also the timing to avoid a baby boom or crash. A stable population, with large numbers of young males and females and fewer older members, is the goal. The SSP is also supposed to work to save animals in their natural habitats—in situ as well as ex situ.

Racing Toward Extinction:
The Cheetah

HUMANS HAVE BEEN bewitched by the cheetah throughout our shared time. Even the pharaohs were spellbound by the glowing amber eyes, the haunting teardrop facial markings, the spotted coat and regal carriage of this mysterious animal. On the plains of Africa, this predatory ballerina performs a spectacular dance of death. But the cheetah, capable of seventy-mile-per-hour bursts of speed, has been racing toward extinction.

The cheetah *(Acinonyx jubatus)* is like no other cat; in fact, it is no longer considered a member of the genus *Felis* (lions, tiger, panthers). It is believed that the cheetah evolved before the lion or leopard—and the original was three times the size of the 80- to 150-pound animals we know today. Once ranging all over Africa to India and the Near East, it can now only be found in fragmented populations in Africa with perhaps a few remaining in parts of southern Asia and the Middle East. Estimates vary, but there were probably about 100,000 at the turn of the century and fewer than 15,000 today.

The cheetah can accelerate from zero to forty-five miles per hour in just two seconds; it is aerodynamically designed for quick sprints but not sustained running. The sleek animal has a powerful heart, oversized liver and lungs, large arteries, small head, enlarged nostrils, large eyes, long legs, a narrow thin body, partially retractable claws that work like cleats and a muscular tail that acts as a rudder. A cheetah at full speed is able to keep its upper body and eyes steady. But the biological price it pays for speed is power. Once the cheetah makes a kill, just about any other predator can steal the prize. The cheetah is too much of a lightweight to fight. With pathetic regularity, even their cubs are taken by lions. As habitats shrink, this shy, unaggressive animal becomes more and more vulnerable to other animal hunters and to human farmers who consider cheetahs vermin.

But the cheetah faces another threat: poor reproduction. And there are at least two schools of thought on why: Is it the way they are built or the way they are kept? The older view, only a few years along, blames the cheetah's genetic makeup. Some theorists believe that about ten thousand years ago, the world's population of cheetahs was squeezed in some kind of genetic bottleneck (climate change? human hunters?), killing off huge numbers of the animals and leaving behind a tiny population with perhaps only 10 percent of its original genetic variation.

Lack of variation produces two problems: one is that dangerous hidden recessive traits are more likely to meet up in a mating and be expressed in offspring that are born dead, defective or infertile. The second is that the homogenization of genes makes all cheetahs, worldwide, susceptible to the same viruses. One virulent strain could wipe the species out completely.

Dr. Stephen O'Brien, a biochemist and geneticist at the National Cancer Institute, discovered this situation. In 1981, O'Brien says, a technician commented to him that she was bored doing studies on cheetahs—the genetic "banding" she was doing all came out the same. "I thought that was very interesting," O'Brien says. Further research with Dr. David Wildt, a reproductive physiologist, and Dr. Mitchell Bush, a veterinarian, involved grafting pieces of skin tissue from fourteen unrelated and related cheetahs onto one another. In every single case, the graft took. This immune response test is crucial. If a human needs a transplant, only one in ten thousand people would be similar enough for tissue to be accepted. O'Brien estimates that cheetahs have ten to one hundred times less variability than other cats—the equivalent of mice that have been inbred for twenty generations.

So what can be done? A certain amount of genetic mutation does occur in any population, but this is a slow process, and sizable portions of these rare mutations are deleterious anyway. What little variation exists must be preserved. Since 1988, members of the SSP for cheetahs have been studying cheetah reproduction, physiology, behavior, nutrition, mortality, genetics and infectious diseases.

But the puzzle of getting cheetahs to breed in captivity has gone unsolved for centuries. Cheetahs were first kept in modern zoos in London in 1829. The first litter born in captivity (since Akbar, the great Indian mogul, in the sixteenth century) occurred in 1956 at the Philadelphia Zoo, but they didn't live. Over the next 30 years, 113 litters (417 cubs) were born in North America, but there was a 37 percent infant mortality rate. Females in captivity rarely came into estrus and were loath to mate.

Seventy percent of cheetah sperm is abnormal (in domestic livestock, animals with 35 percent abnormal sperm are considered sterile), and a cheetah has only a tenth of the ejaculate of a housecat. So researchers are learning how to harvest the good sperm and to use only that in artificial insemination. In 1991, using a mobile lab,

NOAHS (the National Zoo's New Opportunities in Animal Health Sciences) scientists conducted a survey of 128 cheetahs in zoos across North America. The team electroejaculated 60 males and evaluated their semen. They also laparoscopically examined 68 females. Hormone analyses and skin biopsies were taken from all.

That same year, the Caldwell Zoo (Tyler, Texas) and the Fossil Rim Wildlife Center (Glen Rose, Texas) teamed up to produce the first cheetah cub through artificial insemination (AI). Within eighteen hours, however, it was killed by its mother during a violent thunderstorm. Then, on September 29, 1992, Rachel, an artificially inseminated six-year-old cheetah at Fossil Rim, gave birth to four healthy cubs. Days later, another female who received AI bore two cubs. Both of these females had never reproduced before. In November 1995, three cubs were produced at the Albuquerque Biological Park by artificial insemination using frozen semen collected in Namibia in 1994. Only one cub has survived. So far, sixty-three cubs have been born at Fossil Rim since the program began in 1986. But not everyone is convinced that the cheetah's homogenized genes are the cause.

After so much study, the cheetah puzzle—why they are so hard to keep and to breed—is still not fully understood. The majority of captive cheetahs appear capable of reproduction, but only 20 percent have produced offspring. The picture is shifting, however, for captive cheetahs, and there is hope that this new understanding can help those in the wild. San Diego, Columbus and St. Louis zoos have had great breeding successes along with collections at Florida's White Oaks Plantation and at the Fossil Rim in Texas. And at the De Wildt cheetah breeding center, associated with South Africa's Pretoria Zoo, the reproduction program has surpassed expectation: Females are now under birth control, and surplus animals are being offered to U.S. zoos.

These successes have led some to reject the notion that cheetahs are genetically unfit. The April 1994 issue of the *Journal of Animal Ecology* questions not only O'Brien's theories but his science as well. The most damning accusation is that the skin-graft testing was sloppily reported and that, in some cases, conclusions were reached prematurely before it was clear how the body was reacting: "The time is insufficient to gauge acceptance or rejection. . . ."

Experts in San Diego and South Africa believe that homogenized genes may be perfectly normal for the cheetah. They also question the dire reports about the cheetah's immune fitness, and even whether there ever was a so-called genetic bottleneck. This cat, whose body design has been perfected to slip through the wind, may simply be exploiting a narrow niche in nature. Perhaps its very survival depends on similar but breathtakingly well-crafted genetic configurations. Perhaps to craft a living creature capable of reaching speeds of seventy miles an hour, there is no room for variation.

These experts believe that a poor understanding of the requirements for cheetahs in captivity is to blame for the low birth rate. They hope to increase cheetah reproduction through low-tech husbandry. One early change, made long before this debate began, was moving cheetahs out of big cat houses, where they were displayed with their mortal enemies, to more private quarters. But we still have a long way to go.

WERNER HEUSCHELE OF CRES says that if you inspect cheetah semen from San Diego's collection under a microscope, "You'd swear that any male you look at is going to be sterile—abnormal forms, poor motility, low sperm count. Yet every one of those males is a daddy. Every one of our males has sired a litter, at least one. The problem oftentimes may be the female. We've been blaming the male for his poor sperm, but maybe that's natural with the cheetah and for some reason that's all it takes to get a fertile egg *if* you can get a female who ovulates—and therein lies the rub. She may not be functioning normally because she's shut down because there's too much stress around her."

Tim Caro, a field researcher and biologist with the University of California at Davis, believes that larger enclosures and rooms with views may help a female come into estrus. And competition between males for breeding rights may be a vital piece of the puzzle. Watching these animals at the Serengeti National Park in Tanzania, Caro has witnessed coalitions of males—usually brothers—defend small territories. Up to 60 percent of the male population may belong to such groups. He reports that half of the loner male population dies in combat with group males, and the competition for females in the wild can be fierce.

Jill Mellen of the Metro Washington Park Zoo in Portland, Oregon, says that understanding cheetah husbandry is murky. If a zoo is successful in breeding, then everyone tries to follow the model exactly, even though no one is sure what the key elements are: "The secret is, you do it exactly the way I do—OK, you have 126 acres, do I need 126 acres? Well, probably. But I only have 50 acres, is that enough? Well, maybe. You're in Arizona, does it have to be hot? Well, yes. Well, I'm in eastern Oregon, is that OK? Well, maybe . . ."

Mellen is involved in the assessment of big cats across the country—a project that is studying a hundred male and a hundred female cheetahs in North American zoos, half of which have reproduced and half have not. "We're going to throw it all in a big computer," Mellen says, "and see what falls out in terms of the successful animals and the unsuccessful animals." Mellen and others feel, in fact, that the cheetah's problem is more one of management than physiology.

There is one facet of cheetah care that everyone agrees on: The desperate need to understand the infectious diseases that can kill these animals. In 1982, all forty-two of the cheetahs at the Wildlife Safari Park in Winston, Oregon, suddenly showed symptoms of feline infectious peritonitis (FIP). Half of them died. Housecats, too, are vulnerable to this disease, but it kills only about one percent. Fossil Rim is studying a rare copper deficiency, which causes a loss of neurological function in the rear legs, as cases of it show up in other captive populations of cheetahs. Liver disease and reproduction problems menace the captive population.

The obstacles in the path of saving the cheetah are many. As with so many vulnerable species, the zoo must solve a bewildering array of questions, teasing out every detail of what a healthy environment is for this animal. The way we house them, what we feed them and our ability to protect them from disease are vital ingredients. Just getting the data is a tough enough task on its own, but then the facts must be interpreted. Are cheetahs hopelessly inbred or miraculously refined? The scientists can't agree, but for this nimble creature and many other endangered species, time is fleeting.

Elephant Eggs

FOR REPRODUCTIVE EXPERTS, the elephant is an enigma on a grand scale. Scientists have no trouble harvesting sperm through electroejaculation. And though freezing it is not perfected, the success rate is fairly high. Predicting the exact moment of ovulation, however, is a much more precisely refined science for male elephants than for scientists, but the record here is not bad either. Alas, though, not one pregnancy through AI has occurred in elephants. "What we can't get past," explains John Lehnhardt of the National Zoo, "is, we don't know *why* it doesn't work. We don't know what's missing. It may be a social component. It may be that the female needs hormonal feedback from the male, the presence of the male. It may be that intromission is necessary in order for the follicle to kick out the egg. It may be some other chemical imbalance that is physically stimulated. So there's a lot we don't know." Lehnhardt hopes the answer is in getting "the cocktail of hormones" straight. But, he says, "My fear—and this is totally speculative—is that it's a social aspect. If it is, that would be really hard to overcome, because it may require the presence of the male."

It is a serious fear. Moving any elephant is a tough chore, but moving a male can be nearly impossible. Many facilities have several females and not only no males but no restraints to handle a visiting male. Rotating bulls around is dangerous and expensive, Lehnhardt says, and shipping females away from their social group is unnatural.

Perfecting AI and setting up regional facilities with bachelor groups of bulls trained to provide samples would be the best-case scenario for elephant managers. But both solutions will be a long time in the making. And in the meantime, it is difficult to devise a reliable breeding program for North America's population of Asian and African elephants. Females and males live great distances apart; it is difficult to transport the animals; their sperm and eggs cannot meet artificially; and even under the best conditions, they are considered slow breeders: a healthy African cow is likely to give birth to one calf every four or five years.

Clearly, each species has its own mystery to unravel and when we unlock the secrets of cheetah reproduction it will likely provide no clues for elephant management. There may be a cure for cancer, but no single discovery can rescue our endangered species.

The Crowded Ark

ACCORDING TO THE biblical tale, Noah brought seven pairs each of the "clean" animals and two of everything else aboard his ark. Along with tigers, elephants and giraffes, he rescued cockroaches, venomous snakes and snails. But on the modern ark, space is limited and we are more likely to haul aboard lions than lizards. We exhibit and save sexy species. A quick glance at the list of animals in Species Survival Plans says it all: forty-nine mammal programs representing fifty-six species, twelve bird programs representing sixteen species, seven amphibians and reptiles, one fish program for thirty-four species and one lowly invertebrate (four species of the partula snail). So-called charismatic megafauna have won not only the hearts of zoogoers but the flexing muscle of zoo officials. And a study of zoogoers in 1986 by Jacksonville State University found that the larger the species, the longer zoogoers spent watching.

So, really, who can blame zoos? Most people in our culture clearly share these leanings. Dr. Don Coursey, at Washington University in St. Louis, has tracked how much we, as taxpayers, have spent on various native endangered species and how we rank various animals we think are worth saving. It is clear that though we say we believe in preserving the balance of nature, we place a much higher premium on big, beautiful mammals and birds. By sorting out federal preservation spending, Coursey has discovered that each Florida panther alive today is worth close to $5 million; each California condor, $1.5 million; each Bachman's warbler, $1 million; each grizzly bear, $184,000; and each black-footed ferret, $178,000. Here's a rundown of the twenty animals at the top of the spending list: Florida panther, California condor, Bachman's warbler, Puerto Rican parrot, Mississippi sandhill crane, bridled white-eye (a bird), white warty-black pearly mussel, Hawaiian crow, whooping crane, ivory-billed woodpecker, masked bobwhite, Key deer, light-footed clapper rail, grizzly bear, black-footed ferret, woodland caribou, Kirtland's warbler, leatherback sea turtle, Eastern cougar and yellow blossom pearly mussel—eleven birds, six mammals, two invertebrates and one reptile. (The popularity of birds here may be attributed to the fact that eggs make them easier to foster.) According to Coursey, eight of the top animals receive a full half of all money spent, while three-quarters of the bottom-level animals must share 10 percent of expenditures.

Which animals our government chooses to spend money on fits neatly with public perceptions. Coursey also conducted a national survey by mail during the summer of 1993. The 270 respondents (out of 1,000 mailings) were given one of five lists of 50 animals (a total of 247) that are threatened or endangered and asked to indicate the importance of preserving each animal. They were also provided with names, complete descriptions and habitat locations for each animal. The survey did not include fish or ocean mammals. The top twenty were all mammals, large birds or large turtles. The bottom of the list is made up almost entirely of "obscure rodents, snakes, insects and snails." Coursey says it's safe to speculate that these are animals that the public finds "neither 'charismatic' nor 'mega.'" Bald eagles, whooping cranes, green sea turtles, leatherback sea turtles, Southern sea otters and grizzly bears hit the top; Kretschmarr cave mold beetles were at the very bottom, preceded by tooth cave spiders, Tipton kangaroo rats, Bee Creek cave harvestmans (a spider), Eastern indigo snakes and Oahu tree snails.

Ben Beck, a scientist at the National Zoo, coauthored a paper that carefully examined all documented reintroduction programs since the beginning of the century. He found that "mammals constitute about 32% of all reintroduced captive-born vertebrate species, birds about 44%, reptiles and amphibians about 18%, and fish about 7%." In contrast, the paper says, it is calculated that "mammals constitute about 8% of all vertebrate species, birds about 19%, reptiles and amphibians about 21%, and fish about 52%." It is clearly easier to raise money for and attract attention to a program that saves magnetic mammals over repulsive reptiles. With good reason, we have a basic aversion to things that slither, sting and hiss. But, of course, a tiger could do us a lot more harm than a dragonfly, and yet it's still the tiger we care for.

There are those who argue that saving big mammals is fine because they are "umbrella" species. In other words, if you make the African plain safe for the elephant, countless reptiles, birds and bugs will be saved, too. Others say that saving animals should follow the triage system of wartime medicine: Those in the most critical but salvageable condition are served first; those with minor problems can wait and nothing is done for the third group, those for whom there is no hope. With habitat destruction posing the biggest threat to wildlife, it is the largest vertebrates who are in the biggest trouble. These are the animals that need huge ranges in diminishing lands; the animals who consume massive amounts of food in a world of shrinking resources; the animals who need to hide from poachers in an ever more exposed environment. Male Siberian tigers may have ranges of 500 to 620 square miles. African elephants devour 300 pounds of food per day. And living along the Virunga volcanoes in eastern Africa, mountain gorillas are relinquishing more and more habitat to agriculture.

This is the macro- versus micro- dilemma. David Hancocks, director of the unusual Arizona-Sonora Desert Museum, has a few things to say on behalf of the "micro" faction. In a paper entitled "Neglected Minifauna in Zoological Parks: A Dangerous Omission," Hancocks accuses zoos of nineteenth-century thinking as we approach the twenty-first century. Current zoo exhibits, he argues, give us no sense of the "functional role any of these organisms play in their ecosystems." We skip the creepy crawlies in favor of a "very small portion of the animal kingdom, mainly mammalian, principally African, essentially large or colorful or cute." Hancocks sets us straight: "Should all the big mammals become extinct that would be a major catastrophe, but the planet's ecosystem would reorganize and life would continue. Conversely, if insects were wiped out, fungi, or some other group of small organisms, that would be the end of the greater part of all other life forms, including the human race. Even more likely, the eradication of just a few critical species of pollinating insects could have such severe impact on our agriculture as to lead to the collapse of our present way of life and maybe our civilization." More than 95 percent of the world's animals are smaller than a chicken's egg. In Africa, the biomass of termites is greater than that of elephants. Invertebrates compose the largest portion of life on our planet—in weight and numbers. Little things clearly add up to a lot.

Hancocks, in a 1995 AZA paper, points out that there are "about 1639 mammal species in nature, and the average AZA zoo collection contains 53 species. This gives a ratio of 1 in 31. For birds the ratio is 1 in 98. For reptiles the ratio is 1 in 104. Amphibians are represented in a ratio of merely 1 in 2,000 species. And when we get to invertebrates, the ratio is an appropriately miniscule 1 in several millions. . . . The picture we present is a completely upside down version of what really exists in nature."

But William Conway, president and general director of the NYZS Wildlife Conservation Society (which runs the Bronx Zoo), defends current zoo practices. In a 1987 talk delivered to the AAZPA, he argued that "the big animals are often the species most likely to be endangered as well as those of greatest interest to the zoo public." We stand a better chance of saving animals with longer generation times. Zoos use their space more effectively, he says, by concentrating on long-lived bigger animals. And in the wild, slow breeders tend to be the quickest losers to environmental change.

More important, Conway emphasizes, "only habitat preservation has any hope of contributing significantly to the preservation of invertebrates." We simply will not preserve the diversity of life on this planet by capturing everything and sustaining it in zoos; there isn't enough space. There is nothing wrong with the current selection of animals, Conway says. "In the main, zoo propagation should try to save diverse, relatively large creatures, which present-day approaches to habitat preservation cannot accomplish alone; size and generation time are legitimate criteria for SSP programs. . . ."

But we still have the problem of the ark being too crowded. How can we lighten the load? Can we maintain smaller populations of certain species without surrendering that precious genetic diversity?

There are various mathematical formulas at work. Zoos are trying to look at populations and sustain 90 percent of a species' diversity for the next two hundred years. There is less risk to an individual in captivity than in the wild, and so the numbers for healthy population in captive management can be lower. The equations for computing the magic number are quite complex, however, and ever shifting. Some say that for a given species to sustain an ample and diverse pool of inheritable characteristics would require about five hundred individuals. But Michael Hutchins, director of conservation and science for the AZA, says there is really no magic formula, no rule of thumb that would work for all species. "To give you an idea," he says, "five hundred red wolves in a certain area might be a viable population, but five hundred Humbolt penguins is not, because they would all be in one colony that could easily be wiped out. A million penguins might sound like a lot, but it's not if they are all in one spot. It all has to do with context and the nature of the threat that might be facing the animal."

The economics can be staggering. Considering that it costs about $5,000 per year to keep one tiger in captivity, we see that for just one species, five hundred animals in the safety of zoos would cost more than a couple of million dollars. It is unreasonable to think we can preserve the spectacular array of the world's animals inside the walls of our zoos. Problems of space, money and the stunting of wild behavior forbid it. The modern ark is a revolutionary one that must not just ride the waves, it must actually stem the tide.

Subspecies Soup

SOLITARY, SECRETIVE and spectacular, tigers can weigh up to eight hundred pounds and measure ten feet long, not including the tail. They can eat seventy-five pounds of meat in just one sitting. "Tyger! Tyger! burning bright / In the forests of the night," William Blake asks poetically, "Did he who made the Lamb make thee?" These handsome predators are built for the kill, with heavily muscled shoulders and forelimbs, powerful jaws and long canines. Crouching in camouflage coat, the tiger silently stalks its prey in dense forest or vegetation, nimbly approaching before the orange flash of the final rush. Tigers once roamed throughout Asia, out to Turkey, Indonesia and Siberia. Fifty years ago, there were about 100,000 tigers in the world, today there are only 7,000 (two-thirds of which are in India). The tiger population has dropped by 95 percent in this century. These fearless animals are victims of habitat destruction and poaching. Their pelts are valued ($15,000) for their beauty and their bones and other parts used for Asian folk medicine— treating everything from arthritis to ulcers to toothaches—are worth much more. In Taiwan, a tiger soup is made from cooking their penises and served as an aphrodesiac. There are even tiger breeding ranches in China to meet the demand for bone, according to NYZS's *Wildlife Conservation* magazine. (*Time,* however, reports only that "China has considered" ranching tigers.) After years of the wholesale slaughter of tigers in China under Mao Zedong's rule, a surplus of tiger parts in the 1980s created a short reprieve for wild tigers, which ended by the close of the decade. Despite the endangered status of these animals, until the middle of 1993, South Korea brazenly imported tiger parts and the Chinese government sponsored the production of tiger-bone cures. Conservation groups say that tiger products are still quite easily purchased in Taiwan. Today,

a new wave of poaching, along with continued human encroachment, may doom free tigers. The United States imposed trade sanc-
tions against Taiwan in August of 1994, which could help end
poaching, but the biggest threat—habitat loss—remains. Tigers
require more space to survive than any other land animal. Perhaps
captive breeding is the only sure, short-term solution. (The Department of the Interior will spend $50 million over the next five years
on tiger and rhino conservation work.)

We can look at one thick-furred Siberian, the largest of the big
cats, and decide that keeping tigers alive is well worth a few million dollars, but how about five times that amount? There were
eight subspecies of tiger, though probably only five exist today,
four in SSPs. The Bali tiger became extinct in the 1940s, the
Caspian in the 1970s and the Javan in the 1980s. The South China
tiger is close to extinction with only perhaps forty animals in the
wild and as many in Chinese zoos. There are about two to four
hundred Siberians in the wild, four to six hundred Sumatrans, three
to five thousand Bengals and eight to fourteen hundred Indo-
Chinese tigers. To compound the problem, there are only five to six
hundred manageable spaces for tigers in North American zoos,
according to AZA officials.

We face three choices: to maintain each subspecies separately,
to help only one subspecies, or to combine them in what one zoo
director calls a "subspecies soup." Asian elephants could be separated into Indian, Ceylon, Sumatran and Malaysian, but the numbers are so low and keeping elephants so expensive that these
distinctions are dropped. This may turn out to be the case for many
animals. Bob Truett, former director of the Birmingham Zoo, uses
the original Noah story to point out how ridiculous the subspecies
problem can get. Noah herded aboard seven pairs each of the
"clean" animals (ruminants). If he were allowing for today's recog-
nized subspecies, he would have had 546 whitetail deer, 348 dik-
diks (tiny antelope), 98 moose and 826 chevrotains (mouse deer).
For the unclean animals, brought in two by two, Truett estimates
that there would have been 14 tigers, 12 cheetahs, 30 leopards, 16
jaguars, 22 lions, 8 clouded leopards and 58 cougars. "The moral of

this silly fable," Truett says in a paper delivered to the AAZPA in 1987, "is quite simple. If your ark is limited in size, you'd better forget about subspecies and save the species. There is no boat smaller than the earth itself that has the capacity to save everything."

How, then, do we define subspecies? Subspecies are animals within a species that may look different—have a different phenotype—usually because of geographic distribution. They can usually interbreed and produce fertile offspring. The Siberian and Sumatran tigers are good examples. The Siberian is adapted to the cold and is larger, with a much thicker coat than the Sumatran, which is built for the steamy rain forest. The Siberian is pale, beefy and powerful; the Sumatran is dark, sleek and agile. Truett has his own definition: "There is a strange human urge to classify. There is an even stranger academic imperative to write papers. These two phenomena, when put together, result in the human creation known as the subspecies."

Different subspecies do not always look different to us. Truett points to the eight subspecies of jaguarundi, which are impossible to tell apart without knowing the exact area the animal comes from. We can differentiate subspecies through three kinds of information: morphological measurements, molecular analysis, and geographical distribution. Using DNA fingerprinting, it has been determined that the eastern and southern subspecies of black rhino share a large percentage of genes, whereas Asian and African lions are separate enough to be considered different species. Even using state-of-the-art technology, however, we must be cautious in our splitting or lumping. As the Bronx's William Conway has pointed out, considering that humans share more than 98 percent of our genes with chimpanzees, "it is easy to worry about the loss of small differences."

According to Jill Mellen of the Metro Washington Park Zoo, the fact that we can't always see the differences has landed us in trouble. Zoos used to routinely breed Asian lions with African lions, so today American zoos do not have a breeding population of pure Asian lions. There are only two pure Asian lions in this country, both males; and there are thirty-three (fourteen males, nineteen females) "pedigreed" African lions. The problem exists for orangutans, too: There are Bornean orangs and Sumatran orangs. The males of these two subspecies may look almost alike to us, but genetic studies have concluded that the two subspecies are really quite different. There is a greater difference, genetically, than in some animals we classify as separate species. According to Mellen, "The SSP said we have to manage these two populations separately, and what turns out is that with the orang SSP, we have three populations—we have the Bornean, the Sumatran and we have the hybrids. Well, here's an animal that lives for sixty years, and about a third of the population are hybrid orangs. . . . That particular SSP is in big trouble right now. The limiting factor for all of these SSPs is the number of enclosure spaces that are available. The orang spaces are full, and so many of the moves we need to make . . . for example, our female has to go to another zoo to be paired up with an appropriate mate; it took two years to free up that space."

Oliver Ryder, at the San Diego Zoo, and his colleagues have discovered that there is more genetic variation among one subspecies of gorilla—western lowlands—than between the two others—mountain gorillas and eastern lowlands. Considering the reluctance of some gorillas to breed with one another and his recent work, Ryder has begun to question whether there may be some sort of "racial" differences among gorillas that we do not recognize but which they do. I told Ryder about Koko, the famous gorilla who uses sign language, who reviewed tapes of potential mates and had strong reactions, negative and positive, to the males she saw. "I'd like to see the mitochondrial distance between her and the ones she liked and didn't like," Ryder said.

But Truett has argued that nature is not static, and by carefully preserving all subspecies, we may be stopping time and halting wildlife in a freeze frame. "It is a very serious mistake to believe that subspecies are pure and unchanging in nature," writes Truett. "No wild tiger checks the pedigree of a prospective mate. Change is the only constant in nature. The only species that do not change are the extinct species. . . . We can keep our subspecies pure forever by causing them to become extinct, and that may be just what our SSPs are accomplishing."

Many experts and pundits disagree with this point of view. Ulysses Seal, of the Minnesota Zoo and chairman of the Captive Breeding Specialist Group of the International Union for the Conservation of Nature and Natural Resources, worries that in telescoping subspecies we could commit dire and irreversible mistakes. Almost every Asian lion in captivity in North America contains some genes from African lions, rendering the entire population unusable in breeding. Once you join subspecies they cannot be separated. And Conway worries about possible "outbreeding effects" (as is the case of sterile mules from breeding a horse with a donkey). On the other hand, Truett argues, quite persuasively, that interbreeding subspecies will create a high-octane cocktail of fresh genes with a jump in diversity. Instead of splitting spotted hairs to separate various leopards, Truett says to toss them together for a biologically stronger and more robust captive population. If the day ever comes when we can release some of these animals, Truett says, environmental pressures will split them adaptively once again.

Some fresh genetic material was accidentally introduced to the tiny population of Florida panthers, who made the endangered list in 1967 due to habitat loss and hunting. DNA tests have proven that at least some members of the panthers in the Everglades have genes from a different cougar subspecies, of which there are thirty subspecies in North and South America. In the fifties and sixties, these animals, with genetic material from a South American subspecies, were released by private owners who thought they were pure Florida stock. It was an error, but there is no mistaking the fact that these "hybridized" animals are healthier than their pure-bred relatives. Biologists from the U.S. Fish and Wildlife Service lobbied to repeat this "mistake" by cross-breeding the fifty or so Florida panthers with cats from other states, and finally were successful in 1995.

According to the *New York Times,* 80 percent of the small Florida group suffered from heart murmurs; 90 percent of the males have an undescended testicle; and 90 percent of their sperm is abnormal. Hoping that these problems have been caused by recessive genes, the state has brought in healthy female Texas cougars—the closest subspecies genetically—for "genetic restoration," releasing the first two in the spring of 1995.

This genetic exchange is nothing new. Before humans built highways and cities and cut cat populations off into isolated pockets, these various subspecies routinely met up and bred. But in captivity, in cases where we have very few remaining individuals in a population, we are breeding each and every specimen in a desperate grab at retaining the maximum genetic diversity. If we interbreed subspecies, on the other hand, we can be as picky as nature itself in our selection of mating pairs. Nature does not allow the sick and weak to reproduce, and if we want to help a species, argues Truett, neither should we.

Ultimately, the experts say, Truett is wrong. The top experts in the field agree that we are in the dark ages of preserving genetic material. We just don't know up from down right now. Jill Mellen is an eloquent advocate for maintaining genetic diversity. "We don't know what genes a tiger needs to survive in the wild, a red panda needs to survive in the wild and so on. And it may well be that the ones we can overtly see that make this panda dumb as a post, may be linked to another set of genes that are absolutely critical for its survivorship in either captivity or back in the wild. So that's why we try to get everything, because we don't know what that animal or that population is going to need to survive in a wild situation, so we're trying to save everything or as much as we can.

"We're playing God a lot, and it's very frightening. It's just scary as hell."

Leading geneticist Oliver Ryder says he challenges himself with a game in which it is two hundred years from now and he is looking back at his work, asking himself what he did right and what irreparable mistakes he made in handling the fates of exquisite and endangered animals. He states the case bluntly: "What we ought to try to do is screw up as little as possible. And so being clever isn't something we should try to do. We should try to simply say what we've got and have it persist. Persistence should be the highest criteria." Once you interbreed, Ryder points out, you can't shake it out: "Meiosis, completely. You'll never be able to undo it."

The Final Frontier: Return to the Wild

THE HARD WORK, THE commitment and compassion, the years of research and the millions of dollars spent on helping endangered species survive has a shining and noble goal: to place at least some wild animals where they belong—in the wild. Zoos that pick up the last few broken and sickly members of a species, restore their health and blow life back into their spirits, are guided by a vision— opening cage doors and watching a robust animal bound back into the complicated and mysterious realm of nature. John Seidensticker of the National Zoo has written that "the acid test for zoo biology is reintroduction." And though government wildlife agencies con- stitute the real superpower in reintroduction, zoos are important contributors not only of animals but also of expertise.

Releasing captive animals back into the wild is a dangerous endeavor. There have been great successes, as with Arabian oryxes, but the majority have been dismal failures, as is the case with orangutans. Reintroduction can be extraordinarily expensive—a million dollars over seven years for golden lion tamarins and mil- lions per year for the Arabian oryx—and amazingly complex—sci- entists must determine how much information is hard-wired into an animal as instinct and how much of it has to be learned; if preda- tors know how to hunt; if prey animals will know how to hide; can the animal build a home? Mate? Socialize? Forage? Orient itself? Navigate? For these creatures, it really is a jungle out there—no shelter, no scheduled feeding time and no processed medicine. How much of its habitat is left? And are the forces that drove this animal out still at work? Has the local public been educated about the animals?

According to Ben Beck, who recently coauthored a scientific

paper on the subject, of 145 reintroduction schemes involving 126 different species (13 million captive-born individuals total) throughout the world since 1900, only 16 have succeeded. While the other programs are not necessarily failures, some are young projects, for example, success is rigorously measured by a wild population that has reached 500 individuals, "which are free of provisioning or other human support," or where a population analysis "predicts that the population will be self-sustaining." Under this stringent analysis, only reintroduction programs for wood bison, plains bison (two separate programs), Arabian oryx, Alpine ibex, bald eagle, Harris' hawk, peregrine falcon, Aleutian goose, bean goose, lesser white-fronted goose, wood duck, gharial, Galapagos iguana, pine snake and Galapagos tortoise would be considered successful.

Large numbers are often set free with the expectation that only a fraction will survive, and life expectancy for any wild animal is lower than for one in captivity. While captive golden lion tamarins can live up to about twenty years, the life expectancy of wild tamarins is only eight or nine. Over a ten-year period, 136 golden lion tamarins were released in hopes that they would not only survive but reproduce. Yet many died. The first year witnessed a 41 percent mortality. Now, though, the balance sheet, including offspring, boasts 125 living as a result of the reintroduction (most born in the wild). The reintroduction combined with field conservation is working slowly. The wild population when the program began in the early 1980s was around 400. Today, there are 600 tamarins in the wild plus the 125 reintroduced or offspring of reintroduced tamarins. The goal is to reach 2,000 by the year 2025.

The roster of achievements involving zoo-bred animals returned to the wild is short but growing. Soon it should include the California condor, Bali mynah, Puerto Rican crested toad, red wolf, thick-billed parrot and the golden lion tamarin along with the Arabian oryx. The young New York Zoological Society carried out the first zoo reintroduction with the North American bison in 1907.

ONE OF THE EARLIEST accomplishments in reintroduction is the Arabian oryx, which today has reached a self-sustaining population. Completely suited for harsh desert life, the oryx—who may have been the inspiration for the mythical unicorn—once covered the Arabian Peninsula. But herds of these striking desert dwellers, creamy white with black markings, were easily killed in the open terrain. By the early seventies, it is believed, there were none left in the wild.

The introduction of guns and then World War I had already reduced them to just two populations; the knockout punch came in the 1950s when the oil industry swept in on four-wheel-drive vehicles. In 1962, the three known remaining wild oryx were captured in Operation Oryx, conducted by the Fauna Preservation Society. The three were shipped, with six other captives from London, Kuwait and Saudi Arabia, to the Phoenix Zoo. More animals trickled in, and by 1964, there were thirteen Arabian oryx in two groups—the Phoenix Zoo and the Los Angeles Zoo. The San Diego Zoo joined in to help out the "world herd." According to science writer and author Colin Tudge, "We now know that at that time there were quite a few privately owned herds in the Middle East, notably in Qatar, so the position was not quite so dire as it seemed; but that was not known at the time."

The oryx breed quite well in captivity. There are now about eighteen hundred in zoos around the world, and starting in 1982, several individuals were reintroduced to the wild in a reserve in Oman. Similar reintroduction programs are in progress in Saudi Arabia, Israel, Al Ain and Jordan.

Initially, these animals, which had been raised in territory comparable to the desert, were transported to a reserve and kept in pens. To mimic the wild, the ideal herd consisted of ten animals or more, with about an equal number of males and females. Over the course of about two years, the animals got used to the area in pens and then to larger enclosures. They worked out a group hierarchy but were still fed and watered. Finally, in the early part of 1982, within months of each other, the two separate herds were released. Their instincts were right on target. They traveled at night. They were able to map their terrain and to survive on little water—licking rocks and each other after a fog to gather precious drops of condensing moisture. They can walk long distances, and it appears that once a food or water source enters their mental map, the animal can reach it unerringly from any direction. Snakebite, a raven attack and botulism killed a few animals, but none died of thirst or starvation.

ORANGUTANS REPRESENT the other side of the issue. Since 1975, between three and five hundred of these great apes have been set free in Sumatra and Borneo by wildlife rangers. Most of these creatures were rescued from the prolific pet trade, and there is little evidence that any have survived. The forest canopy is quite complex and, because it is alive, changes from day to day. It is full of predators and toxic substances. Many orangs, released without training, refused to even attempt to climb trees. And there is a question as to what diseases these animals bring with them since there is no veterinary screening before release. Details are sketchy at best.

ONE FAMOUS CHIMPANZEE, Lucy, was raised as a human in the United States. Jane Goodall reports that she has witnessed Lucy mixing a gin and tonic, leafing through magazines and watching television. For ten years, Lucy was raised by two psychotherapists as their daughter. She was toilet-trained and learned sign language to communicate.

But Lucy's trusted parents decided to release this pampered pet into the wild. She ended up with some other inexperienced chimps and one well-meaning person on an otherwise uninhabited island in The Gambia. From all reports, Lucy lived another ten miserable years here; she died at the age of twenty-two (chimps can live into their fifties). Lucy completely trusted humans and it is believed that this ape, so beloved by all who knew her or read about her, was shot and skinned by poachers. When she was found, her hands and feet were missing.

It is a glorious dream to release robust captive animals back into the wild, but all too easily, through misguided "humanity," that dream can turn into a nightmare.

Hard-Wiring vs. Software

WE MUST ASK A basic question about the true nature of a zoo animal: Is it wild or domesticated? Over generations of breeding in captivity, what traits have we selected? Can wildness be bred out? What information is instinctual—hard-wired—and how much must be learned? Is that a wily tiger in that cage or just protoplasm with stripes?

Too many zookeepers are maimed and killed every year for anyone to conclude that zoo animals are domesticated. There is a quite reasonable argument that domesticated animals entered into a "partnership" with man long ago. The domesticated species we have today—such as dogs, cows and pigs—are basically the same as those that lived three thousand years ago. Today, we may tame a few individuals from various species, but despite many commercial schemes, and for unknown reasons, domestication has not been possible for some animals. Most wild animals remain unpredictable, especially after sexual maturity. Even in cases where the gentlest members of a species have been selectively bred over many generations, domestication has not been achieved. The ancient Egyptians failed to domesticate the cheetah, hyena and antelope. Native Americans enjoyed bears and moose as pets, but these animals were not domesticated. And more recently there have been failed attempts to domesticate the zebra and the common eland.

John Lehnhardt of the National Zoo argues that even Asian elephants, the ones used in logging camps and generally in circuses, are not truly domesticated. "I don't believe elephants are domesticated, period. The definition for me in domestication is rather strict: that means an animal who, over time, man has changed by breeding in order to fit his needs. And that simply does not fit how elephants have been managed in captivity. Because essentially there has been virtually no captive breeding [working Asian elephants are released into the forest to mate with free elephants]. So there's been no change in the genetic makeup of elephants in captivity. Elephants have been captured and tamed and trained. They have not been domesticated."

But the fact that a chimp would bite a human finger off or that a zoo jaguar would attack with full force certainly does not ensure that either animal would survive in the wild. There are two issues. First, in many cases, particularly where there are only a few remaining individuals, we have bred each and every specimen, regardless of its abilities, in an effort to maximize genetic diversity. The goal is to keep many different elements floating around the gene pool, so every animal available is thrown in. Nature doesn't work that way. In the wild, huge numbers of animals are picked off every day by predators, parasites, disease and accident. Only the most robust survive to sexual maturity and reproduce—the fastest gazelles, the stealthiest lions, the tallest giraffes who can reach those tender leaves way up in the trees. The wild selects those that can run faster and jump higher. What do zoos require of an animal? It mustn't go crazy in captivity; it must tolerate crowds of people close by. It must eat what it is fed. Not much else.

Bob Truett tells a saga that points to the downside of this SSP strategy. "A female snow leopard was recommended to us to reproduce with a designated male. We acquired the female as recommended by the species coordinator. She is a defective animal with a congenital eye condition and behavioral problems, so we returned her. If a species survival plan limits the reproduction of a species, we may find that we have no choice but to breed such defective individuals. Common sense and centuries of agricultural experience tell us this would be unwise. The only way to avoid having to breed defective individuals is to breed abundantly so that all individuals with defects and weaknesses can be culled from the SSP breeding efforts."

This leads to the second issue: What is instinctual to an animal and what is learned?

In 1977, Laurie Marker-Kraus, then with Wildlife Safari in Oregon, took a one-year-old captive-born cheetah to Namibia to see if hunting was learned or hard-wired in this animal. Khayam didn't have a clue about hunting, but did learn. Marker-Kraus spent two months stalking prey with her increasingly predatory pupil. Finally, the day came when Khayam caught a steenbuck—but he didn't know what to do with it. Marker-Kraus had to clamp the cheetah's jaws down on the antelope's neck to kill it.

For golden lion tamarins (squirrel-size monkeys from South America), recognition of predators appears to be hard-wired. As soon as any figure flies above—even a shadow looming overhead can trigger it—captive-born tamarins will sound the alarm and run for cover. When faced with a snake, a tamarin will alert the family by making a lot of noise. Ben Beck, who has followed the arduous tamarin release program from the beginning, says predator recognition was a "wonderful surprise."

The tamarins raised in the National Zoo in Washington and by other participating zoos have been released into a rain forest reserve in Brazil. Within the last twenty years, habitat loss and the pet trade had all but wiped these dazzling little animals out of the forests of Brazil, and there were only about eighty in captivity when the program started in the early 1980s. But north of Rio de Janeiro, the Brazilian government designated 12,500 acres of land for conservation, and in the United States the National Zoo launched a program to toughen the survivors. The goals of the plan are in sight, but the path has been tangled. The captive tamarins were dying more frequently than reproducing until Devra Kleiman, a guru of the zoo world, stepped in. She worked out the bugs in their diet—actually, she worked the protein-rich bugs back *into* their zoo menu, which had consisted of fruits and vegetables. And she split these social animals into smaller groups, since only the dominant female in any group reproduces. The tamarins had a baby boom, and by 1983, there were 370 in captivity.

Now the animals were reproducing, but were they behaving like real tamarins? Beck tells the story of the animals being offered a whole, unpeeled banana for the first time. They sniffed at the fruit and walked away. "This is in 1983, and I said, 'Good grief, this is never going to work.' Imagine having to teach a monkey how to eat a banana!" Beck says, shaking his head and laughing. Nevertheless, a year later, the animals were thought fit for limited release. It was a happy day in 1984 when thirteen were released into the Brazilian reserve. But the euphoria was short-lived. The release was a disaster.

Huge cages were assembled at the forest site as safe refuges for the zoo-raised tamarins in 1984 and 1985. The plan was to acclimatize the animals before freeing them. Beck was there to oversee the project. "I was beaming," says Beck, until a colleague pointed out that the tamarins were avoiding the vegetation inside the cages, and only "locomoting" or moving along the sturdy support beams and wire mesh of the cages. The same colleague said, "Those are plastic monkeys, they will never survive." Beck says he was pretty much right. Of about twenty-six tamarins released over two years, only one was known to survive.

So the zoo created an "outward bound" program designed to teach tamarins about the forest and food. Clearly, the most important thing was to give them the chance to learn how to locomote on real trees. A monkey must move with ease in the jungle in order to find food, avoid predators and socialize. Beck hatched a wild scheme to let the tamarins loose on zoo grounds as part of the boot-camp training. It may have sounded desperate. "Well, my zoo colleagues were quite put off by this," Beck says. Zoo people like animals safe in their enclosures and have nightmares about escapes. Beck had to jump through bureaucratic hoops to do what he knew was right for the animals themselves. Critics were afraid of the "bloody visuals"—a tamarin being splattered on Connecticut Avenue, with the media there to cover it. But Beck had evidence from the first release and other sources that the tamarins would stay close to shelter boxes. He has been overwhelmingly correct, but on the very first day of release, in fact, a female tamarin did disappear. Though it was never proven, it was thought that she was stolen by a zoo visitor. Over the seven years the program has been up and running (with about twenty-five animals), this is one of only two losses (the other being a young, tiny tamarin who slipped into a gibbon cage and challenged the larger primate).

At just such boot camps set up at the National Zoo and other participating zoos, golden lion tamarins now routinely live outdoors in trees during the warmer months, from May through October. They can find insects and fruit up in the trees to live on and they learn cautiously how to map territory. Risk, so much a part of life in the wild, is an element of training. The tamarins who adapt well to these conditions make the cut and are transported to the protected wild. The task is to try to keep them alive long enough in the wild for them to learn some of their own survival skills and, more important, to reproduce. For some reason, which the experts are not sure of, the babies born in the wild fare much better than their well-schooled but captive-born parents. Speaking as a conservationist, Beck says, zoo-born animals are actually a culture medium. "You put them out there, feed them, keep them alive long enough to breed—it's the kids I'm after. Because those kids look like wild-born tamarins and are pretty much self-sufficient." Why? It still mystifies Beck. Zoo-born tamarins don't recognize natural foods. They don't know how to locomote very well. After about eighteen months they come close to being self-sufficient, but not quite. "Their kids are born and—wham!—they're just like wild tamarins. They're locomoting like crazy. They find food. Now these are primates and they are supposed to learn things. Who are they learning this from?"

What's going on? Beck says his favorite hypothesis is that the zoo-born tamarins have to "unlearn a whole bunch of stuff that's appropriate for life in a zoo but not appropriate for life in the wild. The wild-born offspring are not so encumbered."

Today, the emphasis falls less on prerelease training and more on postrelease support. Released tamarins are provided with food, veterinary care and shelter boxes. And though they may be tethered to a support system for a long time, their offspring are not. There is good reason for optimism for these sparkling little forest dwellers.

For black-footed ferrets (the most endangered species in North America), the lesson plan has two items: how to eat (prairie dogs) and how not to be eaten (by owls, badgers, coyotes). Prairie dogs make up the full menu for the black-footed ferret, and when farmers began to poison these "pests," ferrets were nearly wiped out, too. Despite their lovable cartoon appearance, this member of the weasel family can bring down a prairie dog twice its size using powerful jaws and sharp teeth. Each member needs hundreds of acres of prime prairie dog property in order to survive.

On the endangered species list since 1967, the last known group in the wild was devastated by canine distemper in 1985. So the remaining seventeen members were gathered up and a survival plan was born. This program had a rocky beginning, with battles among the agencies "cooperating" in the venture, and the kinks are still being unknotted in the slinky animal's reintroduction. Teaching them to survive in the wild has been a lesson in patience. And there is disagreement over the results.

Experiments involving a radio-operated stuffed badger (RoboBadger) to teach ferrets about predators and another program using outdoor training pens have taught researchers that trained ferrets perform only marginally better than the uninitiated. At this point, it is believed that adolescent ferrets adapt to the wild better than adults and complicated training may be unnecessary. In the fall of 1991, forty-nine black-footed ferrets were released onto a windy plain north of Laramie, Wyoming. Some starved, others got lost or were killed by predators; only nine were known to be alive just a few months after release. A year later, however, young ferrets were discovered, so clearly some animals survived and reproduced. In the fall of 1992, another ninety ferrets were released in the area. Again, the majority disappeared, but of the eleven known survivors, seven had been raised in outdoor "outward bound" pens where they had gained hunting experience.

Today, the count stands at 1,400 living, breathing black-footed ferrets. Altogether, 228 captive-born animals have been released into the wild, though only 7 of those are known to be alive. Coyotes have taken their toll, but so has an unforseen epizootic of sylvatic plague (carried by fleas and known as bubonic plague in humans), which has killed off the majority of prairie dogs in the release area. It is estimated that the prairie dog population has crashed by 90 percent since 1993. And the remaining prairie dogs are hunted. Can the ferrets survive the plague? Are there enough prairie dog colonies left to support the ferrets? Is the captive population—held at the Sybille captive breeding facility in Wyoming and six zoos—stable and large enough to release healthy and fertile females to the unknowns of the wild? The debate about ferret reintroduction rages on.

Extinct in its native habitat for more than twenty years, a herd of Przewalski's horses were returned to the Mongolian steppe in the summer of 1994. There were thirty-one of these thick-necked animals, who may be the ancestor of the domestic horse, at the end of World War II, and today more than a thousand are spread across thirty-three countries. It is expected that these hardy animals will have a self-sustaining population in the wild by the turn of the century.

High-Tech Tracking

UPON RELEASE, biologists do not simply wave good-bye to their subjects and hope for the best. Rather, they rely on sophisticated monitoring and tracking systems.

Bali mynahs have transponders the size of a grain of sand implanted under the skin. A scanner passed near this transponder will reveal the rare bird's identity. This helps field biologists, but in at least one case, it also saved a bird from the pet trade. The leg band had been removed illegally, but the poachers did not know about the hidden transponder, and when the bird showed up at a pet shop, its identity and origin was proved.

Guam rails and pine snakes are outfitted with tiny transmitters. Red wolves can wear old-fashioned radio collars. But because collars are a nuisance to black-footed ferrets, they wear modified radio collars that fall apart in just a few weeks. Trackers have resorted to sweeping bright lights across the plain in hopes of spotting the distinctive emerald green shine of the nocturnal animal's eye, though they are often disappointed by these animals, who conduct so much of their lives underground. Old-fashioned tags, tattoos and body marks are also used.

Small and slippery Puerto Rican crested toads are fitted with high-tech backpacks. In the early 1980s several of these endangered amphibians were collected and sent to zoos. Most had been wiped out by human encroachment and by the introduction of large South American marine toads, who took over breeding ponds and resting sites, and ate not only the crested toad's food but the crested toads themselves.

Inducing these captive toads to reproduce was difficult. Their cycles are triggered by climatic conditions, and zoos had to simulate the long dry spells and spring rains of Puerto Rico and also artificially induce ovulation with hormones. This elaborate process achieved its goal, and by 1991 captive toads were added to the island's wild population. Once the toads leave breeding ponds, biologists can follow their movements with the help of pencil-eraser-size radio transmitters attached to the toads with biobackpacks. These tiny devices allow the toads to carry on a normal amphibian life and to be monitored at the same time by scientists. The goal is to reestablish Puerto Rican crested toads in their natural environment by the year 2000. It is hoped that eventually captive breeding will be phased out entirely. Education has helped in preserving this endangered animal, which may come into contact with the human population in areas as commonplace as parking lots.

The World Is a Zoo

As we think about reintroducing animals to the wild, we may ask ourselves, in all seriousness, what wild? Habitats around the world are shrinking and the little pristine land that is left is being preserved and managed as reserves or sanctuaries, blurring the boundary between zoo and wild.

The untamed Kenya that Ernest Hemingway and Isak Dinesen romanced us with has become a Disney theme park. Safari vans circle lions at a kill, shutters click, tourists shout, and the tawny cats hardly take notice. Another tourist group heads for adventure along the Amazon and finds leveled forest and no animals.

There are critics of the zoo world who would like to see some of the millions spent on species preservation go toward ecosystem preservation. It is a point worth discussing, but obviously the situation is complicated. Should zoos, particularly those hard pressed to stay afloat, close down, sell their land and donate the proceeds to habitat preservation?

As it is, zoo technology is helping wild animals. Tiny, fragmented populations of various species are cut off from one another by highways, buildings, dams and fences. Migratory routes used over hundreds of years are detoured, blocked or impassable. Zoos are ready to deploy their technology to micromanage these remnant populations. Of course, critics suggest that instead of shuttling genetic material back and forth among populations of elephants, we should open up some routes, expand some territory and protect the land and all it contains right now, before it, too, is swallowed up and paved over.

In the meantime, though, these small, vulnerable groups of animals exist, and they need help—environmental, demographic or genetic problems could wipe them out, as a hurricane did earlier this century with a population of whooping cranes. "You can never say, 'We've succeeded,' " says Andrew Rowan of the Tufts School of Veterinary Medicine, "all you can say is, 'We've managed to hold back the tide.' We're still holding back the tide because world events and catastrophes can wipe you out. If a volcano exploded in the Virunga National Park, it would wipe out 50 to 60 percent of the world's mountain gorillas." In tiny populations, demographics can shift randomly and dramatically if there is a sudden imbalance in sex ratios. Quite inexplicably there can be a boom in male or female births. And most important, genetic diversity can evaporate in these stagnant population puddles, leaving unfit individuals and a group unable to adapt to disease or changes in the environment.

In the late 1980s, when thousands of Zambian hippopotamuses began dying, New York's Wildlife Conservation Society was enlisted in an attempt to solve the mystery. Within days, a veterinarian from New York discovered anthrax, a highly contagious and deadly disease. A vaccination campaign saved surrounding wildlife populations. Dr. William B. Karesh of the WCS developed a skin biopsy dart that allows field researchers to gather genetic data without having to capture and stress animals. A barb in the center of the dart's vessel gathers a small sample before the whole unit falls away from the animal.

Biologists who have learned how to collect sperm, eggs and embryos to share among far-flung zoo animals can now use this technology to increase and shore up the stores of genetic material for species such as rhinos held in various sanctuaries. We can build a world gene pool among the captive and the wild. Instead of reintroducing zoo animals back to nature, we can, through artificial insemination and embryo transfer, release their genetic material instead. This exciting approach would not disrupt territories and distribution, and it would not push a captive and uninitiated animal along that treacherous road from pampered shelter to the unforgiving wild. What better reintroduction plan could there be than to transport a healthy tiger embryo with distant and varied genes right into the very womb of the wild—a tigress living an untamed life in the vast pine forest that is the taiga?

Ben Beck at the National Zoo says conservationists used to disdain zoos. "And now all of a sudden you look at what's going on in wildlife management and conservation biology, and it looks real zooey to me. I look out there and here are these guys translocating a rhinoceros in a crate. When they realized there was no longer a corridor between here and there and they had to move this rhino, they said, 'Well how do you move a rhino? We don't know how to do that.' So they got on the phone and called a zoo. You send a zoo vet over, and he darts the rhino." Zoos have helped a great deal in determining tranquilizer dosages, developing exotic vet sciences, diagnosing and treating disease, establishing a database of normal blood values for many species and analyzing the genetics of small population management.

To simply observe secretive species over extended periods of time provides information that would not be possible in the wild without elaborate telemetry equipment. "Many of these animals are impossible or darn near impossible to study in the wild," says Michael Hutchins. "You just can't watch them long enough in order to study them socially, and that's why studies in zoos are so important." I stood and watched three young snow leopards stalk and wrestle one another in their snow-filled outdoor enclosure at the Bronx Zoo and realized how rare it would have been for noted naturalist George Schaller to get this long a glimpse of them in his early studies on the Tibetan plateau. These elusive animals are found in China, four states that were part of the former USSR, Pakistan, Mongolia, India, Afghanistan, Butan and Nepal, but until recently, rough terrain, steep cliffs and transportation problems hampered scientific research.

The Case of the Condor

BECAUSE OF THE unstable environment, we may sometimes be saving animals from the fire and then releasing them into the frying pan. Take the case of the California condor. Biologists can't transform the West back into a wilderness area, but they hope to give these birds a chance by controlling what the released condors eat.

The largest birds in North America, California condors once covered the continent. But by the sixteenth century they could be found only along the Pacific Coast. Throughout the 1800s, the numbers of these scavengers plummeted as they consumed the unclaimed and lead-laden prey of hunters and as they fed on poisoned carcasses put out by farmers trying to reduce the number of predators. They were shot and baited and had their eggs stolen. In our time, high-tension wires and pesticides such as DDT teamed up with lead poisoning to drive condors toward extinction.

Simmering debate during the sixties and seventies boiled over in the eighties as zoos, wildlife groups and the Fish and Wildlife Service battled over a course of action. In 1982, fewer than twenty-five California condors survived. And while zoos, particularly the San Diego Wild Animal Park and the L.A. Zoo agreed with Fish and Wildlife and California Fish and Game that captive breeding was the answer, many conservationists argued, as did the Sierra Club, that these magnificent birds should be left alone or allowed to "die with dignity." Their case was bolstered by an unfortunate accident in June of 1980, when experts from National Audubon and Fish and Wildlife weighed and measured a wild chick and then watched it die from the stress of being handled.

Because of their featherless and wrinkled red heads, these birds may appear grotesque on the ground, but they are a vision of beauty in flight. With a wingspan of up to ten feet, a condor can race across the sky at eighty miles an hour or coast on thermals for an hour with a single wing flap.

There was agreement in the desire to see these birds survive, but not in the way to achieve this goal. Yet with numbers so frighteningly low, action had to be taken. By 1983, there were only three captive condors, and biologists were working on "double-clutching" in the wild to coax population numbers up. If an egg is removed to be hatched in an incubator, the mother condor will immediately lay another—an important development, as mated pairs otherwise tend to produce only one chick every two years. In captivity, condor numbers were finally on the rise.

But in the wild, birds were vanishing, and the reasons weren't clear. Between 1984 and 1985, seven of the remaining sixteen wild condors disappeared. While people argued, the birds in the wild were suffering and dying from lead poisoning. Lead-free carcasses were put out for them in the interim and, finally, after a legal battle, the last remaining wild condors were caught and brought to safety. On Easter Sunday, 1987, the last free California condor was captured.

There were twenty-seven California condors in captivity that year. The first chick conceived and hatched in captivity was produced in 1988. Four chicks were hatched the following year, eight in 1990 and twelve in 1991. In captivity, their numbers swelled. Andean condors were released (only females were released to prevent breeding), like canaries in a coal mine, to see if condors could survive. The pilot program went off without a hitch, and in January of 1992, two captive-born California condors were set free along with two "companion" Andean condors.

The male California condor died from ingesting antifreeze, the two Andean condors were brought back into captivity, and in December of 1992, six more California condors were released, with more releases planned for the future.

Sites and strategies have changed over time—six young condors are being released in Arizona, north of the Grand Canyon at the end of 1996. But today, condors are thriving and breeding in a quiet corner of the L.A. Zoo grounds—in large flight cages called condorminiums—awaiting eventual release. There are 121 living, breathing and flying California condors in the world right now—seventeen living in the wild. Those that don't flourish in the wild are recaptured (as three wayward condors were in the spring of 1994) and others are released in their place. The recovery project is expected to take time—and money; the price tag is hovering at about $15 million.

The only dilemma may sound strange. In order for California condors to survive in the new "wild," their behavior must be altered, because their old behaviors won't support them in this harsh world. Now, chicks are often raised in groups. Instead of free-spirit scavengers, heading out to feed and fly where they please, these released condors are being trained to feed in locations where clean carcasses are set out for them. The foraging areas are sited away from dangerous oil and gas fields and hunting grounds where condors could come into contact with their deadly enemy, lead.

So, zoo release programs are being criticized. Are these really wild animals or merely pets on a long leash? Without the capture program, we simply would not have condors at all, and without providing food to the released birds, we would lose earlier gains. There is still room for improvement; maybe large preserves or sanctuaries that hold cougars and elk and condors can be established. The luxury of truly "wild" condors is one we don't have available at this time; nevertheless, we do have California condors soaring in the sky once again.

Conservation Outside the Gate

SOMEWHERE IN HWANGE National Park in northwest Zimbabwe, as the burning African sun dips below the horizon, a pack of wild dogs, rare animals with bat ears and crazy coats, runs along the treeless plain. Nearby, researchers, partially funded with zoo money, sit in a Land Rover, picking up the beeps transmitted by radio collars fitted to these strange "painted wolves." Scientists are trying desperately to learn about this enigmatic and elusive species whose decline has been breathtaking. African wild dogs have disappeared from nineteen of thirty-two countries where they once roamed. In Zimbabwe alone, their numbers have been halved in the last decade. These rough-and-tumble hunters, who cover huge tracts of land in pursuit of game, are the most endangered large carnivores in Africa. Perhaps only three thousand survive today. And so far, population shifts have been unpredictable, which makes their conservation all the tougher.

The only way to save African wild dogs is to understand them intimately. That means hours of sitting in the bush, a labor-intensive task that is funded in Zimbabwe, at least partially, by the Chicago Zoological Society (which operates the Brookfield Zoo). Researchers studying wild dogs hope to get more than just money out of Chicago's Brookfield Zoo. Working with captive wild dogs, the zoo can contribute information on disease and vaccination, as well as behavioral and endocrinological factors in breeding.

Though it may be problematic for financially strapped zoos to fund conservation projects in the far corners of the world, it is vital—not only for the survival of the species but for the survival of zoos themselves. As Michael Robinson, director of the National Zoo, has written, all the work in high-tech reproduction of endangered species "cannot do more than skim the surface of the problem." Robinson asserts, "We need to save habitats, and that can be accomplished only if we involve concerned people. That, I contend, is our true vocation." While there is much disagreement about the mission of the modern zoo, there is no doubt that zoos must find a way to link themselves with the preservation of ecosystems and habitat. And many smart zoos are doing just that.

"In the past," says Michael Hutchins, "zoos were looked at as modern Noah's arks, and the idea was that if an animal becomes endangered, you bring it into captivity, you breed it, and then you reintroduce it at some unspecified time in the future when human populations have begun to stabilize. We don't buy that paradigm. What we need is action right now. We need to save existing habitats." But Hutchins acknowledges that there are many obstacles to overcome. "Zoos are generally funded by local governments and they're going to ask the question, 'Why should we be getting involved in international conservation?' Well, I think there are a lot of reasons." Hutchins claims both an ethical obligation and a financial incentive. Good conservation work, he says, will give zoos "access to monies and media attention that they have never had access to before. There's just going to be a bundle of benefits that come down the pike."

Along with the wild dog project, the Brookfield Zoo is supporting other conservation initiatives in Australia. It bought land in South Australia and turned a sheep farm into a wombat preserve, eventually donating it to the country's wildlife service. It is involved with other zoos and conservation groups in helping the eastern barred bandicoot and the brush-tailed phascogale (both small marsupials). And Brookfield helps support field research on the duck-billed platypus, an animal that has never reproduced regularly in captivity.

The San Diego Zoo and Chicago's Lincoln Park Zoo have teamed up to establish a research station in Paraguay to stabilize the Chacoan peccary population. The Metro Washington Zoo in Portland sends its veterinarian to Southeast Asia six months of the year to study reproduction with wild and working elephants. They also help with research on drills in Nigeria and Francois's black-leaf monkeys in Vietnam. And Zoo Atlanta has partnered with the Dian Fossey Gorilla Fund, generating revenue and resources to save the world's precious few mountain gorillas.

Philadelphia is trying to preserve one of the last shreds of intact rain forest on the west coast of Africa. Liberia holds the largest remains of the Upper Guinean Forest, and unlike any other West African country, it contains all the climatic conditions necessary for a rain forest. The country's Sapo National Park is a five-hundred-square-mile piece of relatively undisturbed lowland rain forest. This rich and rare park is home to forest elephants, pygmy hippos, chimpanzees, the recently rediscovered Liberian mongoose, bongos, leopards, golden cats and the most uncommon duiker in the world—Jentink's duiker, a large forest antelope—as well as 568 species of bird. Through financial support and field research, the zoo and other conservation groups helped persuade the government to establish Sapo as the country's first national park in 1983.

Sapo National Park has nothing to do with the day-to-day operations of the Philadelphia Zoo; in fact, the zoo contains hardly any species native to West Africa's Upper Guinean forests. But in the worlds of Bill Konstant, formerly of the zoo's One with Nature conservation program, "The 'Adopt-a-Park' concept does not focus upon increasing the number and size of captive breeding programs but upon what zoos can and should do to ensure the survival of threatened species in their natural habitats. It is a partnership effort, formed with the intent that a zoo can provide partial operating support and augment programs managed by government authorities."

Sapo needs to be protected from logging, farming and the hunting of "bush meat." To that end, the zoo will help the park organize awareness and appreciation of wildlife in Liberia, hire and train staff members and restore and replace damaged or lost equipment.

Even tiny Roger Williams Park Zoo in Providence, Rhode Island, finds time and money to devote to conservation. Anne Savage, director of research, is the crusader for cotton-top tamarins. These tiny South American monkeys (weighing less than one pound), from the tropical forests of Colombia, survived the 1960s and 1970s, when U.S. biomedical researchers imported them by the tens of thousands; they are now threatened by ever-increasing habitat destruction. About two thousand square miles of tropical forest is razed each year in that country. Savage works with other groups to preserve as much land as possible; to study tamarins in the wild and in captivity to better understand their behavior; and to work with the local people so that they will care about saving these endangered primates. (Providing people with small cook stoves allows them to use two-thirds less wood than with an open fire.) The zoo also sets aside $8,000 to help fund eight different field projects.

But only one zoo carries the weight and wallop of a five-hundred-pound gorilla: the Bronx Zoo's conservation arm, the Wildlife Conservation Society. From the mountains of Nepal to the jungles of Cameroon, the society has rolled up its sleeves and gone to work. With more than 272 field programs in 46 countries, WCS spends more and reaches farther with field operations than any other conservation organization. It represents almost three-quarters of all field projects run by accredited zoos. In fact, it has been responsible for the creation of more than a hundred parks around the world.

When James Powell, a research biologist with WCS, has trouble locating forest elephants in the wet, dense jungle of Cameroon, he faxes New York. There, in a warm and dry office, curator of mammals Fred Koontz checks a computer and faxes back the longitude and latitude of the large but elusive animals. The computer also picks up the ambient temperature and reports on whether the animal has traveled within the previous twelve hours.

Three elephants in Korup National Park in southwestern Cameroon have been outfitted with radio collars that use ultra-high-frequency signals and are linked to two weather satellites. Tracking these mysterious animals is difficult with conventional telemetry, but knowing their whereabouts is vital—it is estimated that 140 have been killed by poachers in four years and that there may only be 500 left in the park. One-third of Africa's 700,000 elephants are forest elephants, but not much is known about them.

This field research is one of the more recent projects for New York, but the organization was founded on just such conservation. The Bronx Zoo's first director, William T. Hornaday, inspired laws to curb excessive hunting practices and the fashion world's use of bird plumage. The wildlife arm of the zoo society was founded in 1895 and is the oldest of its kind in America. Over time, the organization has contributed a number of initiatives for wildlife: protection of white rhinos in South Africa; the first studies of the mountain gorilla in the wild (1958); aid in coordinating international efforts to protect elephants; the discovery of whale song; leadership in saving the giant panda, the Magellanic penguin of Patagonia and the Komodo monitor; leadership in conserving the largest barrier reef in the Western Hemisphere.

Today, the Society's list of almost three hundred field projects is delightfully dizzying. Recent and current projects include: creating wildlife "corridors" to unite isolated populations in Central America; reestablishing black howler monkeys in the Cockscomb Basin of southern Belize; working to end the trade in rhino horn; tracking snow leopards in Nepal, American crocodiles in Haiti, golden monkeys in China and Stellar sea lions in Alaska; studying the rare okapi and establishing the Okapi Wildlife Reserve in northeastern Zaire; studying survivability and rearing young for dehorned black rhinos in Namibia; studying nutrition as a factor in mass mortality of waterbuck in Kenya's Nakuru National Park; undertaking long-term conservation projects in the tropical forests of Venezuela, Brazil, Peru, Bolivia, Colombia and Ecuador; analyzing the ecology of woodpeckers in India; and monitoring cassowary ecology and conservation in Papua New Guinea.

The strategy, according to the Society, is simple: to gather the field research necessary to devise long-term conservation planning; to open wildlife parks and reserves; and to train local scientists to work in their own countries. Michael Hutchins believes the change must be fundamental. "We're trying to break the idea that the only reason an animal, an endangered species is held in captivity is for its potential for reintroduction back into the wild." Captive breeding, according to New York's Conway, cannot save populations in nature or their habitat, only conservation can. In a speech, Conway said, "A remnant dispersed in a few collections is simply not an adequate fulfillment of a zoo's responsibility." But if zoos refocus on conservation, "it might be that we could really make a difference."

Sex and Morality

AS WE RACE ALONG the fast lanes of high-tech reproduction, we churn up blinding clouds of ethical considerations. What do we owe individual animals in our plans for a species's survival—those that must be moved for mating, and those that are culled because their genetic contribution has been exhausted? Are we rushing in with electroejaculators and scalpels when we should be spending our money and time on creating a suitable and natural environment for animals to mate in? What about breeding unusual animals, freaks of nature that the public adores, such as white tigers?

In 1991, animal rights groups fought to stop the transfer of Timmy, a five-hundred-pound lowland gorilla, from the Cleveland Metroparks Zoo to the Bronx. The thirty-three-year-old ape had been interested in his zoomate, Kate, but she proved infertile. Because lowland gorillas are a threatened species and the aging

Timmy had never before sired offspring, it was decided that he should go to the Bronx Zoo, where he would have the opportunity to mate with four fertile females. Animal rights groups from California and Ohio protested and even went to court because they felt that separating Timmy and Kate was cruel and would cause emotional trauma for both animals. In fact, Timmy had spent most of his life alone and had shared an enclosure with Kate for a little over a year.

A judge granted Timmy's transfer and he has sired four babies: a male named Okpara in July of 1993, with the Bronx's Pattycake; an unnamed female born to Tunko in July 1994; and in August of 1994, rare twins born to Pattycake. Gorillas are remarkably intelligent animals who lead complex social lives, but they are certainly not monogamous. And Timmy's transfer increased the number of these rare animals by at least one. Was there an emotional toll, and can we calculate the cost with these kinds of transfers?

At the Los Angeles Zoo, I stood in the night cages for orangutans with their primary keeper, Rosemarie Weisz. As I served a paper cup of warm cider to the huge male, Louis, and massaged his massive, leathery hand, Weisz told me what a remarkable creature Louis is. She said it took her a long time to realize how subtly he maintained order in his group. At the start of any trouble, Weisz said, a look or gesture from Louis would restore harmony. His cues were so minute and his power so undisputed, that only the sharpest observer could see the strings of his control. The keeper bragged that this thirty-year-old orang is a whiz at untying the knots of string puzzles set up on his cage bars. In fact, he has been known to solve a string puzzle and create a new one himself.

But Weisz's eyes filled with tears as she said that she had just learned that day that Louis was promised to the Toledo Zoo, where his genetic material was needed.

The topic of individual rights versus population needs was explored in March of 1992 at a discussion on zoos and ethical considerations sponsored by Zoo Atlanta, the AAZPA and Georgia Institute of Technology. Dr. Andrew Rowan, director of the Center for Animals and Public Policy at Tufts University School of Veterinary Medicine, said, "It seems to me that the SSP program . . . doesn't pay attention to the individual; the basic priority is the gene pool." Terry Maple of Zoo Atlanta replied in part, "If you sit in on SSP sessions, you can see that increasingly discussions do seem to focus on the response of the individuals that must be moved, and I think that's all for the good. And I do think we're realizing now that the role of behavior is looming very large in the process by which we manage these animals."

As hard as a transfer may be, it is nothing in comparison to the decision to put an animal to death. Survival plans are designed with fairly rigid numbers, allowing for space considerations, so that extra babies from "too large" litters and nonreproductive older animals are considered surplus—they no longer contribute to the plan. Animals whose family tree is uncertain or whose family genes are already well represented in the population are also excess baggage. The unwanted SSP animals are just one part of the larger surplus controversy.

Baby animals attract visitors, so each zoo birth is money in the bank. Just one infant in an enclosure will increase the time zoogoers spend there by more than 100 percent, according to a 1986 study. But every birth also brings another animal to house. Often an older, less attractive member of the species must go to make room. Also, certain species become "hot," shoving others out of the warmth of the limelight and onto surplus lists. Zoos struggle with decisions about the fate of these animals. The choices are to sell to another accredited zoo, to give animals to another zoo (often there are no takers), to sell to dealers or private sanctuaries or to kill the animal.

Accredited zoos and aquariums produce perhaps eight thousand surplus animals a year. Now, consider that accredited zoos make up only a fraction of all zoos—10 percent of the fourteen hundred licensed—and it's easy to figure that eighty thousand animals could be considered surplus each year in North America.

The AZA has strict guidelines about which types of dealers zoos can sell to. "AZA members offering wildlife for sale at auctions attended by the general public are in violation of the AZA Code of Professional Ethics, specifically Mandatory Standards, 2-e," which states, "As a member of AZA, I pledge to . . . make every effort to assure that all animals . . . do not find their way into the hands of those not qualified to care for them properly." Even so, some zoo animals end up as sitting ducks at hunting ranches where "sportsmen" can pay thousands of dollars to walk up to an animal completely habituated to humans and kill it.

During the AAZPA convention in 1991, an animal rights group announced that the San Diego Zoo had sold two Dybowski Sika deer to a hunting ranch and to a game farm that in turn was known to sell to hunting ranches. The zoo claimed that it had made a mistake. In a wire service report, a spokesman for the zoo said, "I'm shocked and disappointed. I'm glad it was pointed out to us." The zoo then went to work to buy the two animals back.

Steve Graham, the former director of the Detroit Zoo, appeared on a "60 Minutes" segment in 1990 scolding other zoos for placing surplus animals with commercial dealers—dealers who in turn might sell to hunting ranches, which Graham called "immoral and unacceptable." Many people in the zoo world consider what Graham did to be immoral and unacceptable. Graham described the practice of killing surplus animals as an "ethical management tool." He had, over the course of his tenure, killed seven Siberian tigers— three old and sick, four healthy but surplus—in the early and mid-eighties. A thirty-one-year-old Asian elephant named Kita was euthanized over a foot infection. And in January of 1990, four scimitar-horned oryxes were killed despite their endangered status because the zoo had run out of room.

But at the Minnesota Zoo, a decision to kill a young and healthy female tiger, not named but numbered 1918, blew up in the press in 1984. For some time, the zoo had tried to sell, and even to give away, 1918 to another accredited zoo, but no one was interested. It was decided that the only solution was euthanasia, and the zoo quietly prepared to cull the animal, whose genes were sturdy but overstocked. Despite precautions, the news hit the press, and the outpouring of condemnation was so great that telephone lines in the community were jammed with protest calls. The tiger lived and was eventually shipped to the Shanghai Zoo.

Zoo officials, geneticists and biologists shake their heads at the sentimental public. There is simply not enough space in zoos and we must choose: Shall we sacrifice a whole species in order to save a few individuals? Zoogoers, they say, must steel themselves to the hard truths of species preservation and not be so attached to specific animals.

Here is the height of hypocrisy. Zoos are built on the public's sentimentality—they bank on it with baby animal parties, adoption programs and name-the-animal contests. Zoos pull on heartstrings to open purse strings, but then zoos are outraged when this emotional public stands between a robust Siberian tiger and a deadly injection. Zoos can't have it both ways. Karen Asis of the AAZPA presents the issue in the 1991 Regional Proceedings: "When are we going to candidly discuss the topics of surplus animals as well as euthanasia, rather than assuming the public won't understand the issues? Face it, we may be able to reduce the number of surplus animals, but, as long as we are doing our job, we are not going to eliminate the surplus situation. It is up to our public relations and education professionals to explain this conservation dilemma to the public." But if what Terry Maple says about the concerns of individual animals being voiced increasingly in SSP meetings is true, then clearly the public has helped educate zoos.

Many zoo people, including Graham, have asked why they should be condemned when millions of unwanted cats and dogs are killed each year in our country. We expect our zoo directors to be more humane and ethical and just plain smarter than the kind of people who dump dogs. The comparison is a good one if zoos want the image of the brute who drowns a basket of kittens.

Terry Maple says that he would never euthanize an animal for so-called management purposes. He believes that zoo animals who have "served humanity deserve to live." In his book *Zoo Man,* Maple says, "We also have provided animals that were too old or infirm to live with others with a comfortable place to retire. Our old male lion Valentino was a case in point. Since he had only one eye we were afraid that if we put him in our new exhibit with younger, female lions, he might be injured. So, we retired him to a renovated, outdoor enclosure in the off-exhibit part of the zoo. He lived out the rest of his life in reasonable comfort."

Zoos simply need to be responsible for the animals they bring into this world. And often they are. Zoos began to use birth control on a regular basis beginning in the mid-seventies. About 4,000 different kinds of contraceptive implants have been used in 100,000 animals worldwide. A bison in San Francisco received an epididymectomy, which stops him from impregnating females but keeps his status as dominant bull. Orangutans are put on the pill (even though it's manufactured for humans). And beavers wear implants. Still there are mistakes, accidents and problems in planning. Despite advances in wildlife contraception, there are still thousands of unwanted zoo animals every year. And the euthanasia debate lives on.

"This is a philosophical conversation that zoo people have ad nauseam over beers, coffee, doughnuts, whatever," says Jill Mellen, Conservation Research Coordinator at the Metro Washington Park Zoo in Portland, Oregeon. "People in the SSP say if we refuse to euthanize the animals that are surplus to the breeding program, the Siberian tiger SSP will collapse. So we can't ignore the surplus issue."

But Mellen talks about Nuri, a tiger who died of old age at her own zoo, who had been "surplused forever" according to SSP guidelines. "I could no sooner have pushed the plunger on Nuri," Mellen says, "than I could go home and shoot my own dog. I can't do it, because I'm emotionally involved with these animals. So I can wear both hats—and I do. And, no, I haven't come to grips with it. I care about tigers. I know that intellectually, to help these tigers, I need to think of the population level. But what's on a computer is not what brings me to work every day, it's Nuri or whoever's doing foofs at me and being able to scratch him through the fence."

"Right now the zoo world is divided," says Oliver Ryder, one of the zoo world's top geneticists. "Increasingly this is something that is going to have to be addressed and will be addressed. And there are fundamentally two ways of addressing it: one is to expand facilities enormously with the associated cost, and the other is to seek public approval or at least not to be castigated for engaging in population control and management practices, especially when it's all done humanely and includes preservation of gene pools. It will be basically not zoos per se that decide . . . it will be societal pressures—how willing the public is and what their proclivities are."

As Ryder points out, zoo professionals are not ghoulish researchers eager to kill animals. "Ask these people how they feel," Ryder says. "Nobody says, 'Oh boy! Today we get to euthanize something.' Everybody goes home on a bummer."

Zoo Freaks

LURKING IN THE DENSE vegetation below a viewing platform at the Cincinnati Zoo, the white tiger was easy to spot: a bright white ghost cat pacing in dark shadows of thick brush. With blue eyes set against a white coat and faint chocolate stripes, these striking animals draw crowds. So it is difficult for zoos to justify killing a healthy but surplused tiger, especially when many zoos are breeding and exhibiting these beautiful oddities.

White tigers are not albinos, their coloring is a naturally occurring genetic variation of the more familiar orange. It is believed, though there is some argument here, that these animals are rarely seen in nature because the few who are born don't last long—the bright white coat makes cubs vulnerable to predators, and if they do survive to adulthood, the lack of camouflage makes it almost impossible for them to stalk prey. Ed Maruska, a white tiger fan and director of the Cincinnati Zoo, maintains that these animals do survive in the wild; as proof, he reports that seventeen adult white tigers were shot in the wild by trophy hunters between 1907 and 1933.

Breeding these animals is counter to what zoos are preaching about genetic diversity. A white coat and blue eyes is the expression of two recessive genes meeting up. To introduce those genes to each other in captive tigers, close relatives had to be mated. The current line of white tigers began by inbreeding—just about all white tigers in zoos today are descendants of one male named Mohan, who was captured as a cub in 1951 by the maharajah of Rewa. Mohan was mated with an orange Bengal and produced a litter of orange cubs. He was then mated with his daughter, and the maharajah got his desired white tiger cub. In 1960, the National Zoo displayed Mohini—a son of Mohan. But it is in Cincinnati where inbreeding takes place as a matter of course to produce more white cubs—perhaps as many as one hundred, though a few white cubs not related to this line have been born in captivity. Illusionists Siegfried and Roy use twenty-three white tigers in their Las Vegas act. San Diego displays a white tiger (a Siberian/Bengal hybrid) that was confiscated at the Mexican border and given to the zoo. New Orleans and Miami also have white tigers. It is said that the inbreeding has caused the usual problems—high cub mortality, birth defects and physical ailments, but Cincinnati denies this.

The Cincinnati Zoo is a leader in breeding endangered species, so it is odd that they would want to be a white tiger cub mill. These freaks of nature, who do not occur in such numbers in the wild, are swallowing up valuable zoo space that should be left to animals in the Species Survival Plan. In fact, Maruska would like an SSP created for these animals, though that is not likely to happen. In 1986, it was reported that virtually all white tigers in North American zoos are hybrids carrying Bengal and Siberian genetic material. Ed Maruska says that is simply not true, that some of his animals are "pure Bengal tigers out of India."

It's hard to find supporters for Maruska's view of white tigers, but he claims the zoo community is merely in lockstep with Bill Conway, the influential director of the Bronx Zoo. Maruska says he respects Conway and considers him a friend, but he doesn't take Conway's "word as gospel."

"White tigers in my opinion are not a freak, they are a mutant, and there's a difference," Maruska told me. "Freaks don't survive, white tigers do. I've got references going back as early as 1834 [of their] being displayed in England. I have a photograph of a male in 1922. I have much information on white tigers in the national parks in India. . . . They have survivability." He says many were collected as adults. He compares white tigers to other big cats with color variation—black leopards or jaguars.

Maruska uses the term *linebreeding* rather than inbreeding and denies that the animals he breeds have any physical deformities, as others contend. Nutritional problems involved with hand-rearing—not genetics—may have caused a few problems, he says.

Most zoos avoid using scientific arguments to defend their use of these animals, because they don't hold up. What these zoos will tell you is that strange or novel animals mean money. And this discussion gives us a glimpse around all the talk about zoos being scientific institutions out to save the natural world, and into the Victorian impulses that have survived to the present in the hearts of many zoo directors. Using animal oddities to lure in zoogoers sounds a lot more like the menageries of old London than the lofty Noah's arks of modern America.

Cincinnati has sold white tigers for as much as $125,000 a pair to circuses, other zoos and to Siegfried and Roy. Zoos may not provide figures or estimates, but clearly white tigers are moneymakers. Maruska says, "They made this zoo, essentially they built our collection here, by demand." Many municipal zoos are under pressure to exhibit these animals for their clear appeal. Maruska says San Diego just took one on loan to cure an attendance slump.

Tony Vecchio, director of the Roger Williams Park Zoo, was offered by the city of Providence to rent a white tiger to boost summer attendance for 1994. Vecchio resisted and compromised by booking a lucrative traveling dinosaur exhibit. Dinosaurs are not this zooman's cup of tea, but, ethically, they were a far better choice, he says, and the revenue from the popular show helped finance a new snow leopard exhibit.

At the financially strapped Philadelphia Zoo, it is white lions—the only ones in North America—who have brought in more than a million dollars in one year. One cub, born in May of 1994, was the result of a great deal of inbreeding. Kanya's parents are brother and sister, and their father, in the words of the *Philadelphia Inquirer,* is "also their grandfather and great-grandfather." Timba, a wild lion from the Timbavati Nature Reserve in South Africa, who was believed to carry a recessive white gene, was mated to an unknown female at the Johannesburg Zoo in the 1970s, then to a female offspring of that union (his daughter), next to the female offspring of that union (his daughter and granddaughter). All white lions exist in captivity and all are the product of the mating between Timba and Bella, his white daughter/granddaughter. Philadelphia bought four lions from Johannesburg.

In the wild, animals tend to know better than to behave this way. Nature has provided a vast array of behavioral mechanisms to disperse brothers and sisters and prevent the kind of inbreeding we force on creatures carrying the moneymaking gene.

Sexual Politics

PANDAS DON'T PRACTICE international diplomacy, gorillas don't respect man-made borders and rhinos can't choose which country's breeding program they'd like to participate in.

But the humans who are deciding the fate of these animals must be as skilled in politics as they are in zoology; they must negotiate an intricate maze within the zoo, the zoo community, federal offices and the politics of international negotiation.

The best portrait of this—in stark black and white—is that of the giant panda. Today, there are fewer than one thousand pandas in the wild. All wild pandas are in China, as are most of the one hundred captives. Because of habitat loss and some poaching, they are on the critical list and could be extinct within fifty years. Everyone agrees pandas should be saved, but just how that should be done is a matter of heated debate, debate that has caused hard feelings among the zoo community, the World Wildlife Fund and the U.S. government. Even the two Chinese bureaucracies responsible for pandas don't get along. At the top of the list of charges is the money issue. Pandas bring a great deal of cash to U.S. zoos, whose attendance swells with the exhibition of these beloved animals, and to the Chinese government, which can take in in excess of a million dollars a year per loaned pair. After a protracted battle and a moratorium on the importation of giant pandas to the United States, which began in December of 1993, the Interior Department hammered out an agreement with the San Diego Zoo in January 1995 that put the profit issue to rest in a dramatic way. In order to receive pandas, the zoo agreed to forgo any and all profits gained from their exhibition. The agreement could prove to be a model for all future loans. There is no better way to prove disinterest in profit-making than to agree to hand all proceeds over to conservation efforts. Whether other zoos can accept such a stark pledge is yet to be seen.

Another problem is that our record with breeding pandas in captivity is dismal—Hsing-Hsing and Ling-Ling were together at the National Zoo in Washington for twenty years, but all five of their offspring died and Ling-Ling herself died in 1992. The zoo community wants another chance, and after new promises have been made, the U.S. Department of Interior's Fish and Wildlife Service may be willing to give it a chance.

These mysterious creatures have beguiled the Western world since the beginning of this century. Reverend J. H. Edgar claimed to have been the first westerner to see one in the wild in 1916, but more definitively, the Roosevelt brothers, Theodore and Kermit, shot one in the spring of 1929 and brought out a body.

Scientific debate has followed ever since. Is it a bear or a raccoon? The panda is as "improbable as a carnivorous cow," says George Schaller in *The Last Panda*. According to some sophisticated DNA tests, giant pandas are bears, but various blood tests bring mixed results. Schaller says they simply cannot be "neatly categorized."

This is a truly odd animal. It has the body of a bear, but unlike any other bear, its pupils are vertical rather than horizontal. Its black and white coloration is distinctive, which may serve as a visual cue to these solitary animals with poor eyesight. Panda vocalizations include a goatlike bleat that would be closer to noises of the raccoon family. They have a sixth digit, or "pseudothumb," unlike any other bear. Bears leave their odor on their surroundings by rubbing their shoulders, neck and head on trees; a panda scent-marks with urine and by rubbing its glandular anal area on trees.

Most peculiar is the panda's diet. The panda feeds almost exclusively on bamboo, a grass that the animal does not digest very well. Pandas have the digestive tract of a carnivore or omnivore but the menu of a herbivore. The giant panda must feed night and day—up to thirty pounds—just to stay alive. It's not a very efficient system.

At the cellular level, plants contain proteins and starches at the center, but surrounding this nutritious core is a strong cell wall. Herbivores—cows, horses, antelopes—have cracked these tough high-security cell walls with large, complex digestive systems that give time and space to microorganisms such as bacteria, which break down and ferment the cellulose and allow the host animal to absorb the now-exposed nutrients. Schaller points out that deer, for instance, can assimilate about 80 percent of the grass they eat this way.

Carnivores and omnivores don't need such an elaborate gut. Our foods are rich in nutrients and easily broken down. Lions absorb about 90 percent of available nutrients in meat. Pandas still have the simple stomach and short intestine of carnivores, but the bamboo they eat is almost all fibrous cell wall. The animal's nutritional efficiency—or inefficiency—is, then, only about 17 percent. Schaller reports seeing pandas pass by much more nutritious vegetation in search of this high-fiber junk food. And no one really knows why. As puzzlingly inefficient as this niche is, it works. Pandas have been around since before humankind as we know it.

But will we let them survive our time? Pandas are poached occasionally—their hides can bring in $10,000 to $40,000—but more often they are inadvertently killed by snares set out for other animals. It has been reported that, so far, six convicted poachers have been executed. The biggest threat, however, is habitat loss—the clear-cutting of China's forests in the once-remote mountain areas where pandas live. During the cyclical die-offs of bamboo (there was one in the mid-1980s), pandas used to migrate to areas where the plant was thriving. But as habitats fragment, this territorial shift becomes impossible.

The first live panda to reach the United States caused "panda-monium," according to reporters covering the event in San Francisco in December of 1936. He made his way to Chicago but died in the spring of 1938; by then the Brookfield Zoo had secured another. That same year, the Bronx Zoo paid $2,500 for a panda. Ling-Ling and Hsing-Hsing were presented to the United States when President Richard Nixon visited China in 1972. Throughout the seventies and into the eighties, pandas visited U.S. zoos through loan programs. The Bronx Zoo, Busch Gardens, Memphis, San Diego, Los Angeles and San Francisco all borrowed pandas during this time. But questions were raised about whether loan animals were wild-caught and how detrimental it was to shuttle them from zoo to zoo. George Schaller wrote to the AAZPA in 1985 suggesting some guidelines for these loan programs, and the AAZPA quickly took them up. But they were ignored by the Chinese, who sent fertile animals on tour, despite the AAZPA's call to accept only pandas that were sterile. As a result, the World Wildlife Fund started opposing these loans. The Convention on International Trade in Endangered Species (CITES) and the International Union for the Conservation of Nature (IUCN) approved of loans if they helped in panda breeding or conservation. In June of 1988, with thirty American zoos and other organizations applying for panda loans, the U.S. Fish and Wildlife Service imposed a moratorium on the import of pandas. In 1991, the agency decided it would once again consider giant panda loans. And zoos began jockeying for them.

It's easy to see why this animal caused such a sensation. Though they can weigh three hundred pounds, giant pandas are the embodiment of what we consider cute and cuddly. With fuzzy beachball bodies, rounded ears and black patches that make their eyes appear large, pandas sit upright and look like darling babies as they munch bamboo held in what look like little hands (a wristbone acts as a thumb). These precious pandas with powerful jaws and sharp claws have mauled zookeepers in Washington, Chicago and London. Schaller calculates that given how few pandas have been held in zoos, proportionately, they are second only to elephants in inflicting

injuries. Nevertheless, the enchantment is inescapable, as zoos fortunate enough to display them have discovered.

During a two-hundred-day loan in 1987 and 1988, San Diego
Zoo's attendance increased by a third—to 3 million—and it was
estimated that the zoo took in $4.5 million from the visit. Two pan-
das spent five months at the Toledo Zoo in 1988 and brought the
city an estimated $60 million in business. Pandas mean money. The
host zoo gets a rocket boost in attendance and makes a fortune on
sales of panda paraphernalia. And China, which charges something
along the lines of a million dollars a year per pair of loaned pandas, profits also.

Zoos have done a great deal to save certain endangered species,
and AZA would like to organize a unified breeding program for
pandas here in the United States. But because of the head-spinning
financial potential of exhibiting pandas, every move toward bringing them here is suspect.

As well it should be. Pandas are gravely endangered, with fewer
than one thousand in existence, their foothold on survival is pre-
carious. Panda reproduction is still largely a mystery to science and
there are no guarantees that if we get a slew of fertile pandas over
here anything will happen. In the wild, pandas are solitary and
come together for breeding about once a year for a two- to ten-day
period. Males cluster and compete for breeding rights. Reproduction in captivity has been very low. Fewer than a third have reproduced, and the mortality rates for newborns and adults is high. The
first captive birth was at the Beijing Zoo in 1963. China had a good
year for births in 1992, eleven out of thirteen infants survived. But
we really don't know why and we don't know that it will be
repeated. For reasons no one understands, Mexico City's Chapulte-
pec Zoo has had the best panda breeding record outside China. It
might be the altitude, or as the zoo itself has joked about the unsci-
entific diet, it could be the Mexican food they are given. Rich
Block, former director of public programs for the World Wildlife
Fund who is now with the Indianapolis Zoo, says, "It could be anything—the food, the altitude. It could be the luck of the draw.

These animals were well socialized. They knew each other. It was not like some big deal where they were smacked together."

Grappling with the issues of starting a serious and unified breeding program in North America is tough enough, but added to the controversy is the fact that a few zoos—San Diego, Columbus and Busch Gardens—have negotiated independently for panda loans from the Chinese government.

The "rent-a-panda" program is a troubling one. There are two issues. One is that since it is so difficult to get pandas to breed, it hardly makes sense to send these sensitive animals from zoo to zoo on a tour that is guaranteed to discourage mating. The other is that we have made it so lucrative for China to ship these animals out, the temptation must be great to pull them out of the wild to fill the ever-increasing demand. Our zoos are not allowed, by international law, to bring in wild-caught endangered species for display unless the capture and export "will ultimately result in enhanced protection for the species." Obviously, this is an important protection for fragile populations. The rule ignited a costly and protracted battle between the San Diego Zoo and Interior Secretary Bruce Babbitt—a fight watched with keen interest from every corner of the zoo world.

When I visited the San Diego Zoo in December 1993, a sign in a large, empty exhibit area lined with snappy graphic boards about the giant panda, read: "This exhibit reserved for giant pandas." It is a reservation that cost more than a million dollars and took three years to fill.

The zoo had negotiated with China to receive a pair of pandas. San Diego pledged a million dollars a year for three years and up to $600,000 for each cub produced there who lived past six months. The zoo applied for a permit for the loan in February 1993, but it was blocked that summer by the U.S. Fish and Wildlife Service, the agency that issues import permits for endangered species. The agency's policy states that loan animals should not be removed from the wild and they should be incapable of breeding either because of age or health. Further, the agency's policy states, "The funds committed in the loan agreement" are supposed to be "used for specific projects designed primarily to enhance the survival of the giant panda."

Interior Secretary Bruce Babbitt said in a letter to San Diego that he felt "the People's Republic of China may not be doing enough to conserve wild pandas." Babbitt also voiced concern that these high-priced loan programs might exert "irresistible pressure for the capture and export of pandas."

There was also debate over the status of the two pandas slated for San Diego. According to officials at the zoo, both animals—the male, Shi Shi, and the female, Shun Shun—were captured in March of 1992 because of injury or illness. But while Fish and Wildlife said documents proved that Shi Shi was removed for medical reasons, the "reasons for the female's removal and retention in captivity remain inconclusive." In fact, the Associated Press reported that an interoffice memo suggested that the female was suffering from nothing more than very treatable roundworms.

But San Diego kept trying. They filed for an emergency permit, saying Shun Shun was extremely ill and could not be treated in China. Babbitt's office expressed concern that the way things are set up, zoos are trying "to work every loophole."

The World Wildlife Fund presented material to the government on the matter. WWF said in its newsletter that it "believes that before long-term giant panda loans should be considered, a number of conditions must be in place. Most importantly, these loans should not involve wild-caught individuals and must be part of an integrated, international breeding program that is designed to complement conservation efforts in the wild panda population."

And it was the work of George Schaller, perhaps the world's top field biologist, who studied pandas in the wild for almost five years and is a very vocal critic of "rent-a-panda" programs, that was cited by Babbitt in his decision. Schaller, who knows the zoo world well as director for science at NYZS/The Wildlife Conservation Society, has charged that zoos have been in danger of seeing pandas as "show animals" rather than an endangered species desperately in need of help. And he has not reserved his wrath exclusively for zoos. Schaller accuses WWF in their panda dealings of caving in to China's demands for fancy structures and high-tech equipment that doesn't get used. He says that Chinese officials do not do enough to stop poaching activity and that their priorities are mixed up. In 1983 and 1984, during a bamboo die-off, the government saved what they claimed were starving pandas. Schaller asserts that these animals were in no danger until they were brought into captivity, where 33 of 108 died.

Because of a lack of accountability, it is feared that money earmarked for conservation may go toward buying hotels or cars in China. Various ministries duplicate each other's work and will not cooperate with one another. And zoos are guilty of greed and stupidity, pure and simple, according to Schaller, who says in *The Last Panda* that he has seen "the greed, politics, lack of cooperation, and undisciplined scramble for pandas that characterized the whole loan program."

Schaller says in the book, "If the millions of dollars that have been raised from loans were spent on anti-poaching and forest protection measures instead of on the construction and maintenance of walls around pandas, the future of the species would be brighter."

With so much to sort through, the U.S. Fish and Wildlife Service announced on December 23, 1993, that it was suspending the review and processing of all future import permit applications of giant pandas for exhibit until a national policy could be developed.

Despite the moratorium, Babbitt directed Fish and Wildlife to give San Diego its permit in January of 1995, saying an important agreement had been reached and that since the zoo had started the whole process before the moratorium, it could now be granted. Though it would cover only the first five years of the proposed twelve-year loan.

The guidelines negotiated had to do with which animals would be allowed in (thirteen-year-old Shi Shi, a male injured in the wild; and three-year-old Bai Yun, a female born in captivity). What kind of research would be conducted (behavioral and chemical communication through scent marking) and whether it would enhance the survival of the species in the wild. There were also assurances that there would be a global network in place with institutions in the United States and China, as well as the Zoological Society of London, the Mexico City Zoo and other zoos cooperating and sharing data.

But by far the most important part of the package, the compromise that struck at the very core of all the wrangling (but curiously was buried as the penultimate paragraph on the press sheet released by the Department of the Interior) concerns money: "Net revenues derived directly or indirectly from the public display activity will be invested in panda conservation activities within the PRC [the Fuzhou Giant Panda Research Center]. Special accounting procedures have been agreed to by the Zoo and the PRC Ministry of Forestry to ensure that this research activity will not generate economic incentives for panda imports and to maximize the investment of net revenues derived from public display in specific, high-priority conservation projects in China." For years, zoos had claimed that they were interested in saving pandas and not in profiting from them, but for the first time ever, a zoo was willing to put its money where its mouth is: pouring all the cash from T-shirts and toys and increased gate receipts back into pure panda conservation.

Now, Babbitt suggested, the moratorium might end within months, if these guidelines could be solidified in a national policy. San Diego did get the pandas, but not until September 1996. Shi Shi, now sixteen, and Bai Yun, now five, are committed to a twelve-year stay. The zoo has pledged to focus on the study of how pandas communicate sexual willingness by scent and keeping the two animals from one another most of the time in order for them to live a more realistic solitary existence.

It all sounds promising, but groups such as the Humane Society of the United States are skeptical and there is still much to settle. Pandas have caused all-out war in the zoo and conservation world before. The loan of two pandas to the Toledo Zoo in 1988 caused WWF and the AAZPA to join forces in a lawsuit against the Fish and Wildlife Service for commercial trafficking in pandas. Toledo countersued. (Toledo got their pandas for five months and WWF got $50,000 in legal fees out of the Justice Department to settle the lawsuit.)

George Bush and an Ohio congressman were instrumental in helping the Columbus Zoo get its panda loan in 1992. Although Fish and Wildlife was giving out permits by then, conservation groups were against short-term loans. Columbus got its pandas in May of 1992, but its accreditation with the AAZPA was suspended over the incident. And there was another round of legal battles involving the zoo and WWF.

Rich Block has been involved with panda issues for many years and thinks things are getting better. A consortium formed among accredited zoos in the AZA has been working to come up with a cogent conservation program for pandas, which would bring eight to twelve breeding pairs to the United States. Block sees this as a good sign. And, he says, he believes that people of integrity, such as Devra Kleiman of the National Zoo, truly love pandas and want to make a contribution. Block believes we've grown more sophisticated since the 1980s, when zoos were bringing pandas over in the name of friendship, not conservation.

Certainly San Diego has done just that through its Center for Reproduction of Endangered Species. This impressive scientific unit has diligently spent eight years trying to unravel the enigma of panda reproduction. They have worked in China to monitor the ovarian cycle of the giant panda because pinpointing her rare ovulation is critical to captive breeding. Their endocrinology expert, Nancy Czekala, is the first human to do what male pandas have always been able to do—pin down through urinalysis the moment when the female is reproductively ready. CRES is also hard at work at determining paternity of pandas through hair samples (a method already perfected for rhinos and mountain gorillas). This simple, noninvasive DNA test would help make sure that no inbreeding takes place. Currently, Chinese researchers use both artificial insemination with semen from one panda and natural breeding with another with each receptive female, and consequently, paternity is unclear. The method will also help determine paternity of wild pandas and breeding success of individuals. And they are studying hormone levels and the behavior of breeding pandas.

There is no question that zoos in the United States are better financed and equipped than the Chinese government. Consequently, our scientists are more sophisticated. But does the solution to the panda problem lie in laboratory science? And we must ask what exactly is in the best interest of the pandas. Wouldn't it be easier to send our science and scientists over to China than to ship pandas here? After all, fewer biologists have died from the stress of transit than wild animals.

"It's a simple question," Block says. "Why is it better here than there? If there are things that can be done in China, why aren't they done in China? If you have a set pot of money to spend to get a job done, do you want to spend all this money bringing a few Chinese over here and the pandas and spending a lot of dough to rent those pandas, or do you want to send a team and some equipment over to China and work with the people there and make that happen? Now, the other argument says to not put all your eggs in one basket, but China is a big place, you know. Give me a break."

Suspicion and disagreement is still rampant in this debate. When I attended the annual zoo conference in Omaha, Nebraska, in 1993, it was only at the Panda SSP meeting that I was required to stand and identify myself as a reporter. When I asked if the zoo association was in support of San Diego's private dealings with China, I was asked to come back later for a more private talk. The private talk yielded little. The next year, I was not allowed into the closed panda conference. And Block says he receives a lot of mail from people in San Diego who hold him responsible for Fish and Wildlife's decision not to issue a permit.

Not guilty, Block says, it was not his decision. But he is happy that we have a system of checks in place. "I love CITES," Block says, "because just like the Endangered Species Act, it protects us from our own worst vices. The biggest one of which is greed. And that's why people don't like those laws—they run against the dark side in each of us. And the spirit of CITES is that we won't exploit these endangered species for commercial purposes."

Considering the political problems, Providence's Tony Vecchio says he wouldn't take a panda "even if it were free."

San Diego's agreement takes a giant step away from profiteering and toward the conservation of pandas in the wild. These next years are crucial for the giant panda, and we can only hope that this is the wave of the future and that the wrangling stops long enough for work to be done.

Rhinos: On the Horns of a Dilemma

EMI WAS THE DARLING of the zookeepers in Los Angeles. This gentle two-horned Sumatran rhino, whose calls are a mixture of Julia Child and a whale song, is among only eighteen of these endangered animals living outside Indonesia. They are the most primitive of rhinos and relatively petite. Though solitary in the wild, Sumatran rhinos in captivity often seem like overgrown shaggy lapdogs. They have hairy coats, but in the wild, dense vegetation shaves it off. Small, shaggy, vocal and fond of people, the Sumatran in a zoo seems more Muppet creation than wild rhinoceros.

Emi may be popular with the keepers and the public, but with fewer than five hundred in the world, it's her fertility that is of great interest to the scientific community. When I scratched her hard armor coating of skin, I realized that I had gotten closer to her than a male Sumatran rhino ever had. Emi was removed from the wild for the good of her species, and today, she is at the Cincinnati Zoo to be mated with a male there.

Sumatran rhinos and their even more endangered Javan cousins are at the center of a heated conservation debate. Clearly this species is in crisis, but the question is how best to save it. Is high-tech assisted reproduction in Western zoos the answer, or better protection and increased field biology?

It took two years and $1 million to catch the first pair of Sumatran rhinos in 1985. They were sent to England, where they have never reproduced. And since that time, twenty-seven have been brought into captivity, nine dying during or after capture, and not one baby to show for it. Considering that it costs about $200,000 per animal for capture and shipment, many believe the money could be better spent in fieldwork.

The situation is even more dire with Javan rhinos. There are only about sixty animals living in a park called Ujung Kulon, a tiny peninsula on the western tip of Java. And there are no Javan rhinos in captivity. Here, field biologists such as Kathy MacKinnon or Charles Santiapillai of WWF argue that, given the track record of the Sumatran rhino project, money would best be spent on protecting the remaining Javan rhinos in Ujung Kulon. If a captive population is to be established, they say, it should remain in Indonesia.

In the other corner, we have Ulysses Seal of the Minnesota Zoo and chairman of the Captive Breeding Specialist Group. Seal wants the population to blast up to two thousand in a short amount of time, and he feels the best way to do that is to remove about half the population from the reserve. The population has been fairly stable, which may mean that the numbers are up to capacity for the tiny park. Seal has conducted a computerized Population Viability Analysis, which has concluded that given the chances for environmental disaster, genetic drift, space limitation and other factors, Javan rhinos if left alone will die out.

Field biologists question the data fed into the computer. Of the five rhino species, the least is known about Javans. The true population size, the sex ratio of the group and the age structure are unknown.

What is known is that this group cannot expand significantly in its current home. It is also known that digging pits for capture and transporting these animals will cause a certain number of injuries and deaths. If we used the viability computer to analyze the number of births and deaths of rhinos in captivity, would it tell us that population is also doomed? After all, only black rhinos have reproduced with any regularity in captivity.

Part of learning is making mistakes, and if we are to assist rhino reproduction artificially or through old-fashioned husbandry, there have to be some animals to work with. Biologists cannot perfect artificial insemination or embryo transfer techniques before animals are placed in captivity.

The situation is dire because all five species of rhinoceros are in jeopardy. According to *Wildlife Conservation* magazine, "During the past 25 years, 85 percent of the world's rhinos have been killed for one thing and one thing only, their horn." The horn, used in folk medicines and to make ceremonial dagger handles in Yemen, is worth about $7,000 a pound.

One experiment that held much promise has proven unsuccessful. Dehorning wild rhinos seemed like the perfect solution. But the horns grow so quickly that it would cost as much as $1,400 a year per rhino to keep them trimmed. And, worse, initial studies in Namibia indicate that dehorned mothers are unable to adequately protect their young. *Wildlife Conservation* reports that "In areas with predators such as spotted hyenas and lions, all the calves born to dehorned mothers died before the age of one; whereas mothers *with* horns were 100 percent successful in rearing calves. In addition, the calves of mothers with the shortest horns had a tendency to be missing tails or ears, indications of unsuccessful predation." The horns grow back at a rate of about three inches a year, and in Zimbabwe it was discovered that poachers continued to kill these massive animals even for a tiny stump. Besides, the operation itself is not always simple. In December 1990, the Audubon Zoo in New Orleans decided to trim the horn of a thirty-two-year-old white rhino in order to allow smaller-horned males to mate with her, but she died during the procedure.

IF THE ZOO TRULY is a modern ark, it is just beginning an important voyage. There is rancor and disagreement over which animals to save and how to save them. And zoos must navigate international seas and negotiate global politics. Yes, we have to rush in when needed, but, just as important, we must also resist the temptation to net every live creature and haul it on board.

The ark is a scientific ship and it is developing startling new technologies to assist in the reproduction of endangered species, but it is also learning that all the problems cannot be solved in its laboratory.

The zoo community may have occasionally steered in circles, but even that brought lessons. Now that we have the mechanics down, we must chart the course for the future, looking ahead, rowing in synchrony.

The modern ark has the potential to save the planet's biodiversity, it is poised to rescue a natural world under siege, but as we look out to the horizon, we must not forget to keep our own ship in order. Creating a rich life for the animals on board is as complicated, expensive and contentious as any issue the zoo world faces.

5

THE FUTURE: REVOLUTION IN
STYLE AND SUBSTANCE

IT IS THE YEAR 2020, and a raven-haired matriarch named Gigi has become a media sensation. She has five children, each with a different father. She bore seven, but lost two in infancy. She has lived through good times and bad. She has survived famine and enjoyed plenty. She has seen leaders come and go, coalitions built, and dynasties destroyed. Today, she is pleased that her oldest son rules the community after a very rough campaign. Though she is surrounded by grandchildren, she is still sought after and quite active sexually. She is patient, kind, loving, wise and, above all, strong—perhaps three times stronger than a man.

Gigi is a chimpanzee in Tanzania, and her daily existence is carried via satellite to huge theater screens in zoos around the world. Her life is one of many that the zoo channel zooms in on. There are polar bears hunting in the Arctic. Penguins waddling off Patagonia. Hyenas waging war in the Masai Mara. Giant pandas nursing young in China. The zoo channel is dramatic, immediate and ever-changing. And though the airwaves may be invisible, they are the strongest link imaginable between vulnerable wild places and powerful civilization. The zoos that pick up the network have a financial stake in the protection of habitat. The viewers, people who have always shown a remarkable capacity for the care of individual animals, have an emotional stake in their well-being.

There are currently plans for just such a high-tech zoo in London, but even if this exact scheme never comes to pass, we know that if zoos are to survive in the coming century, they must zealously make conservation their most urgent priority.

The World on a String

THERE IS A MONSTER loose in the world that is gobbling up every green inch and chopping down every forest. The beast, of course, is the planet's human population. Every year another 97 million human beings join the crowd—90 percent of whom are born in less developed tropical countries, where the bulk of the remaining wildlife lives. By 2050 the world's population could reach 12 billion. That's 12 billion people who need roads and houses and land for crops and domestic animals. Who need fuel and food and wood.

Because of that, the nonhuman, nondomesticated animal portion of the planet's biomass is being squeezed out of existence. The statistics are too much to fathom. According to E. O. Wilson, we are reducing biological diversity to its lowest level in 65 million years. We have probably named about 1.4 million species of animals, but that is a tiny fraction of the 4 to 30 million species that actually exist. Through deforestation we may be killing off four to six thousand species a year, with perhaps six species of plant and animals being doomed to extinction each hour, according to Wilson. William Conway, president and general director of NYZS and WCS, has made up a staggering laundry list of our consumption: We pull 100 million tons of fish from our seas each year. More than 5 billion animals are killed for food each year in the United States. Worldwide,

10 to 15 billion domestic animals are using up space that was once wildlife habitat. Cows and other ruminants have staked out turf nearly the size of Africa. Half that amount again is dedicated to crops. Only about 4 percent of the earth is protected land. Each year, Wilson says, we are losing rain forest cover at the rate equal to the area of Switzerland and the Netherlands combined.

Can we console ourselves with the thought that many of these species are just little bugs we don't even have names for? It's even more frightening to think that we'll never know the magnitude of our loss. But the clues are everywhere. Many very big, very charismatic animals are in decline. There are fewer than one thousand giant pandas alive today. Not one species of rhino can be counted in numbers higher than five thousand. Half of the bird species in Polynesia have disappeared. There may have been as many as 10 million elephants in Africa in 1930, but poaching and habitat loss have hacked that figure down to just half a million.

It is all completely irreversible. The great, huge pool of genes is now a puddle. And vast tracts of land are just fractured and fragmented pockets of wilderness. Increasingly, these pockets are "managed" areas, where soldiers guard against poaching and biologists monitor the health of the inhabitants. The wild world is becoming a series of megazoos.

The zoo community is uniquely qualified to manage and preserve these precious pools of biodiversity. Nutritionists, biologists, wildlife veterinarians, population specialists, geneticists and behaviorists are already assembled and on staff. Zoos can be what Bill Conway calls "your full-service conservation organization." And who else should be doing this? As Conway also points out, "No powerful government anywhere on earth has placed environmental conservation among its top priorities."

Saving and preserving a wild area is complicated business. Conway uses the example of Florida's Everglades National Park. In 1947, the park was established. Hunting stopped. Encroachment ceased. But shockingly, by 1989, the population of large wading birds had been reduced by 90 percent. "Refuge management by benevolent neglect does not save wildlife communities when their ecosystems are too small or are modified by activities outside their borders." says Conway.

In 1976, it was discovered that three to five Javan tigers, a species previously thought to be extinct, were alive in the Meri-Betiri Reserve in eastern Java. The 190-square-mile park is the last area of lowland rain forest in Java. A plan was proposed for their survival, but by the early eighties, none of these tigers, known for their distinctive narrow stripes, was alive. The Javan tiger slipped through our fingers and is gone forever.

"All kinds of conservation activities ultimately come down to buying time," Conway says during an interview in his office at the Bronx Zoo. "And in some instances all we can do is buy time. We successfully bought time for the American bison. Successfully bought time for Arabian oryx. There aren't many examples [but] there are others—we may have been successful in buying time for the Mongolian wild horse, Przewalski's horse. When you can buy time for the land itself, for nature, then you're not simply buying time for a species, you're buying time for an entire community of species. If you are successful in getting large spaces, you may even be able to help save functioning ecosystems, which is what you want to do. The living animals in your collections, for the vast majority of human beings, provide the only contact they're ever really going to have with wild animals. So the significance of the zoo animal in a municipality can do nothing but increase. They will become rarer and rarer. And the horrible thing is that as they become more valuable in human eyes, they become less valuable ecologically, because they can no longer fulfill ecological functions as their numbers decline. This gets into a catch-22 situation.

"I believe that we are moving away from a time when people can afford to simply sit back and care about animals; we have to care *for* them. Increasingly, the wildlife reserves will be too small to maintain viable populations of animals. Those that are big enough will have to be managed with increasing intensity. Because within the limited spaces we are able to accord them due to our own over-procreation, they cannot sustain their numbers in relation to one another in viable ways. In many a reserve today there can be a male rhino who dominates a whole reserve. No other male can breed. He'll kill them. He'll run them out. So the population will not be viable. If we continue to modify the environment adjacent to our reserves, we're going to run into all kinds of problems."

Standing at the Crossroads

ZOOS HAVE THE potential to save more biodiversity than any other private organization. But it is a huge responsibility, and the commitment in money and labor is staggering. And the overwhelming majority of zoos are financially strapped. The roof to the ape house is leaking. The elephant has a foot infection. A zoogoer who tripped in the bathroom is suing. The keepers aren't being paid enough. The giraffe fencing blew over in a storm. And yet they are being asked to save the entire planet.

Zoos have the weight of the world on their shoulders, and they may just shrug it off. The zoo community is at a dramatic crossroads. It is truly a time for a new direction, and not everyone in the zoo community is willing to go.

Bill Conway, the visionary of the zoo world, the man referred to as "god" without a trace of sarcasm, says the mission is clear. "There isn't any question about the future of zoos at all," Conway says with confidence. "It is not to be a simple museum of living creatures. It is to be a proactive conservation organization that is directly acting to preserve nature and wildlife." Conway asserts the way to accomplish that is not the issue; the hardest part, the most important part, is deciding to try. "The situation has become so desperate with regard to wildlife and nature that the future of zoos is evolving very, very rapidly, and they are destined to become conservation organizations attempting to preserve wildlife and nature. And that is very straightforward and simple, and after you've gotten that far in your thinking, it's simply a matter of detail."

But it may take precious time. Michael Hutchins is pushing his organization toward the future and he may be a little frustrated.

"Anything that is that revolutionary takes some time to trickle down to the lowest common denominators, and this is going to take some time. Cultures don't change very fast generally, and we're talking about a culture that has evolved out of the sixteenth and seventeenth centuries. There will have to be some major changes if the institution is to survive. And I personally have strong feelings that it can make the transition, at least in North America."

Whether it is a matter of design or detail, most zoos simply don't come near New York—in zeal or impact. The AZA boasts of hundreds of field projects run by accredited zoos. But if one were to weed out the baggage—projects listed several times because many zoos participate in it; or those of only marginal conservation value—Conway estimates that, in 1993, there were only 425 legitimate field projects left to count and 272 belong to New York; the rest were scattered among the nation's 160 zoos and aquariums. Conway is blazing the trail, but his parishioners are a bit timid.

In a pamphlet entitled "A Hidden Value," celebrating its upcoming eightieth birthday, the San Diego Zoo points out—in facing pages in bold red type—that it has spent $55 million in the last ten years on public relations and in that same amount of time only $17.6 million "in support of internationally acclaimed wildlife conservation studies conducted by CRES scientists."

Michael Hutchins, the respected director of conservation and science at the AZA, concedes that these figures "are probably true," but maintains that the scenario is "changing very rapidly."

Rick Barongi, director of Disney's planned five-hundred-acre Animal Kingdom theme park in Orlando, Florida, and has served as director of the children's zoo within the San Diego Zoo, also believes the zoo world is evolving in the direction of conservation work, but he is blunt in his assessment of the current situation. "The Bronx has pretty much done it alone. And Conway is strong enough and smart enough and powerful enough that he can insulate his researchers from the day-to-day, mundane problems that zoos have to deal with. But a Conway comes along only once in a generation. Zoos need to concentrate on conservation more than preservation and Conway is definitely the true visionary of the field."

Tony Vecchio, director of the Roger Williams Park Zoo in Providence, Rhode Island, says, "Most zoos are not doing enough in situ work. And yet the biggest crisis is in conservation. We're running out of time and losing more than we're winning. So there's a great sense of urgency."

Yet it is clear that many in the zoo world are stuck in the past. In contemplating "the challenges of the twenty-first century," one zoo director spoke, at the 1991 AAZPA annual meeting, about the importance of entertainment. "Let us also not forget animal rides such as elephant, camel or even pony rides. Although they may seem like pure entertainment, there is an element of education through the impressions that are gained by the close association of man and beast."

The serious, not the silly, will survive in the next century. In a prescient paper delivered in 1972 at the AAZPA annual meeting, naturalist Roger Caras asked, "The world is changing, are you?" Caras, who has written more than sixty books on nature, said, "If you think you are going to remain the same while all institutions and all values around you evolve with the speed of an atomic explosion, you are in for a shock. You may wake up and find your zoo is not only obsolete in architecture but in purpose." Caras stood before zoo leaders and took them to task for not having a futuristic think tank, for not being an educational institution, for not listening to the concerns of zoogoers, for not marketing and merchandizing themselves and for not reaching out to the community. "I know many of you who are fifty years behind the times at a time in history when the only way to survive is to be ten years ahead of the time in which you live. . . . I look ahead and see how many of you could be phased out. Because, with many of my affiliations, I deal with gift and bequest situations, and I see where that money is going. When it doesn't go to you, I despair." Caras's comments are all true today. Zoos that think they cannot afford to change will ultimately find out they can't afford not to.

A Tour of the New Zoo:
As Different as Night and Day

YOU HAVE JUST finished an exquisite meal—a salad of wild greens and goat cheese, pasta tossed with wild mushrooms and braised baby vegetables, with crème caramel for dessert—and you are seated on a balcony in a white-cushioned rattan chair and sipping a brandy. Now the excitement begins. The watering hole below is coming to life. An African elephant matriarch, her young baby and three other females have charged in to drink and swim and wallow. Low clouds of dust churn up before the massive beasts as they come to a halt. Two of the females had been apart earlier, and a sort of gleeful greeting pandemonium breaks out. There is trumpeting, ear flapping and the tender touching of bodies and trunks. Fluid leaks from their temporal glands, signaling their great joy. There is a murmur among the fellow diners on the balcony, but it is quiet and reverential. Hardly anyone stirs as the matriarch leads her baby to the edge of the water and coaxes him in by placing her trunk along his back. He is timid and calls out, but she reassures him and he clumsily splashes in. Last week, the entire balcony, turned out in their finest evening wear, were sprayed by one playful elephant. It was a night to remember and brag about.

A short time later, after one of the trees in the back of the area is knocked over by the matriarch, the elephants leave the area and a pride of lions enters—four females and a male. Their tails are twitching and they snarl, caught up in the electricity of smelling the essence of elephant left behind.

So many of the animals at the zoo are awake at night. Wild lions hunt at night; elephants sleep only a few hours a day. Terry Maple, director of Zoo Atlanta, wants to make use of that. He'd like to see just such a zoo restaurant and nightclub come into existence. Ecotourism is big business. And zoos should lure some deep pockets inside their gates for a little adventure.

Zoos have not adequately welcomed the demographic that has made ecotourism and retailers such as the Nature Company so profitable. The crowded and noisy daytime zoo is still available to huge numbers, but the nightclub allows a more intimate and more expensive portal to the wild.

Perhaps an exclusive gift shop that sells safari jackets and field guides and the romance of adventure would open in an exotic-looking building nearby.

A Day of Adventure and Education

The future zoo will be about connections—to the wild, to other humans and to a kind ethic of conservation and care. In many zoos you won't see elephants or polar bears or gorillas. There will be fewer animals with more space. Smaller, active animals such as meerkats and monkeys will interest you in the way a lone elephant in a dusty corral never could. Zoos will let go of the notion that you have to see certain species to care for them. Dr. Andrew Rowan, head of the Center for Animals and Public Policy at the Tufts University School of Veterinary Medicine, responds, "I see no data indicating such a notion. It is much more likely that the zoogoer will care for elephants, not from seeing a surly-looking one at the local zoo" but from watching them on TV or reading about them in books.

Expensive and notoriously unreliable electronic, interactive signs will be gone, and the zoo's best-kept secret—the keeper—will give you an intimate glimpse of the animal you see and its role in the world. The new zoo will have to pay keepers more and beef up their numbers as an investment in the future.

Rick Barongi says zoo management "has missed the boat with keepers." They remain an untapped resource in most zoos. Disney's keepers, he says, will be comfortable "in three hats"—caring for the animals, training them and dealing with the public. "The majority of keepers in this country would love to close down the zoo to the 'stupid' public," he says, laughing. "That's their dream, to have a zoo where they can take care of and love their animals to death and not have to deal with those 'idiots' who make all the comments." Barongi says the keepers he hires will be able to shovel dung and be good humored enough to laugh about it with the zoogoers.

Time and again, low tech is what really works. As Bill Conway points out, often children learn more about technology than about animals through "modern" video displays. Max Frisch, Swiss novelist and playwright, has said, "Technology is a way of organizing the universe so that man does not have to experience it." The new zoo will not distance the zoogoer from nature. Personalizing contact with masses of people is the challenge.

Zoos are critical of zoogoers who pour concern into individual animals, real or fictional, such as Bambi, Keiko (the killer whale) or Lassie. Zoos of the future will be smart enough to take advantage of that dynamic. When the orangutan keeper in Los Angeles tells you that Louis, the huge red male, savors a cup of warm apple juice in the evening, you might just stick around to hear about how many of these animals are doomed to the pet trade. You might even be moved to drop some change, or your charge card, into a slot next to the exhibit that is taking donations to save wild orangs.

"You could have a VISA machine right there, where you could plunk the card in and make a donation," says Michael Hutchins.

But our new zoo hasn't dismissed technology. It uses it to make powerful and intimate connections between the center of the city and the heart of the wild. That is what the Worldlife Center is currently planning for central England. It will take $67 million to complete this high-tech zoo. William Travers, son of Bill Travers, star of the film *Born Free,* has told reporters that "Three o'clock feeding time at the zoo will be replaced by a satellite link with the Amazonian rain forest, the Great Barrier Reef, Antarctica or Africa and allow people to interact with that environment through our guide on the spot."

Travers is planning a "sensorium," where virtual-reality technology will allow visitors to see the world as a fruit bat or a spider would. A headset and wired glove will link the human with the image.

Huge, rounded theater screens can take millions on virtual safari with little impact on the environment. Without leaving your seat, you'll soar to a giraffe's height or jet down to a lizard's-eye view.

The thrill of adventure is clear, but the planners will also build a library and database that will bring the latest information on endangered species and the efforts to save them to an interested visitor.

However, Travers's group would have no live animals on the grounds. They feel that any education is compromised by viewing animals in unnatural settings, and that the captive animals are placed under too much stress this way.

One of the best exhibits in this country has no animals. The "thirsty animal" trail at the Brookfield Zoo is a wooded maze in which the visitor must think and behave like a wild animal to get to the watering hole alive. As the visitor trips motion detectors, lions roar or birds squawk or a musky odor is given off. At each station, the zoogoer must decide whether to stay still or proceed. At the very end, there are three water fountains with three pictures of zebras over them. You must decide by the photos which water source is safe to drink from—only that bubbler will deliver water.

Barongi has given a great deal of thought to the future of zoos, and he is building his dreams. Though the powerful corporation is still secretive about plans, Barongi talked about his vision. A big portion of the park will be a safari adventure. Vehicles that look like Land Rovers will guide zoogoers through a veld of biodiversity and walk them through a storyline (perhaps about catching poachers). This safari may not look so different, but Barongi is hoping a revolution will be taking place within the exhibits. There will be enough money and space, Barongi says, for the collection to "eat the landscape." Proper social groupings will also be maintained.

Unlike most zoos, with dark and dingy nightquarters that the public never sees, Barongi plans to open all of the animal areas to the public (sometimes through cameras) so that everything can be monitored.

Barongi is honest, he says Disney's "mission" is to make money,

249

but nevertheless, conservation is part of the goal. After the "immersion" experience of the safari, zoogoers will enter a "conservation station," and engage in conversations via live satellite with field biologists all over the world. "We want to get kids to identify with field biologists like George Schaller, Russ Mittemier and Jane Goodall and see them as role models to the same degree as they see athletes and rock stars. We have to market conservation much better—even if that does take 10 percent of our budget. San Diego spends 10 percent to market themselves and that's not right." Barongi says these far-flung researchers might write dull scientific papers, but they can also tell amazing stories of hanging off cliffs and running from charging elephants in order to collect that dry data.

Barongi also plans to create an endowment foundation to be run by a small staff with little overhead. Rather than hiring field biologists, Barongi's idea is to form a granting agency that can get quick cash out to those already in the field. To those who might scoff at the idea of donating money to Disney, Barongi points to the success of the philanthropic Ronald McDonald House.

What Barongi may have a hard time doing is providing the opportunity for engaging the mysterious link between humans and animals. While small zoos can allow visitors to touch and interact with some of the animals, he can't promise that experience to the millions who generally attend Disney parks.

Thinking back to the most delightful zoogoing experience, the visitor will almost always remember an intimate connection, a brief moment when the zoo animal looked up, followed or reached out. The chimpanzee who peeked through the glass at you. The snow leopard who stalked your stroller. The sea lion who did a water ballet while following you along a glass viewing panel. John Lehnhardt at the National Zoo gets tears in his eyes when describing the mystical bond that takes place between his elephant Shanti and the children who visit and sometimes touch her. It is not an elephant ride. It is not scheduled. It takes place when Shanti herself indicates that she wants to make the connection. That's a magic that no camcorder or satellite can compete with.

Our connection with the natural world can also get our adrenaline pumping. Some aquariums have built clear, acrylic tubing straight through tanks so that visitors can walk through shark territory. Our new zoo would place one of these tubes through the cheetah exhibit. By slanting the tube, a few zoogoers will be allowed to slide through, with the sight-hunting cheetah in hot pursuit. A reward system (dropping every twentieth zoogoer out into the exhibit?) could be set up to keep the big cat's interest.

The new zoo will be a place of meditation and thought and learning. While zoo officials complain about visitors spending mere seconds per exhibit, they do nothing to encourage a longer stay. At a crowded zoo, you must elbow your way to a viewing area and once there look briefly and leave so there is room for others. Even when the zoo is quiet, it's difficult to stay with an exhibit—there are few benches, and those that are scattered about generally face away from exhibits and toward the path.

At the Brookfield Zoo, I stood for at least fifteen minutes watching a troop of sixty-four very active baboons. The architecture of Baboon Island is dismal (it's basically a mountain of gunite), but the animals are riveting. Zoogoers on either side of me spent just as long, but we all turned away eventually when our legs grew stiff. Stadium seating at such an open and popular exhibit will allow zoogoers to spend real time with such engaging animals.

Quiet outposts, viewing areas restricted to those who wish to sit in silence for an extended period, will be created over most exhibits. Perhaps for a fee, the zoogoer can enter a tented viewing platform and use binoculars and field guides at the site. A biologist or naturalist might be on hand to explain behavior.

Conservation is complicated. Answers to environmental problems may be counterintuitive, and many of us need guidance. Bill Conway points out that while many people have rallied around the antifur campaign, "we're doing more damage—much more damage—with wool. Environmentally we're killing many more animals by raising sheep than by harvesting domestic mink." Is recycling paper as damaging to the earth through water use and chemicals as is making new raw paper? What about the diaper dilemma? Is the cleaning of dirty cloth diapers worse than burying tons of plastic ones? Conway wants to see an end to shallow, easy and misguided answers and a beginning of environmental sophistication.

Conway is currently planning a multimillion-dollar Congo Rain Forest exhibit that will cover seven acres and embody the spirit of the new zoo. Wrapped around the Congo forest habitat that contains gorillas would be three levels of walkways and awareness. The first floor would offer inspiration and discovery, seeing the animals themselves. Conways says, "Someone has said that Rembrandt painted 750 paintings in his lifetime, and all 3,000 of them are in the United States. There are no fake elephants, no fake pythons—that's the real thing."

The second level would be an explanation of natural history and ecology: teaching how nature works. And the third level, the one Conway is wrestling with, is the conservation level. This floor would be an adventure, a game, in which the zoogoer would become more sophisticated environmentally as he or she went through. At the end, this enlightened zoogoer could donate money (with matching funds from corporate sponsors) and decide directly how that money should be spent.

Here in the plans for one exhibit is the challenge of the new zoo: To allow living, breathing animals to inspire wonder and awe of the natural world; to teach us that animal's place in the cosmos and to illuminate the tangled and fragile web of life that sustains it; to open the door to conservation for the millions of people who want to help save this planet and the incredible creatures it contains. To enrich, enlighten and empower the people who care, so that through huge numbers and sheer willpower we save the beetle and the snail and the alligator along with the panda and the rhino and the condor.

No one knows exactly what the zoo of the future will look like. But with so much at stake, it is clear we desperately need zoos to help save the diversity of life. The question is not whether the world will have zoos in the future; the question is: Will the world have animals?

INTO THE WOODS . . .

W E SHOULD STRIVE to be the stewards of the animal kingdom, not its jailers.

Like the Victorians, we can prove our intelligence, power, pres-
tige and wealth to the rest of the world through our zoos. But this
will not be achieved by imprisoning sad and tired animals; it will
not be achieved by killing old animals; it will not be achieved by
driving active, migratory or intelligent species crazy with boredom;
and it certainly will not be achieved with plastic enclosures molded
into "naturalness." We can enhance our status by doing the right
thing: understanding and protecting nature for its own sake.

The zoo is not a window on nature but rather a prism that
bends the light according to the culture it is set in. And our view
of nature accords us a clearer view of ourselves. We have always
defined man in comparison to other animals. We thought we were
the only tool users, but Jane Goodall and others dispelled that
notion. Today, our place as the only true language users is being

questioned. But human beings are not defined by what we do with our hands or our vocal cords but by what we do with our hearts. As George B. Schaller wrote in *National Geographic,* "For one species to fight for the survival of another, even in times of stress, is something new in evolution. In this, more than all our technology, lies our claim to being human."

Arguments can be made for preserving nature because it may hold medical and technological secrets that could cure cancer or provide more efficient solar energy. Arguments can be made that we must preserve the fragile web of life because changing one small thread could alter the whole world. But the best argument for putting so much money and energy into preserving nature is for the sheer, breathtaking, poetic beauty of the diversity of life. This is an argument that is at once selfish and altruistic.

Throughout history, zoos have entertained and educated; now they have a staggering opportunity before them: to tip the global balance back in favor of nature. To work toward the restoration of harmony in the living world. Zoos, which have provided so much joy to people, can now breathe life back into moribund populations of wild creatures.

For the modern ark, the rains may never cease, the tide of extinction may always lap at its bow. The voyagers fighting to save the planet's biodiversity may sail on an endless sea, forever working to hold on, to buy time, to keep animals alive. Today, zoos keep generations of healthy tigers, elephants, rhinos and gorillas, suspended in time as a gift for our grandchildren's grandchildren. It is a treasure we all have a stake in.

Bibliography

AAZPA/AZA. "Annual Proceedings and Regional Proceedings, 1972–96."

Angier, Natalie. "Cheetah's Appear Vigorous Despite Inbreeding." *The New York Times*, 10 November 1992.

AZA. "Who Visits Zoos and Aquariums—A Demographic Profile." A Composite Survey of zoo and aquarium demographics.

Beck, B. B., et al. "Reintroduction of Captive-Born Animals." In *Creative Conservation: Interactive Management of Wild and Captive Animals,* edited by P. J. Olney et al. London: Chapman & Hall, 1994.

Begley, Sharon. "Killed By Kindness: We Nearly Wiped Out the Beast of the Field." *Newsweek*, 12 April 1993.

———. "New Life for an Old Bird: The Condors Will Go Free." *Newsweek,* 12 August 1991.

———. "Wilder Places for Wild Things." *Newsweek,* 17 July 1989.

Bendiner, Robert. *The Fall of the Wild, The Rise of the Zoo.* New York, N.Y.: E. P. Dutton, 1981.

Bostock, Stephen St. C. *Zoos and Animal Rights: The Ethics of Keeping Animals.* London: Routledge, 1993.

Berger, Joel. "The Return of the Takh." *Science* 266 (November 1994).

Berger, Joel. and Carol Cunningham. "The De-horning Dilemma." *Wildlife Conservation,* January/February 1994.

Berreby, David. "Where the Wild Things Are." *Discover,* August 1991.

Bitgood, Stephen et al. "Control of Public Feeding at the Birmingham Zoo." The Center for Social Design, Jacksonville, Ala., 1988.

Block, Richard. "Giant Pandas: Black and White in a Gray World." Paper presented at annual AAZK conference, Tuscon, Ariz., 1988.

Bibliography

Blunt, Wilfrid. *The Ark in the Park: The Zoo in the Nineteenth Century.* London: Hamish Hamilton Ltd., 1976.

Caras, Roger. *A Perfect Harmony: The Intertwining Lives of Animals and Humans Throughout History.* New York: Simon & Schuster, 1996.

"California Condors Released in the Wild." *Science News* 141 (25 January 1992).

Carter, Janis. "Freed from Keepers and Cages, Chimps Come of Age on Baboon Island." *Smithsonian,* June 1988.

Caughley, Graeme. "Directions in Conservation Biology." *Journal of Animal Ecology* 63 (1994).

Cherfas, Jeremy. *Zoo 2000: A Look Beyond Bars.* London: BBC Publishing, 1984.

Cohn, Jeffrey, P. "Decisions at the Zoo: Ethics, Politics, Profit, and Animal-Rights Concerns Affect the Process of Balancing Conservation Goals and the Public Interests." *BioScience* 42, no. 9 (October 1992).

————. "The Call of the Wild: Reintroduction of the Red Wolf into Protected Natural Areas Is a Milestone for Conservationists." *Zoo Life,* Winter 1991.

Coursey, Don. "The Revealed Demand for Public Good: Evidence from Endangered and Threatened Species." Paper presented for national meetings of the American Association for the Advancement of Science, San Francisco, Calif., February 1994.

Crowcroft, Peter. *The Zoo.* Milson's Point, Australia: Phillip Mathews, 1978.

Dale, Steve. *American Zoos.* New York, N.Y.: BDD Promotional Book Company, 1992.

DeBlieu, Jan. *Meant to Be Wild: The Struggle to Save Endangered Species Through Captive Breeding.* Golden, Colo.: Fulcrum Publishing, 1993.

Dembeck, Hermann. *Animals and Men.* New York, N.Y.: The Natural History Press, 1965.

de Waal, Frans. *Good Natured: The Origins of Right and Wrong in Humans and Other Animals.* Cambridge, Mass.: Harvard University Press, 1996.

————. *Peacemaking Among Primates.* Cambridge, Mass.: Harvard University Press, 1989.

Fisher, James. *Zoos of the World: The Story of Animals in Captivity.* London: Aldus, 1967.

Fossey, Diane. *Gorillas in the Mist.* Boston: Houghton Mifflin, 1983.

Gavzer, Bernard. "Are Our Zoos Humane: Two Movements Clash over an Emotional Issue." *Parade,* 26 March 1989.

Gibbs, Nancy. "The New Zoo: A Modern Ark." *Newsweek,* 21 August 1989.

Goddard, Donald, ed. *Saving Wildlife: A Century of Conservation.* New York, N.Y.: Harry N. Abrams, Inc., in association with the Wildlife Conservation Society, 1995.

Goodall, Jane. *The Chimpanzees of Gombe: Patterns of Behavior.* Cambridge, Mass.: Harvard University Press, 1986.

Grandy, John W. "Zoos: A Critical Reevaluation." *HSUS News,* Summer 1992.

Greene, Melissa, "No Rms, Jungle Vu." *The Atlantic Monthly,* December 1987.

Hagenbeck, Carl. *Beasts and Men.* London: Longmans, Green, and Co., 1910.

Hahn, Emily. *Animal Gardens.* New York, N.Y.: Doubleday, 1967.

Hanna, Jack and John Stravinsky. *Monkeys on the Interstate and Other Animal Tales.* New York, N.Y.: Doubleday, 1989.

Harrigan, Stephen. "Nature of the Beast." *Texas Monthly,* July 1988.

Harris, Roy J. Jr. "Panda Loans to Zoo Cause Ruckus." *The Wall Street Journal,* 8 June 1993.

Hediger, Heini. *Wild Animals in Captivity: An Outline of the Biology of Zoological Gardens.* New York, N.Y.: Dover Publications, 1950.

Hutchins, Michael et al. "Strategic Collection Planning: Theory and Practice." *Zoo Biology* 10 (1991).

"The Hybrid's Dilemma." *Discover*, November 1993.

Kleiman, Devra G. et al. eds. *Wild Mammals in Captivity: Principles and Techniques.* Chicago: University of Chicago Press, 1996.

Keller, Bill. "Cheetah's Race with Fate: U.S. Couple to Rescue." *The New York Times*, 17 May 1993.

Kisling, Vernon N. Jr. "The Origin and Development of American Zoological Parks to 1899." In *New Worlds, New Animals: From Menagerie to Zoological Park in the Nineteenth Century,* edited by Robert J. Hage and William A. Deiss. Baltimore: Johns Hopkins University Press.

———. "Libraries and Archives in the Historical and Professional Development of American Zoological Parks." *Libraries and Culture,* Summer 1993.

Koebner, Linda. *Zoo Book: The Evolution of Wildlife Conservation Centers.* New York, N.Y.: Forge, 1994.

Laxon, Andrew. "Zoos on Trial." *Animals International,* Autumn 1992.

Linden, Eugene. "Tigers on the Brink." *Time,* 28 March 1994.

Lipske, Mike. "Fast Cat in a Marathon: What We're Learning About Cheetahs May Enable These Troubled Sprinters to Compete in the Long Race for Survival." *International Wildlife,* September/October 1993.

Litchfield, Linda. "Panda Politics." *Zoo Life,* Summer 1992.

———. "Save the Tiger." *Zoo Life,* Summer 1991.

Luoma, Jon R. *A Crowded Ark,* Boston: Houghton Mifflin, 1987

———."Two Pandas Bound for U.S. May Be Just First Wave." *The New York Times,* 17 January 1995.

———. "Born to Be Wild: Captive Breeding Can Coax Animals Back from the Edge of Extinction. But in Rescuing Them, What Have We Lost?" *Audubon,* January/February 1992.

Macdonald, David, ed. *The Encyclopedia of Mammals.* New York, N.Y.: Facts on File, 1984.

Maple, Terry L. and Erika F. Archibald. *Zoo Man: Inside the Zoo Revolution.* Atlanta, Ga.: Longstreet Press, 1993.

Marshall, Anthony D. *Zoo: Profiles of 102 Zoos, Aquariums, and Wildlife Parks in the United States.* New York, N.Y.: Random House, 1994.

Mellen, Jill D. "A Comparative Analysis of Scent-Marking, Social and Reproductive Behavior in Twenty Species of Small Cats (Felis)." *American Zoology* 33 (1993).

———. "Effects of Early Rearing Experience on Subsequent Adult Sexual Behavior Using Domestic Cats (Felis Catus) as a Model for Exotic Small Felids." *Zoo Biology* 11 (1992).

———. "Factors Influencing Reproductive Success in Small Captive Exotic Felids (Felis spp.): A Multiple Regression Analysis." *Zoo Biology* 10(1991).

McKenna, Virginia, Will Travers and Jonathan Wray, eds. *Beyond the Bars: The Zoo Dilemma.* Wellingborough, Northamptonshire: Thorsons Publishing Group, 1987.

Mullan, Bob, and Garry Marvin. *Zoo Culture.* London: Weidenfeld & Nicolson, 1987.

Norton, Bryan G. et al., eds. *Ethics on the Ark: Zoos, Animal Welfare, and Wildlife Conservation.* Washington, D.C.: Smithsonian, 1995.

Nyhuis, Allen W. *The Zoo Book: A Guide to America's Best.* Albany, Calif.: Carousel Press, 1994.

Page, Jake. *Smithsonian's New Zoo.* Washington, D.C.: Smithsonian, 1990.

———. *Zoo: The Modern Ark.* New York, N.Y.: Facts on File, 1990.

Preiser, Rachel. "Back to Mongolia." *Discover,* January 1995.

Bibliography

Quigley, Howard B. "Saving Siberia's Tigers." *National Geographic*, July 1993.

Radetsky, Peter. "Back to Nature." *Discover*, July 1993.

Ritvo, Harriet. *The Animal Estate: The English and Other Creatures in the Victorian Age.* Cambridge, Mass.: Harvard University Press, 1987.

Robinson, Michael. "The New Zoo and the Old Adam." *Museum News*, January/February 1994.

Roper Organization. Poll commissioned by Sea World, Public Attitudes Toward Aquariums, Animal Theme Parks, and Zoos, October 1992.

Ryder, Oliver A. "Panda Paternity: The DNA Evidence." *Zoonooz*, July 1995.

———. "Przewalski's Horse: Prospects for Reintroduction into the Wild." *Conservation Biology* 7, no. 1 (March 1993).

———. "DNA Investigative Technologies: Application to Endangered Species Preservation." *Clinical Chemistry* 38, no. 3 (1992).

Ryder, Oliver A., et al. "Analysis of Relatedness in the California Condors, from DNA Fingerprints." *Molecular Biology Evolution* 10, no. 3 (1993).

Ryder, Oliver A. and L. G. Chemnick. "Chromosomal and Mitochondrial DNA Variation in Orang Utans." *The Journal of Heredity* 84 (1993).

Ryder, Oliver A., and Phillip A. Morin. "Founder Contribution and Pedigree Inference in a Captive Breeding Cology of Lion-Tailed Macaques, Using Mitochondrial DNA and DNA Fingerprint Analyses." *Zoo Biology* 10 (1991).

Ryder, Oliver A. et al. "Sequence of the Mitochondrial Control Region, tRNA(Thr), tRNA (Pro) and tRNA (Phe) Genes from the Black Rhinoceros, Diceros Bicornis." *Nucleic Acids Research* 21, no. 18 (1993).

Ryder, Oliver A., and Karen J. Garner. "Some Applications of PCR to Studies in Wildlife Genetics." *Zoological Symposium* no. 64 (1992).

Schaller, George B. *The Last Panda.* Chicago: University of Chicago Press, 1993.

Sedgwick, John. *The Peaceable Kingdom: A Year in the Life of America's Oldest Zoo.* New York, N.Y.: Ballantine Books, 1988.

Seidensticker, John. "Bearing Witness: Observations on the Extinction of Panthera Tigris Balica and Panthera Tigris Sondaica, and Managing Tigers in the Sunderbans: Experience and Opportunity." In *Tigers of the World: The Biology, Biopolitics, Management, and Conservation of an Endangered Species,* edited by Ronald Tilson and Ullysses S. Seal. Park Ridge, N.J.: Noyes Publications, 1987.

———. "Big Bear with Big Problems." *The Wall Street Journal*, 28 May 1993.

———. "From Field to Zoo: Basic Considerations for Wild Animals in Zoos." Paper presented at the Conference on Environmental Enrichment, Portland, Ore., July 1993.

———. "Large Carnivores and the Consequences of Habitat Insularization: Ecology and Conservation of Tigers in Indonesia and Bangladesh." In *Cats of the World: Biology, Conservation, and Management,* edited by S. D. Miller and D. D. Everett. Washington, D.C.: National Wildlife Federation.

Seidensticker, John, Kathy Carlstead, and Janine L. Brown. "Behavioral and Adrenocortical Responses to Environmental Changes in Leopard Cats (Felis Bengalensis)." *Zoo Biology* 12 (1993).

Seidensticker, John, Kathy Carlstead, and Robert Baldwin. "Environmental Enrichment for Zoo Bears." *Zoo Biology* (1991).

Seidensticker, John, et al. "Genetic Variation in Sri Lankan Leopards." *Zoo Biology* 10 (1991).

Bibliography

Seidensticker, John, and Kathy Carlstead. "Seasonal Variation in Stereotypic Pacing in an American Black Bear Ursus Americanus." *Behavior Processes* 25 (1991).

Seidensticker, John and John F. Eisenberg. "The Tangjiahe, Wanglang, and Fengtongzhai Panda Reservese and Biological Conservation in the People's Republic of China." *Biological Conservation* 28 (1984).

Seligmann, Jean, and Lynda Wright. "How to Handle an Elephant: Zoos and Animal Abuse." *Newsweek*, 14 November 1988.

Shepherdson, David J. et al. "An Enrichment Device for Great Apes." *Animal Welfare* 1, 1992.

Shepherdson, David J. "Environmental Enrichment in Zoos." *RATEL* 16, no. 3 (June 1989).

Shepherdson, David J. et al. "The Influence of Food Presentation on the Behavior of Small Cats in Confined Environments." *Zoo Biology* 12 (1993).

Shepherdson, David J. et al. "A Mealworm Dispenser for the Slender-Tailed Meerkat (Suricatta Suricatta) at London Zoo." In *International Zoo Yearbook*, London: Zoological Society of London, 1989.

Sunquist, Fiona. "Cheetah's: Closer than Kissing Cousins." *Wildlife Conservation*, May/June 1992.

———. "Should We Put Them All Back?" *International Wildlife*, September/October 1993.

Thompson, Sharon Elaine. "A Shaggy Rhino Story." *Zoo Life*, Spring 1991.

Travers, Kathi, and Philip Haworth. "Changing Stripes: Are Zoos Saving the World or Just Saving Themselves?" *Animal Watch*, Summer 1993.

Tudge, Colin. *Last Animals at the Zoo: How Mass Extinction Can Be Stopped.* Washington, D.C.: Island Press, 1992.

———. "Captive Breeding of Endangered Species." *Swara,* July/August 1991.

Wiese, Robert J., and Michael Hutchins, eds. *Species Survival Plans: Strategies for Wildlife Conservation.* Bethesda, Md.: AZA, 1994.

Wiese, Robert J., et al. "Is Genetic and Demographic Management Conservation?" *Zoo Biology* 13 (1994).

Willis, Kevin, and Robert J. Wiese. "Effect of New Founders on Retention of Gene Diversity in Captive Populations: A Formalization of the Nucleus Population Concept." *Zoo Biology* 12 (1993).

Wiseman, Carter. "The New Zoo." *New York*, 18 July 1988.

Zhi, Lu. "Newborn Panda in the Wild." *National Geographic*, February 1993.

Zuckerman, Solly. *Great Zoos of the World: Their Origins and Significance.* London: Weidenfeld & Nicolson, 1980.

Index

Index